GROUNDING CRITIQUE

Studies in Critical Social Sciences Book Series

Haymarket Books is proud to be working with Brill Academic Publishers (www.brill.nl) to republish the *Studies in Critical Social Sciences* book series in paperback editions. This peer-reviewed book series offers insights into our current reality by exploring the content and consequences of power relationships under capitalism, and by considering the spaces of opposition and resistance to these changes that have been defining our new age. Our full catalog of *SCSS* volumes can be viewed at https://www.haymarketbooks.org/series_collections/4-studies-in-critical-social-sciences.

Series Editor
David Fasenfest (York University, Canada)

Editorial Board
Eduardo Bonilla-Silva (Duke University)
Chris Chase-Dunn (University of California–Riverside)
William Carroll (University of Victoria)
Raewyn Connell (University of Sydney)
Kimberlé W. Crenshaw (University of California–LA and Columbia University)
Raju Das (York University, Canada)
Heidi Gottfried (Wayne State University)
Alfredo Saad-Filho (Queen's University Belfast)
Chizuko Ueno (University of Tokyo)
Sylvia Walby (Royal Holloway, University of London)

GROUNDING CRITIQUE

Marxism, Concept Formation,
and Embodied Social Relations

GÖKBÖRÜ SARP TANYILDIZ

Haymarket Books
Chicago, IL

First published in 2024 by Brill Academic Publishers, The Netherlands
© 2024 Koninklijke Brill NV, Leiden, The Netherlands

Published in paperback in 2025 by
Haymarket Books
P.O. Box 180165
Chicago, IL 60618
773-583-7884
www.haymarketbooks.org

ISBN: 979-8-88890-557-9

Distributed to the trade in the US through Consortium Book Sales and Distribution (www.cbsd.com) and internationally through Ingram Publisher Services International (www.ingramcontent.com).

This book was published with the generous support of Lannan Foundation, Wallace Action Fund, and the Marguerite Casey Foundation.

Special discounts are available for bulk purchases by organizations and institutions. Please call 773-583-7884 or email info@haymarketbooks.org for more information.

Cover design by Jamie Kerry and Ragina Johnson.

Printed in the United States.

Library of Congress Cataloging-in-Publication data is available.

Dedicated to
Himani Bannerji and Cem Eroğul

Contents

Foreword XI
   Terrell Carver
Acknowledgements XIV

Introduction: The Living Individual and the Marionette

- I   The Predicament of the Marxist Sociologist   3
- II   A Marxism Made to the Measure of Life   5
- III   The Principle of Sociability for Social Relations   6
- IV   The Specificity of Social Relations in Marx   8
- V   Embodied Social Relations under Capitalism   10
- VI   Embodied Social Relations in Contemporary Marxist Social Thought   12
- VII   A Brief Note on Intersectionality   13
- VIII   A Marxist-Feminist Symposium on Intersectionality   13
- IX   Embodied Social Relations in Social Reproduction Theory   15
- X   A Conceptual Ground Clearing to Return to Marx   17

PART I
Embodied Social Relations in Contemporary Marxist-Feminism

- I   Introduction   21
- II   Intersectionality   23
- III   Some Methodological Propositions for a Marxist Engagement with Intersectionality   25
- IV   The Generalization of Embodied Social Relations as the Categories of Subjective Human Life   28
- V   The Framing of the Marxist-Feminist Engagement with Intersectionality   33
- VI   The Analytic Primacy of Class and the Transformative Pedagogies   34
- VII   The Ideological Techniques of Bourgeois Management   36
- VIII   The Concept of the Mode of Production   38
- IX   The Methodological Tension between the Phenomenology and Ontology of the Social   39
- X   The Need for the Recovery of the Concept of Experience in Its Lived Sense   41

XI   Embodied Social Relations and the Levels of Analysis in Social Sciences   42
XII Class Burdened with the Difficult Conceptual Task of Reconciling History with the Social   45
XIII Mistaking Critical Marxist Epistemologies for a Sociology of Knowledge   48
XIV A Quasi-transcendental Framework of Explanation Premised upon a First Principle   52
XV   Marxism and the Non-identity of the Law and Life in Contemporary Capitalist Societies   54
XVI Supra-racial Epistemology of an Aleatory and Subjectless Conception of History   57
XVII Marxist-Feminist Aporetic of Description versus Explanation   62
XVIII 10+1 Theses on Feuerbach   64
XIX The Non-coincidence of Experience and Explanation   68
XX   Marxist-Feminist Inscription of the Binary of the Idiographic versus the Nomothetic   70
XXI Why 'Race' Cannot Be Accommodated within a Marxist-Feminist Analysis as an Embodied Social Relation?   72
XXII Conclusion   74

PART II
Embodied Social Relations in Social Reproduction Theory

I   Introduction   77
II   What Is the Relationship between Social Reproduction Theory and Intersectionality?   79
III   Social Reproduction Theory's Ambiguous and Inadequately Self-Reflexive Relationship to Intersectionality   82
IV   Social Reproduction Theory as a Marxist-Feminist Alternative to Intersectionality   85
V   Social Reproduction Theory's 'Methodology' and Its Articulation and Selection of Social Problems   87
VI   'Race,' Racialization, and Experience in Social Reproduction Feminism   90
VII   Vacillating between Supplementing and Supplanting Intersectionality   95
VIII Inauguration of Socialist-Feminist Political Economy as a Unitary Social Theory   99
IX   One-Sidedness of Experience in Social Reproduction Theory   101

CONTENTS IX

    X   The Values, Facts, and Factuality of Oppression in the Quasi-transcendental Structure of Social Reproduction Theory   104
    XI   Social Reproduction Theory as Sublated Intersectionality   108
    XII   Metaphorizing Concepts, Criticizing Metaphors   112
    XIII (Hegelian-Marxist) Totality in Social Reproduction Theory?   115
    XIV Severing Methodology from the Rest of the Theoretical Framework in Social Reproduction Theory   117
    XV   Co-constitutivity in Social Reproduction Theory   119
    XVI 'Additive Method,' Anti-additivity, and Social Reproduction Theory   121
    XVII Liberalism, Ontological Atomism, Social Newtonianism, and Intersectionality according to Social Reproduction Theory   126
    XVIII An Alternative Outlook on the Relationship between Intersectionality and the Critical Import of Newton's System into Liberal Bourgeois Social Thought   128
    XIX The Pitfalls of the 'Methodology' of Analogical Argumentations and Battling Metaphors   133
    XX   Towards a Marxist Social Theory of Embodied Social Relations   135

Coda: A Long Day's Evening

    I   A Critique of Concept Formation   139
    II   Through Intersectionality to Concept Formation in Contemporary Marxist Social Thought   139
    III Dissolving Intersecting Lines in Favour of Parallel Planes Bereft of Social Existence and Life   140
    IV Conceptual Conditions of Dialectically Overcoming Intersectionality   140
    V   The Finality of Conceptual Judgement?   141
    VI Tarrying with Marxist-Feminism and Social Reproduction Theory   142
    VII Quo Vadis Social Reproduction?   144
    VIII Social Reproduction Qua Method   146
    IX Returning to Marx to Study Embodied Social Relations   148

Afterword   149
    Himani Bannerji
Bibliography   151
Index   163

Foreword

Grounding Critique: Marxism, Concept Formation, and Embodied Social Relations makes a major contribution to social theory across a very wide range of disciplines and sub-disciplines as we have them in the global academy. These include sociology, political studies, cultural studies, human geography, policy studies, women's studies, and no doubt other stops in the A-Z lists of universities and colleges. However, that kind of claim, across that kind of list, sets up precisely the kind of tendentious parcellation of understanding and knowledge that Tanyildiz challenges.

The title references Marxism as an on-going intellectual tradition, but for me the primary identification in the book is with Marx himself. Marx had no interest in, or patience with the (very few) academic boundaries of his day. In *Grounding Critique*, however, Tanyildiz has considerable interest in, and patience with, the sub/disciplinary empires within which the primary contemporary readership lies. However, his project here is not to address readers in familiar terms and comfort zones. Rather the goal is to stretch our minds across society as a subject, by including ourselves in it as participant-observers. In that way – as Hobbes advised, quoting the ancients – *nosce teipsum*: we read ourselves. How then does this work?

Central to *Grounding Critique* is a way of looking at how methodology is understood and used within social theory, the social sciences, and human studies more broadly. Hence in the book we are offered a 'view' [*Ansicht*] or 'outlook' [*Aussicht*] or 'conception' [*Auffassung*]. I am quoting Marx's own self-characterisations here, which, as Tanyildiz makes clear, stand opposed to the deployment of an already validated set of ontological presumptions and epistemological protocols. On that conventional model 'a researcher' 'applies' these methodological 'tools' to an 'external' object of study, and truthful results are supposed to emerge. Tanyildiz's argument, however, is that research objects in social theory are not 'external' but rather internal to the researcher who is part of, but necessarily intervening within, the conflictual and reparative activisms of the moment. That approach rules out the deployment of ontological and epistemological presumptions and claims as 'givens,' or are unselfconsciously and factitiously 'deployed' – an understanding which is also integral to Marx's own method.

Tanyildiz's approach arises through the nexus of subject-formation, rather than disembodied subjectivity-formation, because subject-formation takes place as human embodiment in social relations. The embodied subject is thus enacted conceptually as lives-the-way-they-are-actually-lived, including the lives of author and reader. Tanyildiz's inspiration is in Marxism, but understood as a mode of political thinking, drawing particular inspiration from those works, passages, and theorizations in Marx which focus on praxis as everyday activity.

However, it is also the case that Tanyildiz's approach derives just as much from feminist, and particularly from women-of-colour and Black feminist understandings of embodiment. This latter encompasses racializations, as well as gendered and sexualized differences, including further conceptualizations of physically experienced and socially referenced identifications, commonly understood as 'identities.'

Tanyildiz is rightly critical of the use of intersectionality in relation to liberal, social-democratic and other 'inclusive' critiques of exploitation, exclusion, and oppression in so-called liberal-democratic or 'free market' capitalist societies. Alternatively, the book points us to the political utility of intersectionality, if understood within its original context, as subverting the race-only/gender-only modes of legal and policy reasoning. The argument of *Grounding Critique* emerges so effectively because the objects of interest are concepts, such as oppression, intersectionality, and social reproduction, that are currently both controversial in themselves and reference points in practice. This focus on everyday sensuous practice as embodied social relations, a covering-term through which gender, race, class and ability are variously articulated, holds the author's critiques together.

Indeed, that focus fosters a novel critique of the meta-critiques of intersectionality. The author's edifying discussions of embodied social relations, sensuous practical activity, and contingent processes of subject-making, speak very directly to how the reader sees and re-visions the social world. This is a powerful contribution to scholarship.

Tanyildiz's argument emerge with great clarity from critical engagement with two specific bodies of work. One is a selection of contemporary Marxist-feminist treatments of intersectionality, where critique is misunderstood as a process of negation and clarification. And the other is with articulations of social reproduction theory, where critique is contrarily misconstrued as a process of positivity and sublation. Tanyildiz argues instead for a kind of theorizing that explores the gap between the objectified and ideological forms of life – just as Marx was doing when exploring the materialized sensuousness and symbolically effectual character of 'the commodity.' Thus, Tanyildiz urges us to reject foreclosure and purification, and explanation as tautology, and get to grips with the 'excess' in society-making as knowledge-making. In a revisioned social theory, we should be seeing not just the praxis that lives the capitalist life but crucially how lives are *unlived*, explained away as capitalism reproduces the inhuman.

Thus, *Grounding Critique* redefines concept-formation in a way which transcends the usual distinction between methodology and application, and makes reflexive sense of embodiment and agency. That analytical capstone demonstrates exactly why the author's critical examination of the two intersecting theoretical/political positions holds together so well.

Critique is a cliché in social theory. But whose work is 'uncritical'? *Grounding Critique* resolves that issue synoptically and convincingly.

Terrell Carver
Bristol, UK

Acknowledgements

Grounding Critique: Marxism, Concept Formation, and Embodied Social Relations is a congealment of my relations, an archive of my orientations. The titular ground is not simply a relic of foundational ontologies. Rather, it is the ongoing struggle between the gravitational pull of the social world, sedimented as it is through power struggles in history, and the subject's freedom, will, dignity, creativity, and resistance. Thus, this grounding is individual, transindividual, and collective all at once, and this book is both an expression and a product of the process of this grounding. While the bibliography itself should be read as an acknowledgments, there are some people whose person –not just work, or mind– have been integral to *Grounding Critique,* and it is a particularly gratifying experience to inscribe their names here as part and parcel of the book.

An earlier version of *Grounding Critique* was written as my PhD dissertation under Himani Bannerji's supervision. Himani's existence in my life began as textual presence. I read her work before meeting her. I started my PhD at York University just so I could work with her. She first became my professor, then my PhD supervisor. That way, the textual presence was appended with administrative categories. However, one of the first lessons I learned from Himani was that her citational authority and our institutional relation were the practico-inert context of our encounter, and that they had to be sublated in order for the actual possibility of learning and knowledge to arise. This meant a shift towards mutual intellectual curiosity, pedagogical solicitude, and living attention. It is through this shift that, for the last decade and more, Himani and I have become real presences for one another. Being-with-her and thinking-with-her make the world anew and generate that rare and exhilarating feeling of recognizing myself as a part of all generations past, present, and future – both as the wreckage of history is piled and hurled before one's feet, and as the liberation struggles of the world catches in the wings of one's spirit, as Himani's beloved Walter Benjamin would have it. I am truly fortunate to continue to be and think with her.

It was about two decades ago, when I was only seventeen, that I went to Cem Eroğul's office and asked him to help me become a marxist. He was, and remains, one of Turkey's foremost marxists and orginial thinkers. I am grateful that rather than indoctrinating me with formulaic clichés and platitudes, he said no! Becoming a *marxist* was not a matter of simple identification, he explained to me. Marx had set a bar for himself to become himself, and I had to meet that bar for myself if I were serious about becoming a marxist. With that objective, Cem and I discussed a book every week for four years during my undergraduate degree. Having thus completed studying major works of French social and political thought, British political economy, and German philosophy that made Marx Marx, I turned to focusing on my own contemporary context. This, for me, meant reading feminist, anti-racist, queer, and decolonial literatures. Through all this, I was able to become myself, and, therefore, a marxist at last! Without Cem, this would not have happened.

Linda Peake is the best collaborator, mentor, and friend one could ask for. In the North American academy, it is hard to meet someone like Linda, who has turned her feminist and anti-racist ethics of care into everyday praxis. Terrell Carver is a belatedly found and cherished kindred thinker. His versions of Marx and Engels are always surprising, dynamic, and fascinating, much like his company and methodological camaraderie. David Fasenfest is the very best editor. His enthusiasm and support for *Grounding Critique* prevented the undue anxiety often associated with publishing.

Friendship fulfils its concept in Dalia Kandiyoti. Her humour, kindness, and intelligence have been indispensable and grounding for me in moving forward with life and with this project. Athena Colman is my grey-eyed goddess. Feminist philosophy and Frankfurt School come alive in her company. I have been living in thought with her. Sue Ruddick sees the argument I make right in the eye and reflects it back to me in abundance. David McNally and Sue Ferguson are my socialist Toronto. Their friendship and comradeship have been invaluable. Their thinking started me off in this project.

My wonderful friends and comrades replenished my life and intellectual energies as I worked on *Grounding Critique*: Rebecca Lock. Wiley Sharp. Azim Remani. Donya Ziaee. Eva-Lynn Jagoe. Radhika Mongia. Michael Kuttner. Souvankham Thammavongsa. The late Donald Goellnicht. Adrie Naylor. Emrah Öztürk. Chris Webb. Aziz Güzel. Asha Jeffers. Cansu Dinçer. Elspeth Brown. Pacinthe Mattar. Thy Phu. Michael Tang. Brian Sune Sandbeck. Ratiba Hadj-Moussa. Lina Nasr El Hag Ali. Selmin Kara. Sedef Arat-Koc. Mustafa Koc. Robert Latham. Ebru Ustundag. Nicole Leach. Gülay Kilicaslan. Malissa Phung. Aaron Surty. Tim McCaskell. Richard Fung. Tamara El-Hoss. Ju Hui Judy Han. Jennifer Jihye Chun. Ronald Cummings. Stefan Kipfer. Karen Anderson. Andil Gosine. Raju Das.

The Department of Sociology at Brock University was my institutional base during the preparation of this manuscript. I have been lucky to be surrounded by many generous and brilliant colleagues, as well as curious students. In particular, I am grateful to my following colleagues for their interest in and support of my project: Nancy Cook, Michelle Webber, Margot Francis, Janet Conway,

Hijin Park, Lauren Corman, Ifeanyi Ezeonu, Kevin Gosine, Tamari Kitossa, Julie Ham, Mary-Beth Raddon, Dennis Soron, and Tom Dunk.

I thank Nagehan and Ünal Tanyildiz, my parents, for always encouraging and supporting my pursuits in life and in academia. Hien Nguyen and the whole Nguyen family showed great care and support as I worked on this project. Gökbige Tanyildiz, my sister, has the sharpest judicious mind, psychoanalytic insight, and lively humour – all of which have been vital for me to be able to carry out this project.

Vinh Nguyen is the horizon of this project. He is life to which concepts can only approximate. He is love that propels life into its excesses. He is my innermost.

Like all books, *Grounding Critique* presupposes life. When there is no life, there is no concept formation, embodied social relations, the social, and society. Unfortunately, as I write these acknowledgements, the genocide in Gaza and Palestine is still ceaselessly raging. Palestinians everywhere are trying to reproduce life and liberate themselves and, therefore, the rest of us. All around the globe, students are trying to help them in encampments. And us faculty in Canada, through the Faculty4Palestine networks, have been standing in solidarity with Palestine and its peoples. The world's one hope lies in the compassion of the oppressed for the oppressed, as Bertolt Brecht said. It is my one hope that by the time the reader reads this book, we will all be jubilantly celebrating a free Palestine and witnessing the punishment of the genocidal fascist regime in our righteous dignity.

*Introduction: The Living Individual
and the Marionette*

∴

> As if the task were the dialectic balancing of concepts, and not the grasping of real relations!
>
> MARX, 2005: 90

∴

> Mode of production must not be considered simply as being the reproduction of the physical existence of the individual. Rather it is a form of activity of these individuals, a definite form of expressing their life, a definite *mode of life* on their part. As individuals express their lives, so they are.
>
> MARX AND ENGELS, 1976: 31, emphasis in original

∴

> Our politics must sidestep the paradigm of 'unity' based on 'fragmentation or integration' and instead engage in struggles based on the genuine contradictions of our society.
>
> BANNERJI, 2000: 120

∴

1 The Predicament of the Marxist Sociologist

Life, society, politics, relations, and concepts are the keywords of our collective and individual existence. Only in history is their meaning constructed, comprehended, and contested. However, as Marx and Engels remind us, "[*h*]*istory* does *nothing*, it 'possesses *no* immense wealth,' it 'wages *no* battles.' It is *man* [sic], real, living man [sic] who does all that, who possesses and fights; 'history' is not, as it were, a person apart, using man [sic] as a means to achieve *its own* aims; history is *nothing but* the activity of man [sic] pursuing his [sic] aims" (Marx and Engels, 1975: 93). Therefore, it is in the course of living and struggling that people make history, as well as the meaning of these keywords, which are but the self-reflexive tools for assessing and understanding of this making.

It is this activist, in-process, and formational conceptualization of history and the subject that constitutes marxism as a *Weltanschauung*, a worldview – my worldview in any case. It instills within me "a system of generalized sensibilities, of intuitive notions and theoretical views of the surrounding world" (Spirkin, 1990: 23), and my place and relationalities in it. This worldview has long ago oriented me towards sociology and social thought, which inquire into the relationship between history and the subject through the mediation of society.[1] I believe that such inquiries into the social prevent this worldview from rigidifying and, thereby, becoming dogmatic. Rather, the knowledge that these inquiries into the social produce keeps marxism attuned to the ever-changing and contradictory realities of social life and existence, thereby helping to maintain its activist, in-process, and formational spirit.

I have found, however, that fulfilling this spirit is easier said than done. This is especially the case in the realms of sociology and social thought. For "the first premise of all human history" (Marx and Engels, 1976: 31), which is "the existence of living human individuals" (Marx and Engels, 1976: 31), may be misinterpreted in the manner of "childishly naïve and purely mechanical view of history held by the subjectivists, who contented themselves with the meaningless thesis that history is made by living individuals, and who refused to examine what social conditions determine their actions" (Lenin, 1960: 411). Such is the predicament of the marxist, the sociologist, and the marxist sociologist: Understanding the relationship between history, subject, and society without historicism, subjectivism, and sociologism.

Echoing Marx, Lenin offers "a reliable criterion" (Lenin, 1960: 408) for those who find themselves in this predicament. He writes that "when I investigate *actual* social relations and their *actual* development, I am in fact examining the product of the activities of living individuals" (Lenin, 1960: 408), whose "'thoughts and feelings' had already found expression in actions and had created definite social relations" (Lenin, 1960: 408). Missing this criterion of focusing on social relations runs the danger of rendering the place of living individuals and their praxis in history into a platitude and a truism.

Should we like to avoid the pitfall of such platitudes and truisms, we must take Lenin's critique of Narodnik sociology[2] seriously as a cautionary methodological tale for all of us who identify as a marxist, a sociologist, and a marxist sociologist. Lenin admonishes those who forget social relations even if they may have a focus on living individuals:

---

1 Adorno argues that "the concept of society, is itself not an object but a category of mediation" (Adorno, 2000: 103).
2 For brief entries on Narodniks and Narodism, see: "Narodniks," in *Encyclopedia of Marxism*, https://www.marxists.org/glossary/orgs/n/a.htm; "Narodism," in *Encyclopedia of Marxism*, https://www.marxists.org/glossary/terms/n/a.htm#narodism.

But though you talk of 'living individuals,' you actually make your starting-point not the 'living individual,' with the 'thoughts and feelings' actually created by his [sic] conditions of life, by the given system of relations of production, but a marionette, and stuff its head with your own 'thoughts and feelings.' Naturally, such a pursuit only leads to pious dreams; life passes you by, and you pass life by.

LENIN, 1960: 408–409

11   A Marxism Made to the Measure of Life

Grounding Critique: Marxism, Concept Formation, and Embodied Social Relations is a product of my scrutiny of the above predicament. It is driven by the desire to reckon with this predicament, learn from those who have been doing so for much longer, and contribute to ongoing discussions about how best to understand the relationship between history, subject, and society. Above all, my book searches for the conditions for the possibilities of a marxism that is made to the measure of life. That is, one which is capable of grasping real social relations, the expressive mode of people's lives, and the genuine social contradictions of our contemporary moment – rather than, one that endeavours to fit life into its own theoretical boundaries through scholastic maneuvers.

I suggest that Lenin's above emphasis on investigating social relations is as crucial for our time as it was for his. Indeed, I forward that in our time it is imperative for a marxism that does not 'pass life by' to have a rigorous account of social relations. In *Grounding Critique*, I hope to contribute to developing such an account. Only the examination of social relations may provide us with a thorough analysis of the increasing economic subsumption of all aspects of social life, which is the main characteristic of contemporary capitalism. It is this subsumption that alters our relationships to the self, others, and the world – the ensemble of which constitutes our practical sensuous activity in history. Therefore, what is at stake in studying social relations is to discern the shifts and transformations in our mode of life, to understand the differential consequences of these shifts and transformations for people, and to consider the ways of making a better mode of life possible.[3]

---

3 Immediately observables of these shifts and transformations may be found in daily papers, including ongoing wars, ecological crisis, the threat of extinction, acts of everyday violence, and severe global inequality. I suggest that these are not merely events but the variegated moments of our species-becoming and -unbecoming.

It is, however, important to highlight that in pointing out the economic subsumption of life under contemporary capitalism, I do not intend to reproduce a commonplace economistic misinterpretation of Marx's thought. To be sure, all relations of economic production are social relations; yet, not all social relations are relations of economic production. Marx does not conflate these relations with one another. Rather, I suggest that what makes Marx indispensable to any social inquiry is that he superbly and with great precision investigates how the production of life assumes an exclusively 'economic' character under capitalist mode of production and forms a particular social organization.

It is within the spirit of this inquiry that we can make sense of Marx's argument that "[t]he relations of production *in their totality* constitute what is called the social relations, society, and, moreover, a society at a definite stage of historical development, a society with peculiar, distinctive characteristics" (Marx, 1847: n.p., emphasis is mine). Social relations, however, constitute the context and subtext of relations of economic production. For instance, Marx writes that "[i]n order to produce, they [human beings] enter into definite connections and relations to one another, and only within these social connections and relations does their influence upon nature operate – i.e., does production take place" (Marx, 1847: n.p.). Thus, I argue that a marxist social theory must reject the conflation of these relations with one another and examine their relationship through the study of the constitution and organization of society and the social.

III The Principle of Sociability for Social Relations

This rejection, however, does not mean that in *Grounding Critique*, I adopt the Weberian conceptualization of social relations, which is commonly used in contemporary sociology and social thought. 'Social relations' attains a conceptual status in Max Weber's usage. In the "Basic Sociological Concepts" chapter of his *Economy and Society,* Weber explains that:

> Social 'relationship' shall refer to the meaningful content of the mutual disposition of several persons, and comportment arising from such an orientation. A social relationship therefore consists entirely and quite exclusively of the *Chance* that action will be social in a (meaningfully) manifest sense, leaving to one side for the moment the basis of this *Chance.*
> WEBER, 2019: 103

The chief characteristic of social relations for Weber is "the existence in the relationship of a minimum of mutual orientation one to another" (Weber, 2019: 103). In other words, social relations are about the interconnectedness of social action. In this conceptualization of social relations, human actors behave in a fashion that is "sensibly oriented" (Weber, 2019: 99) towards the anticipated behaviour of other actors. These 'other actors' may be "individual and familiar, or indefinitely numerous and quite unfamiliar" (Weber, 2019: 99). Social relations may be "transitory, or long-lasting" (Weber, 2019: 105). However, for Weber, what makes a behaviour into an action is that it is "linked to a subjective meaning on the part of the actor or actors concerned" (Weber, 2019: 78). Relatedly, what makes this behaviour into a 'social' action is that "the meaning intended by the actor or actors is related to the behaviour of others, and the action is so oriented" (Weber, 2019: 79).

I argue that Weber's conceptualization of social relations is valuable in so far as he does not uncritically allow every interaction between people to be a social relation. Moreover, he shows that social relations are subject to change, and what once was a social relation might cease to exist *qua* social relation. Therefore, the great merit of Weber's conceptualization of social relations is that it does not derive the concept from the fact of our being. We do not socialize, sociate, and associate simply because we are social beings. Rather, Weber offers a principle of sociability. That is, through the action of meaningful behaviour, we orient our sociality towards others, and if they, too, are disposed towards us within an interpretive expectation of our behaviour, then – only then – a mutuality between us emerges, and the interconnectedness of our social action becomes a social relation.[4]

Despite this great merit and conceptual clarity of his conceptualization, Weber's narrow principle of sociability generates a restricted understanding of society, which is determined by the subjective meanings that actors attach to society. In fact, Weber has no concept of society. As Richard Swedberg and Ola Agevall note, Weber only "occasionally uses the term 'society' in his sociological writings, but it plays no analytical role in his general (interpretive) sociology" (Swedberg and Agevall, 2016: 321). David Frisby and Derek Sayer argue that "this avoidance of the concept of society is justifiable for Weber given his commitment to the methodological individualist position" (Frisby and Sayer, 1986: 68). Pointing to the extent of this commitment, Frisby and Sayer explain

---

4 Weber does not stipulate any one-to-one correspondence between different subjective meanings in social relations and is well-aware of the asymmetry within social relations. See, Weber, 2019: 78–138.

that, according to Weber, "recourse to collective concepts by sociologists was only justified on the grounds that they referred to the actual or possible social actions by individuals" (Frisby and Sayer, 1986: 68).

Weber's conceptualization of social relations is, thus, helpful in studying the forms of rationality that actors employ in their processes of creating these meanings. However, I argue that when it comes to explicating the conditions for possibility of these meanings themselves – in other words, the constitution and organization of society – their usefulness ceases. This marks the conceptual limits of Weberian sociology and constitutes the rationale as to why I cannot adopt this conceptualization in this book. Put simply, my interest does not lie in investigating the constitution of singular social relations through the sociality of human action. Rather, it lies in examining the constitution and organization of society through the relationship between social relations that expresses the identity between history and the subject.

This relationship of identity is achieved through concord and discord among definite social groups that are formed by human subjects in response to the contradictions in their modes of life, the necessities of production and reproduction of their lives. Thus, the principle of sociability for the social relations I examine in *Grounding Critique* cannot be that of Weber. Instead, it must be one that is capable of explaining both the subjectivity of the subject, and formation of collective subjects, as well as the tension between these modalities of life expression within the context of the making of history.

IV   The Specificity of Social Relations in Marx

With this analytical awareness about the concept formation of social relations in mind, I began my book project. Initially, I had planned to work on the social relations of sexuality, building on my earlier attempts to put marxist social thought, critical feminisms, and queer theory in conversation (Tanyildiz, 2013). I hoped that this project would contribute to the growing literature on 'queer marxism.' Being a relatively new academic field of study at the time, queer marxism was not self-referential. Unlike many other established fields, it could not afford a certain oblivion concerning its own intellectual and political history and genealogy. Therefore, making sense of queer marxism demanded that one study marxist social thought altogether, especially those literatures that focused on the social relations of gender, race, and sexuality.

In these literatures, I expected to find a conceptualization of social relations which is neither economically reductionist, nor narrowly subjectivist. During the course of my research, however, it became clear to me that although the use of 'social relations' was ubiquitous in contemporary marxist social thought, the term often simply functioned as a synonym for the relations of economic production. Various efforts to undo the economic reductionism of this usage, on the other hand, ended up resorting to an unspecified, commonplace meaning.[5] In these literatures, social relations came to merely stand for "any relation between actors within a social space of some kind" (Nassehi, 2006: 567). For me, this represented not an advance, but a regression on even the economistic uses of social relations. This was because, at this level of generality, 'social relations' could not serve in any analytical capacity and fulfill a conceptual function. The principle of sociability was naturalized. People were simply assumed to be always in social relations due to our nature as social beings. Thus, such a regressed usage de-conceptualized the term.

I soon realized that this ubiquity of social relations, which left the term bereft of any conceptual capacity and clarity, *supposedly* replicated Marx's approach to studying capital. At least in three different places, Marx emphasizes that capital is a social relation of production. In *Wage Labour and Capital*, he writes that "[c]apital also is a social relation of production. It is a bourgeois relation of production, a relation of production of bourgeois society" (Marx, 1847: n.p.). In Chapter Thirty-Three of *Capital Volume I*, in his critique of the colonialist Edward Gibbon Wakefield, who "discovered, not anything new about the Colonies, but ... discovered in the Colonies the truth as to the conditions of capitalist production in the mother country" (Marx, 1887: n.p.), Marx notes that "capital is not a thing, but a social relation between persons, established by the instrumentality of things" (Marx, 1887: n.p.). And in Chapter Forty-Eight of *Capital Volume III*, Marx explains once again that:

> [C]apital is not a thing, but rather a definite social production relation, belonging to a definite historical formation of society, which is manifested in a thing and lends this thing a specific social character. Capital is not the sum of the material and produced means of production. Capital is rather the means of production transformed into capital, which in themselves are no more capital than gold or silver in itself is money. It is the means of production monopolised by a certain of society, confronting living labour-power as products and working conditions rendered

---

5 For a good typological examination of these efforts and the epistemological tensions to which they have given rise, see Bakan, 2012.

independent of this very labour-power, which are personified through this antithesis in capital.

MARX, 1894: n.p.

As ought to be clear, when Marx submits that capital is a social relation, he demonstrates the specificity of the social relation he analyzes. His demonstration is not aimed at issuing epistemological self-validity for his claims. When he counterposes things and relations and argues that relations are not the sum of things, Marx does not engage in a dialectical balancing or overcoming of these concepts. Nor does he outsource the labour of explanation to mathematical metaphors. Rather, Marx shows how the social relation in question is established by revealing the principle of sociability operative in the definite society that he examines. For me, recognizing the marked difference between the methodological manner in which Marx mobilized the concept of social relations and the de-conceptualized way in which it was used in contemporary marxist social thought was the moment I decided to pursue this present project for this book.

v Embodied Social Relations under Capitalism

In *Grounding Critique*, I argue that mobilizing social relations as an entry point into investigating the constitution and organization of the social and society, and taking these relations for granted with an assumption that they themselves possess a universal explanatory capacity, are two very different projects of knowledge production, although both these approaches bore the same epithet, 'marxism.' Thus, it is imperative for me to scrutinize the ways in which 'social relations' are treated in contemporary marxist social thought to thematize these usages and demonstrate their shortcomings through a set of methodological close readings. In this way, I hope to contribute to marxist projects of transformative knowledge production by instilling a conceptual and methodological vigilance so that the dominant contemporary usages of social relations do not overdetermine more productive uses of Marx's thought and stymie the possibilities of returning to him and his writing.

In this study, I am interested in exploring what I call embodied social relations under capitalism. All social relations are experienced in and through the body. For we are our bodies. Therefore, I must clarify that in terming my interest in this way, I do not intend to offer a redundant qualifier, or a truism. Rather, by embodied social relations, I mean those social relations that contribute to the constitution of society through the social organization of particular bodies. In other words, embodied social relations are those that organize the subject's passage between the individual and the collective, and the particular and the universal, in the making of history. They are the modes through which subjects experience, express, contest, and change their own sensuous human practical activity – with its possibilities and restrictions alike. Embodied social relations are historically contingent and sedimented; subjectively transitory and affecting; and socially operant and involuntary. In our contemporary class society, they include gender, race, sexuality, and ability.

The rationale for the focus on embodied social relations under capitalism in this book is threefold:

1) Embodied social relations and their relationship to class are often deemed of secondary importance in marxism. As a result, while marxism flourished in the areas of political economy and philosophy of the categories of political economy, marxist sociology and social thought lagged behind in responding to the exigencies of our time. What is at stake here is not a disciplinary interest, but the rigidification and reduction of marxism into a one-sided praxial project – especially, at a historical moment when all its insights are required to illuminate the way forward, lest we descend into life-denying global right-wing barbarism.

2) The socio-political realities of our time find their expressions more and more in gendered, racialized, and sexualized forms of consciousness. Even a cursory look at daily papers, social media, and cultural productions suffices to demonstrate this increasing tendency. Therefore, it is of utmost importance that the conceptual and methodological place that embodied social relations occupy in contemporary marxist social thought is clarified and assessed in order to determine whether this existing place constitutes an epistemologically valid ground for the production of transformative knowledge.

3) The focus on embodied social relations under capitalism offers a particular analytical vantage point because it requires the examination of the ways in which the relationship between embodied social relations and class is established in the works of different contemporary thinkers. From this vantage point, conceptual practices of contemporary marxist social thought can be productively conducted. Such an examination reveals whether these practices actually belong to Marx's thought, or they impose themselves onto various marxist-identified theories from non-marxist sources of thought. It is important to note that what is at stake here is not some theoretical purity, but mistaking these external sources for Marx's thought, thereby forsaking a thorough exploration of

what his thought can offer to understanding and changing the problems of our present historical moment.

VI Embodied Social Relations in Contemporary Marxist Social Thought

In the last decade, two related developments in marxist social thought have proved particularly apposite for the critique I undertake in *Grounding Critique*. The first has been the increasing marxist engagement with intersectionality. The salience and ascendency of intersectionality has brought race, gender, sexuality, and other social relations to the fore of contemporary intellectual and political agendas. In response to this, contemporary marxist feminists, who have been long dealing with gender as an extra-class social relation, have begun to elaborate on how they understand embodied social relations under capitalism in a more theoretically sophisticated and informed way.

The second development has been the emergence and popularity of social reproduction theory. Building on earlier political economy analyses of marxist feminism, social reproduction theory has claimed to be a unitary theory of exploitation and oppression. This passage from political economy to the realm of social thought has been accomplished through intersectionality. By fashioning itself as a marxist-feminist alternative to intersectionality, social reproduction theory has declared its remit to be encompassing not only class and gender, but race and other social relations as well.

Combined, these recent developments in marxist social thought have provided me with the investigative objects of this book, the epistemological locales through which I conduct my examination of the ways in which embodied social relations are mobilized in contemporary marxist social thought. Therefore, instead of undertaking the impossible task of examining the whole of marxist social thought, in Part I of *Grounding Critique*, I focus on contemporary marxist feminism, and, in Part II, on social reproduction theory. Admittedly, these two bodies of knowledge are too vast and expanding to pronounce any exhaustive and final judgement upon. However, considering the objective of my research, which is not to pass such pronouncements, but to critically explore the most common and dominant uses of embodied social relations and their conceptual consequences, the inexhaustible nature of the field does not pose a methodological problem for my study. Rather, it obligates that I provide the rationale for my choices of the particular texts and thinkers for the critical examination I undertake in this book.

VII A Brief Note on Intersectionality

Before such a necessary provision, however, it is imperative that I offer a brief note on intersectionality. Both the contemporary marxist-feminist theorists and social reproduction theorists with whom I engage in this book are occupied with intersectionality. In their work, intersectionality functions as the academic and political common sense of our time to which contemporary marxist social thought responds. It is during their critique of intersectionality and efforts to supplement and supplant intersectionality that their accounts of embodied social relations under capitalism take a definite form and content. This form and content, in turn, clarifies these theorists' mobilization of Marx's and marxist social thought. It also reveals the non-marxist, classical sociological sources of their thinking, even though these sources often remain imperceptible when cloaked in a language of marxist politics.

I must, thus, register that, in *Grounding Critique*, I do not perform a critique of intersectionality. Nor do I proffer an analytical defense of it. Rather, I scrutinize marxist-feminists' and social reproduction theorists' critiques of intersectionality in order to understand their concept formations of embodied social relations under capitalism, as well as the analytical consequences of these formations. My engagement with intersectionality is conditioned by this objective of this book and the methodological close reading through which I accomplish this objective. Therefore, in this book, I do not assess the validity of the various analytical charges that are launched against intersectionality by contemporary marxist-feminists and social reproduction theorists. Instead, I examine what these charges reveal and from what conceptual standpoint they are rendered possible. However, considering the importance of ethical politics of knowledge production, I do refer the reader and the critics to the intersectional literature in my footnotes when contemporary marxist-feminism's and social reproduction theory's charges are factually incorrect and display a severe lack of knowledge of the literature.

VIII A Marxist-Feminist Symposium on Intersectionality

Having provided the note on intersectionality above, I now turn to the explanation of the choice of the bodies of knowledge with which I engage in Part I and II of *Grounding Critique*, and to the themes of my exposition in these parts. Across both parts of this book, I exercise a methodological close reading that reveals the concept formation of embodied social relations and their relationships to class. In Part I, where I examine the embodied social relations in contemporary marxist feminist thought, I focus on *Science and Society*'s 2018 symposium on intersectionality. The reason for my decision is that, to the present date, *Science and Society*'s symposium remains the only special issue of a journal of marxist thought and analysis that focuses on intersectionality.[6] Furthermore, the contributors to this symposium whose work I examine have been at the forefront of marxist-feminist knowledge production for decades, and are considered to be some of the most theoretically robust contemporary thinkers of this tradition.[7] As it can be seen in Part 1, their articulations of embodied social relations are not only the analytical distillation of their important work. These distillations also represent the main theoretical formation of contemporary marxist-feminism in the way that these theorists mobilize the foundational concepts of social thought. The analytical coherence of these contributions, which is achieved through the intertextuality between them, moreover, allows for a methodological examination of the conceptual whole in which contemporary marxist-feminism produces its knowledge claims.

In the course my exposition in Part 1, I first establish a framework of methodological inquiry that focuses on concept formation to analyze contemporary marxist-feminist engagements with intersectionality. Then, I demonstrate that during these engagements, contemporary marxist-feminist thinkers, whose contributions I examine, produce analyses of embodied social relations and

---

6 Considering the omnipresence of intersectionality, this claim is rather unbelievable. However, to the best of my knowledge, it is true. It is important to note that, to be sure, my claim is limited by the language in which it is expressed. The possible existence of non-anglophone special issues and collections on the subject is beyond the remit of the truth content of this claim. The same year as the Symposium, in 2018, *Historical Materialism: Research in Critical Marxist Theory* published a special issue on identity politics, in which some articles discussed intersectionality. Although this conflation between identity politics and intersectionality is often exercised, it constitutes scant reason as to why one should consider this issue to be on intersectionality.

7 These contributors are Hester Eisenstein, Martha E. Gimenez, Barbara Foley, and Lise Vogel. The only contribution to the Symposium that I do not examine in Part 1 is that of Shana A. Russell, "Intersectionality: A Young Scholar Responds." The reason for this is that Russell's response does not focus on the use of embodied social relations in contemporary marxist-feminist thought. It does not, therefore, meet the criterion of engagement for the objective of this book. However, Russell's response is worth reading on its own merits. In her response, Russell reminds that "[w]hile the majority of the world's workers are people of color, the most visible and celebrated theorists, past and present, are, with a few exceptions, white men. This is not a challenge that can be overcome by reasserting the primacy of Marxist theory. Marxism's answer to intersectionality should be to consider the ways that gender and race, as social dimensions of difference, broaden our understanding of capitalism and class exploitation" (Russell, 2018: 291).

their relationship to class through the mobilization of core concepts in social and sociological thought. Staying with the analytical tension present within these texts and tracing the unfolding of these thinker's knowledge claims and propositions, I show that contemporary marxist-feminism operates through a set of conceptual binaries. In my exposition, the themes through which I analyze these binaries include: the base versus the superstructure; mode of production versus social formation; class-as-structuration versus class-as-culture; critical marxist epistemology versus general sociology of knowledge; theory versus practice; understanding versus action; and the nomothetic versus the idiographic. Through the analysis of these themes, my critique in Part I demonstrates the following:

1) The concept formation and conceptual practices in the works of these contemporary marxist-feminists rehearse the well-known antinomies of classical sociological reason.
2) Contrary to the claims of these theorists, these formations and practices do not belong to Marx's social thought. And they summon marxist class politics only to deliver them out of the aporias these formations and practices produce.
3) Contemporary marxist-feminist thought, as represented by these thinkers, separates history, society, and the subject. This separation stymies the possibilities of both understanding embodied social relations and producing transformative knowledge for social change.

IX   Embodied Social Relations in Social Reproduction Theory

In Part II of *Grounding Critique*, I examine social reproduction theory to assess whether it contributes to a marxist understanding of embodied social relations. The rationale for this decision of the object of analysis is social reproduction theory's claim to be a unitary social theory of exploitation and oppression. This claim suggest that social reproduction theory offers an account of embodied social relations and their relationship to class. In fact, it is this claim that accounts for the recent and increasing popularity of social reproduction theory within contemporary marxist social thought as an alternative to intersectionality. Social reproduction theory's intellectual and political relationship to socialist- and marxist-feminism, and its self-conscious efforts both to come to terms with this relationship and to include race and racialization into its analytical framework render it a particularly appropriate object of analysis for this book.

In Part II, I forward that social reproduction theory's claim to be a unitary social theory of exploitation and oppression hinges on its relationship to intersectionality because the move from gender-class analytics to an integration of race and racialization is effected in response to intersectionality. Yet, I show that social reproduction theory's relationship to intersectionality remains unelaborated and less than clear in the literature. In the course of clarifying this relationship, I conduct a methodological close reading of concept formation in the works of the main progenitors of social reproduction theory.[8] This close reading analyzes the following themes in social reproduction theory: the specific analytical moves through which it attempts to remedy the structuralist and functionalist accounts of embodied social relations in earlier social reproduction analyses; the ontological, epistemological, and methodological propositions of its unitarian structure; social reproduction theory's constant separation between method and systems in the bodies of knowledge with which it engages; its conflation between ontology and politics as a way of issuing validity for its knowledge claims; and the steps it takes to effect a dialectical overcoming of intersectionality. Through the analyses of these themes, my critique in Part II demonstrates the following:

1) Social reproduction theory cannot be validly and soundly argued to be a social theory because its concept formation and its selection and articulation of social problems do not methodologically integrate embodied social relations – in particular, race and racialization – into the theory's analytical framework.

2) Social reproduction theory merely imports embodied social relations from intersectionality without undertaking the necessary conceptual labour. Therefore, while it recognizes the existence of these relations and the systems of oppressions they stand for, social reproduction theory does not produce a marxist account of these relations through which sensuous human practical activity and their genuine contradictions may be grasped.

3) The unitarian character of social reproduction theory is constructed formalistically through the ontological entrenchment of a quasi-transcendental structure of explanation; the epistemological deployment of a unitarian phraseology in this structure; and the resultant methodological circuit in which all social phenomena, irrespective of their

---

8 Although there has been a proliferation of publications on social reproduction theory, Susan Ferguson's, Tithi Bhattacharya's, and David McNally's works remains as the constant reference in virtually every piece of writing on the subject. It is the works of these thinkers that I mainly focus on in Part II.

specificity, are conjugated into the initial metacritical structure using unitarian phraseology. Yet, this unitarian theory does not help explain the relationship between history, society, and the subject. Instead, it corroborates its own analytical presuppositions and propositions.

x   A Conceptual Ground Clearing to Return to Marx

In closing this introduction, I hope that the methodological close reading that I perform in *Grounding Critique* contributes to the project of knowledge production for transformative social change. The shortcomings I identify in these literatures belong more to our collective conceptual consciousness in marxist social thought than to the works of the individual theorists I examine. My intention, in carrying out this project, has been to demonstrate that we must cultivate a methodological self-reflexivity in relation to the concepts we use and the social problems that we should like to address.

Therefore, I hope that this book serves as a critical exhortation to re-evaluate the core concepts of marxist social thought and to realize that these concepts function more according to their meanings in mainstream social and sociological thought than according to Marx's social thought. Given the rigidification and misapprehension prevalent in contemporary marxist social theory, I argue that a conceptual ground clearing is imperative to return to Marx. Such a return is possible only collectively. I would consider my training in social and sociological thought to have been put to a good-enough use if I were able to begin fulfilling my part of this collective responsibility with *Grounding Critique*.

PART I

Embodied Social Relations
in Contemporary Marxist-Feminism

∴

1 Introduction

The year 2024 marks the 35th anniversary of Kimberlé Crenshaw's coining of the term intersectionality. Since the coining, there has been volumes of engagement with intersectionality from many different theoretical and political orientations. Even a cursory library catalogue search proves the existence of an ever-growing literature on intersectionality. The aim of this first part of *Grounding Critique*, however, is not to offer a historiography of intersectionality. Nor is it to perform an engagement with the intersectionality literature in its entirety. Rather, this part focuses on contemporary marxist-feminist engagements with intersectionality. To be sure, over the years some marxists have been in dialogue with intersectionality, mostly through the critique of identity politics. However, it was not until recently that this engagement came to the fore of marxist knowledge production in the field of social theory.

I celebrate the proliferating marxist-feminist engagements with intersectionality not only because it helps to establish the categories of experience as genuine objects of knowledge and investigation within marxism and, therefore, once again makes marxism relevant in the contemporary political landscape. But also –and even more importantly– I believe that such engagements help us reorient marxism back to non-ideological considerations of life as it is actually and concretely lived. Marx's thought and marxism, which I consider to be offering a profound methodological orientation towards the production of knowledge for revolutionary social transformation, are most fecund when we turn to comprehending how the embodied social relations of sensuous human praxis, as the necessary condition of making history, are actualized.

In this part of the book, I thematize, problematize, and critique the recent uses of intersectionality in contemporary marxist-feminist social theory. Rather than offering an alternative or another 'corrective' account to intersectionality, I cultivate a methodological vigilance to the phenomena intersectionality reveals. That is, understanding and analyzing embodied social relations – such as, race, class, and gender – under contemporary capitalism. I take this methodological vigilance to be a historical materialist reckoning with our time, and I understand my own work as shifting the conceptual ground of the marxist discussions examining embodied social relations – the need for which becomes clear in what follows. In order to sharpen the framework within which I argue for this shift, I provide a brief sketch of how I understand embodied social relations and their relationships with one another in contemporary class societies. However, this sketch remains necessarily incomplete because I believe that prior to the thorough critique of existing marxist accounts of embodied social relations, one cannot produce a novel substantive account of these relations. The process of concept formation for such an account methodologically demands that the labour of critique is completed. Therefore, the account I proffer is a preliminary one that helps generate questions for the critique I undertake in *Grounding Critique*. Having set up the problematic of this part, which is the relationship between contemporary marxist-feminism and intersectionality, and offered a preliminary account of embodied social relations, I perform a methodological close reading of important recent marxist-feminist critiques of intersectionality. This reading follows the internal unfolding and structure of these critiques and reveals the conceptual presuppositions and methodological problems in contemporary marxist-feminisms.

In Part 1, I demonstrate that concept formation and conceptual practices of contemporary marxist-feminism operate more through the antinomies of classical sociological reason than through Marx's thought. Thus, I suggest that contemporary marxist-feminist theorists separate Marx's thought and marxist politics, and summon the latter only when their analysis reaches a conceptual impasse as they analyze embodied social relations through a critique of intersectionality. Specifically, I examine the symposium on intersectionality that appeared in *Science and Society: A Journal of Marxist Thought and Analysis*, which "is the longest continuously published Marxist scholarly journal in the world."[1]

This symposium contains the most comprehensive, crisp, and consistent marxist-feminist critiques of intersectionality. The symposiasts, with whom I engage, are considered to be among the most renowned marxist-feminists. They include Hester Eisenstein, Martha Gimenez, Barbara Foley, and Lise Vogel. Their decades long contributions to marxist-feminism have helped broaden the focus of marxist social analyses. I treat their contributions to the symposium on intersectionality as the distillation of their thinking on embodied social relations and suggest that engaging with these texts offers an important opportunity to revise and re-evaluate the often-used-but-unelaborated concepts in marxist social theory. Below I begin my analysis by problematizing the relation between intersectionality and marxism, through which embodied social relations as an object of knowledge emerges in contemporary marxist-feminism.

---

1 "Science & Society: A Journal of Marxist Thought and Analysis," Guilford Press, accessed 21.09.2019, https://www.guilford.com/journals/Science-Society/Editor/00368237/summary.

II Intersectionality

Intersectionality has been an important concept since its inception in the 1980s, coinciding with the projects of deconstructing the supposed singularity of the subject. It has been taken up by many, sometimes indicating a methodology, an epistemology, or a theory. Intersectionality has been used in courtrooms, policy debates, activist meetings, and in academia. Independent of the different contexts and goals in which it has been situated, intersectionality both emphasizes the multiplicity of social identity categories, and the experiential convergence of these identities in individual and collective bodies. It has been oriented towards fighting the injustice, exploitation, oppression, and domination that are inflicted on these bodies in the everyday accumulation of ongoing violent histories. In other words, in its every evocation, intersectionality has been undeniably political.

Intersectionality has usually been associated with identity politics because it disrupted the ideological functioning of some identity categories by supplementing them with other identity categories. In so doing, intersectionality has sought to generate a better mapping of the social landscape of power dynamics. For instance, the proclamation "all women are white, all blacks are men, but some of us are brave" (Hull, Bell-Scot, and Smith, 1982) served as a corrective to the constant erasure of the experiences of Black women in different institutional and political settings, nuancing these categories by bringing the lived reality of social injustices. Intersectionality has provided an actionable and operationable language to the marginalized who do not always find a room or representation, even in left politics and marxist theory that address issues of social injustice.

In this respect, intersectional politics might be argued to be a thorough reconsideration of new social and political movements of the 1960s in which each category (e.g., women's movements, civil rights, gay rights, etc.) was thought to be representing the interests of a more or less undifferentiated group of people. Within this historical context, intersectionality usefully showed how each category and embodied social relation was in relation with another. According to intersectionality, in order to address the issues of social injustice we need to grapple with the inter-relations of these social relations. This model of identity politics necessarily incited a response from the marxist-identified left, which, during the 1960s, had pointed out the weakness of social atomism at the core of new social movements and asserted the primacy of class as a response to this social atomism.[2] However, intersectionality was able to address this weakness of identity politics not by positing class as primary, but by acknowledging it as an axis of social injustice. By this move, class was dethroned, although still preserving the possibility of being, at best, a *primus inter pares* under peculiar circumstances.

Any critical engagement with intersectionality ought to realize that intersectionality does not have a singular meaning. This is not the customary rejoinder that 'such and such is never a monolith.' To be sure, there are different strands in the conceptualization of intersectionality. However, what I want to draw attention to is not this conceptual heterogeneity, but the heteroglossia of intersectionality – the multiple standpoints, locales, discourses, and genres from which intersectionality is effected. For instance, depending on where it is brought about, intersectionality might become a principle of political organizing; an institutional(ized) tool of bureaucratic reason; another name for identity; an individualistic concept; a collective concept; a struggle concept of epistemology; a methodological approach in research design; an ethical imperative; a token in neoliberal management strategies; a philosophical concept; an adjective of the zeitgeist; an indicator of political sensibility; a desire and invitation for openness; a worldview; and a transformative tool for social justice. These different uses of intersectionality are, of course, not completely indivisible from one another. They pass into one another in their auxiliary kinship; they themselves are intersectional in their deployments. However, these different meanings are not fully coincident with one another either. And, therefore, I argue that it is often quite possible to discern these different meanings during the temporal unfolding of the narrative structures in which they are situated.

Because marxist social theory is not a mere exercise in logomachy and picture-thinking, I suggest that marxist engagements need to exercise great analytical caution so as not to conflate these very different and often contradictory uses of intersectionality. As I show in this part of *Grounding Critique*, the predominant modes of engagement with intersectionality in contemporary marxism-feminism are: 1) adopting neoliberal mobilizations of the concept and reducing every other possible meaning of intersectionality to this function;[3] 2) fixating on the metaphor of intersections and substituting the critique of concept with that of the metaphor; and 3) focusing on the additive

---

2 For the relationship between marxism and new social movements, see Boggs, 1986, and Crossley, 2022.
3 To be sure, the 'institutional capture' of intersectionality, like any other nominal and ideological uses, calls for an immanent critique, and this critique is already conducted within the intersectionality literature itself.

deployments of intersectionality and arguing in favour of non-additive modalities.[4] Throughout this book, I demonstrate that these are neither the most politically fecund way of engaging with contemporary activist communities, nor a rigorous way of producing the knowledge necessary for revolutionary social transformation.

III   Some Methodological Propositions for a Marxist Engagement with Intersectionality

Rather than rehearsing the above three modes, I argue that a marxist engagement with intersectionality must organize itself in the orbit of the following fundamental questions:

1. How are intersectional phenomena in general (as opposed to in particular) possible?
2. How do the relations that intersectionality point to appear as constructive of social phenomena?
3. In what kind of societies and under what historical circumstances, does intersectionality appear?
4. How do intersectional phenomena show up in particular?
5. Why do so many activists, who genuinely desire a better world, feel that intersectionality captures their political imagination?[5]

I suggest that these questions help shift marxist social theory from remaining within the conceptual field intersectionality sets up and being forced to assume an unproductive for-or-against stance towards intersectionality. Rather, they forward the need for marxist social theory to develop a robust account of embodied social relations and their relationship with one another under capitalism.

Needless to say, within the capitalist mode of production, the economy and the economic have an epistemic privilege. This has often been a point of confusion and contention both within marxist and non-marxist social theory,

---

[4] These modes of engagement are not peculiar to contemporary marxist-feminism. As I demonstrate in Part II, social reproduction theorists also operate within these modes in their relationship to intersectionality.

[5] In these questions, by appearance, showing up, and phenomenality of intersectionality, I do not inscribe a hackneyed, non-Hegelian appearance vs. reality dichotomy, according to which the concerns of intersectionality would be at best only symptoms, or at worst illusions of a deeper reality. For me the phenomenality of intersectionality is as essential as the so-called deeper reality.

resulting in the well-worn *base and superstructure metaphor* and its clarifications and critiques from multiple theoretical positions. In fact, the history of marxist social theory could be read productively through this debate. For instance, the Stalin-era Soviet marxism's defence of base/superstructure (Buzuev and Gorodnov, 1987); Plekhanov's embrace of the metaphor (Plekhanov, 1940); Lifshitz's critique in relation to Marx's philosophy of art (Lifshitz, 1973); Pashukanis' work on legal superstructure (Pashukanis, 1978); Gramsci elaboration of political society and civil society (Forgacs, 1988); Althusser's overdetermination and determination in the last instance (Althusser, 1977); Williams' clarification via the dominant, residual, and emergent (Williams, 1977); Hall's rethinking of the formulation (Hall, 1977); Rodney's analysis of superstructure in the colonial context (Rodney, 1972); Cabral's reflections on the role of culture in anti-colonial struggles (Cabral, 1974); Poulantzas' analysis of the state (Poulantzas, 1978); Laclau and Mouffe's semiotic marxism (Laclau and Mouffe, 1985); the Frankfurt School's and its American versions' rejection of the term (Lijster, 2017); and Freudo-Marxism's and Left Lacanians' focus on the relationship between desire, sex, and economy (Stavrakakis, 2007). To be sure, this list is not at all comprehensive and is only meant to be a reminder of some classical marxist positions, and the unresolved nature of ongoing debates.

In these debates, while the base stands in for the economy and class, which is the unit of analysis for economic relations of private property and exploitation, the superstructure names different social structures, such as the state, culture, education, law, arts, the political, colonial domination, family, and even the human psyche itself. The explicit subjective categories of the former are the bourgeoise and the proletariat, whereas the implicit subjective categories of the latter are, first and foremost, gender, race, and sexuality. What is important to note is the shift in which the way the economy and class are counterposed to what latterly has become the categories of difference, such as gender, race, and sexuality. In the classical elaborations of the base and superstructure analyses, embodied social relations of gender, race, and sexuality were always moored to – if not an effect of – those social structures. After the new social movements, or what others might call the turn to identity politics, these categories came to be counterposed to class directly, without the mediation of those social structures. This does not mean that the critical analysis of structures was abandoned. Rather, I suggest that this unmooring is an indication of the material and discursive change in the social organization of life, which further subsumed these social structures into the demands of the capitalist economy by way of privatization, deregulation, neoliberalism, and financialization, and consequently launched embodied social relations into society itself, rendering them to be the *general* experiential categories of life.

Put differently, it is not the autonomy of those social structures, which was the focus in the above cited debates on base and superstructure, but the very heteronomy of them, which is achieved through specific forms of ongoing primitive accumulation, e.g., the decimation of welfare states, that generalized the embodied social relations as actual – not, ideological – categories of human praxis under contemporary capitalism. However, this is not a mere levelling of these social relations vis-à-vis class. In my analysis, class is an immediate social relation, whereas others are mediated social relations in their relationship to the contemporary capitalist mode of production. And their mediation takes different shapes in the course of social life.

It is important to highlight that by this distinction, I do not mean to reinscribe the analytic primacy of class. The problematic of 'analytic primacy,' for me, needs to be commensurate to the object of social inquiry in question. To put simply, my methodological contention is that one cannot begin their critical analysis already knowing what the primary unit of analysis will be prior to a thorough examination of the given social situation. For this would be simply an act of self-corroboration: positing an explanatory concept in an *a priori* fashion, which then delineates the limits of legitimate explanation itself as the subtending reality of social phenomena.

This is not a simple interdiction against tautological structure in the processes of knowledge production. In fact, I would unequivocally defend, not the primacy, but the presupposition of the actuality of class as an entry point into social inquiry in order to discover the conditions of its possibility. In such a methodological structure, what is arrived at would no longer be *how class effects the 'totality' of given social formation*, but rather it would be *how class is affected and mediated by other social relations in the social formation in question*, and *how this affecting and mediating would enable and disable its capacity of effecting and impacting upon the given social formation of life*. Here, class does not require an anxious alibi under the auspices of analytic primacy, but is recovered as a concept through which we can better comprehend how living human praxis is achieved, as Marx himself intends it to be.

If I do not mean to reinscribe the analytic primacy of class by suggesting that class is an immediate social relation, whereas the others are mediated social relations, what do I mean? Mediation and immediation are intercessory passages through which different social relations form their significations in the capitalist mode of production, which is marked by an ongoing superimposition of the economic on the non-economic and extra-economic, or the latter's subsumption by the former. Before moving any further, a clarification of terms is in order: I do not use the economic as a synonym for the material and, therefore, its other is not immaterial. Under capitalism, the economy is often understood as the reality, or the material base of life; however, as Marx shows us, it is merely the ideological double of reality, which exists by striving to annex all aspects of life through violence and super/exploitation. Class, on the one hand, as a social relation of private property and exploitation cuts across all other social relations without compromising its own haecceity. On the other hand, to be sure, all other social relations too are motile and dynamic in their relationship to one another and to class, such that their passages in and through one another renders an ipseity of their own impossible.

If the historical actualization of embodied sensuous subjective human praxis as life is our beginning point for a historical materialist social investigation (Marx and Engels, 1976) it would then follow that the foundation of the economy consists of the immanent realities of embodied subjective experience, despite the fact that ongoing capitalist processes of dispossession and exploitation substitute the economic ideal – in the capitalist sense – for the real.[6] My argument here is not one of simple reversal of the base and superstructure metaphor. Namely, the real is social relations of gender, race, sexuality, ability etc., and they are the real base, or the substrata of life. Such an interpretation would constitute the re-inscription of the autonomous spheres thesis that animates classical debates on base and superstructure. It is, therefore, of cardinal importance to remember that my analysis arrived at this point by arguing that any presupposition that institutions of the so-called superstructure are autonomous particularizes the social relations of embodied experience (gender, race, sexuality etc.) to the specific institution in and through which they are operationable. On the contrary, I argue that it is the heteronomy of these institutions that generalizes these relations as categories of embodied sensuous subjective human praxis.[7]

IV The Generalization of Embodied Social Relations as the Categories of Subjective Human Life

This generalizing is a result of a continual historical process. Thus, it *is* real. However, positing these categories of embodied experience as *the real* would be mistaken because the condition of their possibility is indeed inflected by

---

6 Here my argument draws on Michel Henry's phenomenology of Marx's thought. See Henry, 1983.
7 With the characteristic analytical and strategic acumen of his conjunctural imagination, Stuart Hall reflects on the history of generalization in a 2008 interview with Les Black. See, Hall, 2019. For my elaboration of Hall's conjunctural imagination see, Tanyildiz, 2024.

the capitalist subsumption of life by the economy, as the ideological double of reality. Therefore, I submit that social relations that are congealed as the categories of embodied sensuous human praxis have a twofold nature – that is, ideological and real. Because it is so easy to slip back into the customary ways of practical and theoretical thinking, I must underline that here the ideological and the real do not belong to two different archeological planes to be dissected, discovering the real beyond the ideological. They are the copula of how we actualize our human praxis. In other words, it must be emphasized that the inflective work of the capitalist subsumption of life by economy does not merely generate the categories of embodied experience by conjugating them in accordance with economic imperatives. If this were to be the case, we could in fact, like some marxist-feminists do, talk about articulating or disarticulating social relations of class, gender, race, sexuality etc. in and through one another.[8] In my analysis, the generalization of the social relations of embodiment as the categories of subjective human life is inflected through the ideological economic double. This inflection is morphological, altering and mediating how we experience our embodied social relations. And it is this morphological inflection in our sphere of immanence that generates the content of social relations of class, which otherwise is an empty eidos of capitalism in its irreducible immediacy. Summarily put, I suggest that through the generalization of the categories of embodied experience, their twofold nature, and morphological inflection, the relationship between class, gender, race, sexuality, etc. could be reconsidered.

To be sure, such reconsiderations have been done time and time again. In order to draw attention to the differences of the account I proffer here from that of other reconsiderations, let me provide a brief overview of them in social thought. When the first symptoms of this generalization of embodied social relations demonstrated itself in the streets as the new social movements of the 1960s, each category of embodied experience (e.g., women's movements, civil rights, gay rights, etc.) was interpreted as representing the interests of undifferentiated groups of people. As mentioned earlier, an important strand of marxist responses to this new development was to point out the weakness of social segmentation at the core of these social movements and to assert the primacy of class as a response to this social segmentation. Critical strands of post-structuralist feminism and queer theory were able to capture the aporetic impossibility of thinking of these categories as atomistic, as having an ipseity of their own. However, these post-structuralist analyses often did not consider

---

8 See, Mojab and Carpenter, 2019.

the formation and deformation of the categories of embodied social relations in history and with respect to capitalism. In turn, they were often dismissed by the majority of marxist literature with the charges of linguistic idealism and, ironically, for committing to identity politics. Against this 'retreat from class' (Wood, 1986), marxist-feminists sought a unitary analysis of oppression and exploitation. Such a unitary analysis was considered to be possible because of an imputed totality of capitalism, which required the analytic primacy of class to be reasserted. Not only was this reassertion far from capturing the *generality* of experiential categories of life, but also the emphasis on unitary analysis and totality did not help uncovering the capitalist subsumption of life by the economy. Intersectionality emerged as an attempt to consider all embodied experiences and social relations in the analysis of social injustice. In this framework of analysis, class was but an axis of injustice, among many other axes.

The above overview, to be sure, is only meant to be a cartographic groping towards a cursory sketch, rather than a thorough historiography, of such reconsiderations. I suggest that each of these above reconsiderations respond to the base and superstructure metaphor either directly, or indirectly. This is not due to some analytical superiority of the metaphor itself, nor is it due to a lack of sophistication among the social theorists. Rather, it is because the twofold character of the general categories of embodied sensuous human praxis (i.e., of them being ideological and real *at once*) is not adequately emphasized and analyzed.

Contemporary anti-racist, feminist, and anti-oppression strands of marxism, under the auspices of dialectical and/or historical materialism, focus on the general categories of embodied sensuous human praxis as ideological. They do not in the least deny the violent realities of patriarchy, sexism, racism, and heteronormativity. On the contrary, they recognize the necessity of abolishing such atrocities everywhere in society. However, in their analyses, these categories, in whose name people are violated *and* defend themselves, are considered to be ideological outcomes of real material processes. Such analyses are most robust when gender and race are under scrutiny, whereas they tend to become tenuous when it comes to sexuality and other embodied social relations. For instance, in these analyses, gendered power relations originate in the sexual division of labour (Ebert, 1996); race and racism originate in slavery and other imperialist and colonialist practices of capitalism (Meyerson, 2000); and heteronormativity and homonormativity are connected to the history of capitalism by materializing the research done by mainly post-structuralist and other sexuality scholars (Hennessy, 2000; Drucker, 2015).

In short, contemporary marxist social theory accepts the materiality of these social relations, but only through the stripping their ideological functions in relation to an originary historical process of class relations. While such genetic structural analyses are important, the phenomenological aspects of embodied social relations often remain unelaborated in these analyses. Historical accounts of genetic origins do not explain how they are lived concretely, in the here and now. These relations are not generated for once and for all. They are remade in people's subjective lives in an ongoing fashion, thereby themselves becoming generative of other social relations. It is this generalization of these embodied social relations as subjective human praxis that is the historical mark of our times. And contemporary marxist social theory often leaves them unelaborated. As a result, in Himani Bannerji's words, the 'feminist,' 'anti-racist,' 'anti-oppression' components of these marxisms become "an uncritical adoption of an essentialist or idealist subjectivist position, just as much as the 'marxist' component [becomes] an objective idealism" (Bannerji, 1995: 80).

Intersectional analyses, on the other hand, do focus on the categories of embodied social relations as material relations. Different categories of these relations interact as a relationship of *inter pares* in an open ended matrix, always in anticipation of the emergence of a different category, or permutation of existing ones – as though, these relations are "spontaneous, or found objects on the ground of ontology" (Bannerji, 2001: 3). It is precisely because of this undetermined openness and the representation of these material relations as the absolute real of life that intersectionality leaves the subsumption of life by the economy under the capitalist mode of production unelaborated. The levelling of the social relations of embodied experience and class in the sphere of materiality might be argued to be a genuinely important political move, which helps to bring traditionally neglected and omitted social relations to the fore. However, I argue that such a move universalizes these social relations, as opposed to help us investigate the generalization of them as the experiential categories of the corporeal sensuous subjective human praxis in relation to our actualization of life.

Contrary to common sense, solely focusing on the reality of these categories and leaving their ideological aspects unelaborated does not help us produce a better phenomenological account. Such a framework of analysis cannot adequately capture the generalization of these categories as the ongoing double passage between the particular and the universal. Each intersection is particular and situated; however, the constituents of these intersections are universal. For otherwise we would not be able to locate and name the specific place of each intersection in the matrix. As a result, subjects are rendered to be merely the incarnation of categories of embodied experience, as opposed to experiencing social beings. This reduction of the phenomenological notion of experience into a structure of experience also produces a temporal capture in the future anterior by already having a room for possible subjects and their experiences in advance of their appearance. The absolute coincidence between subjects and categories of embodied experience diminishes the possibility of an ontological pluralism, which can resist the subsumption of life in different forms and makes possible a production of knowledge for revolutionary social transformation.

To summarize, I argue that both contemporary marxist social theory's affirmation of the analytic primacy of the economy and class relations as being material and capable of generating other material relations, and intersectionality's opening of the sphere of materiality up to other embodied social relations reproduce, albeit unintentionally, the base and superstructure metaphor. Furthermore, both approaches circumvent the conceptual role of lived experience in comprehending the actualization of embodied sensuous human praxis. This unintentional reproduction results in the positing of a series of totalizing coincidences between life, the economy, and embodied experiences in contemporary marxist social theory, and between experiences, bodies, and their conceptualizations in intersectionality.

In the context of the growing inequality, immiseration, and proto-fascistic politics on a global scale, of course, we must politically mobilize the insights of both contemporary marxism and intersectionality (notwithstanding their limitations) to defend the rights and freedoms of the oppressed everywhere. Against these growing atrocities, we must unite urgently under whatever strategies and tactics are possible. However, we must at the same time remember the disjointed gap between political action and philosophical comprehension. This gap cannot be simply covered over through the force of pure action, nor pure understanding. In this way, action and its comprehension are always historically embedded and always in relation to one another, yet never coincident with each other. The failure of recognizing this gap often results in sectarianism and other purist approaches, and, therefore, stymies political action itself.

I argue that despite the difficult times we find ourselves in globally, we need to develop an account of the relationship between class and other social relationships that would overcome the base and superstructure metaphor. This account ought to be able to conceptualize the generalization of the embodied social relations of experience as the sensuous subjective human praxis, their twofold nature, and morphological inflection. As I have demonstrated above, neither contemporary marxist theory nor intersectionality are fully capable of such a conceptualization. I suggest that this conceptualization of embodied social relations under capitalism might be possible only by rediscovering class as the irreducibly immediate social relation of private property and exploitation, which is the empty eidos of the capitalist mode of production. Moreover, class, in this account, ought to be understood as actualized in and through the intercessory passages of embodied human praxis as life. And these embodied social relations themselves, in turn, are mediated in the plasticity of their interactions with one another under capitalism.

The spirit of my above consideration of embodied social relations has been exploratory. As I mentioned earlier, rather than offering a fully-fledged marxist theory of embodied social relations under capitalism, here I have provided the conceptual background of previous efforts of examining these social relations, foregrounded the need for producing another account that does not operate within the base and superstructure logic, and investigated the conditions for the possibility of such an account. Thus, my consideration here serves as an incomplete but necessary reference point for the critique of contemporary marxist-feminism's critique of intersectionality in the *Science and Society* symposium.

v   The Framing of the Marxist-Feminist Engagement with Intersectionality

In their very brief exordium, the editors of *Science and Society* identify intersectionality to be "a central concern of much current thinking in critical social science" (Laibman et al., 2018: 248). They explain that the participants of this Symposium seek "a dialectical (recuperative) critique, from the standpoint of a fully elaborated and structural class analysis" (Laibman et al., 2018: 248). A methodological consideration of this aim orients my reading of the Symposium towards the following twofold consideration:

1) It ought to be clear that in seeking a dialectical critique, the editors presuppose the relationship between "race, gender and class, and indeed among these and other sources of social oppression such as sexuality and disability" (Laibman et al., 2018: 248) to be contradictory and internally connected. Moreover, the qualification of this dialectic with a parenthetical recuperation points to another presupposition that undergird this symposium. That is, the belief that separation of these categories is a result of exertion, illness, or loss, and therefore needs to be recovered by a sublated unity.

2) Situating this 'dialectical (recuperative) critique' in "the standpoint of a fully elaborated and structural class analysis" (Laibman et al., 2018: 248), the journal editors reveal their substitution of analytics for subjects. Standpoints as epistemological loci are usually mobilized in relation to the consciousness of individual and collective subjects in (marxist)

social theory – for instance, the bifurcated consciousness of women (Smith, 1990), the double consciousness of African-Americans (Du Bois, 2008), or the revolutionary consciousness of the proletariat (Lukács, 1971). Through the editors' substitution, however, subjects and their consciousness are twice removed from their lived experiences. Put summarily, subjects' relationship to their own experiences is made accessible only by the conceptual representation of their experiences, which constitutes an ideological methodology of social inquiry. Moreover, the adjectival qualification of class analysis being fully elaborated and structural also points out to a potential stricture of the proletarian experience itself vis-à-vis its gendered, racialized, sexualized, and other embodied social relations. Therefore, such a standpoint runs the risk of foreclosing any new (and possibly revolutionary) experience prior to its arising within a given social formation.[9]

Having introduced the Symposium, the journal editors end their exordium with the following question: "Can intersectionality be seen both as an advance over naive identity politics and 'single issue' thinking, and as a barrier to be overcome on the way to a complete Marxist understanding?" (Laibman et al., 2018: 248). It may be argued that the leading marxist-feminist symposiasts contemplate this question in their individual contributions. Below I analyze these contributions by focusing on the ways in which these symposiasts conceptualize embodied social relations and their relationship to class under capitalism.

VI   The Analytic Primacy of Class and the Transformative Pedagogies

The renowned marxist-feminist sociologist, Hester Eisenstein begins her contribution to the Symposium, "Querying Intersectionality," with an anecdote that is rather fitting with the characteristic convivial extemporaneity of the original Greek form of symposiums:

> Imagine my shock and surprise, on opening the November 2016 issue of *Monthly Review*, to find an article entitled 'Intersectionality and Primary Accumulation: Caste and Gender in India under the Sign of Monopoly-Finance Capital' (Whitehead, 2016). OMG! Has the austere Marxist journal of the late Paul Sweezy and Harry Magdoff conceded space to the

---

9 Here it must be emphasized that my argument is not directed at class analyses *per se*, but at their ideological mobilizations.

I-word? This might be a signal that we Marxist–feminists had better get our house in order and decide what to do with this very troubling word/concept.

EISENSTEIN, 2018: 248–249

For Eisenstein, contemporary marxist-feminism's need for a thorough engagement with intersectionality is prompted by its unexpected appearance in one of the most highly regarded marxist journals. And this need does not arise because marxist-feminism should have an account of embodied social relations that is attuned to the lived experiences of the sensuous subjects of history. I suggest that this privileging of the conceptual universe of marxism over the actuality of lived universe of human-beings-in-struggle is consonant with the editors' privileging analytics over subjectivities. The question Eisenstein asks is not: 'does intersectionality help us better understand (and, therefore, help us change) our social organization in this given history and geography?' Instead, her question is: "do we see the widespread use of this concept as a progressive advance in the realms both of scholarship and activism? Or do we see it as a reactionary, misleading and dangerous retreat from Marxist analysis?" (Eisenstein, 2018: 249).

Eisenstein's main issue with intersectionality is "that it undermines the primacy of class" (Eisenstein, 2018: 255). Citing global gendered struggles against ongoing "accumulation by dispossession" (Harvey, 2003), Eisenstein argues that "to make sense of current struggles one cannot overlook the fundamental category of class, defined as our relationship to the means of production" (Eisenstein, 2018: 256). Intersectionality, according to Eisenstein, "obscures class, or more precisely, it muddies the waters so that one can't see clearly the fundamental lines of force that are dividing the planet" (Eisenstein, 2018: 256). In this way, Eisenstein takes the explanatory analytic power of class for granted. However, as I have explained above, for me, class needs to be explained as *founded* upon and *grounded* in the ongoing social division of labour at multiple local and extra-local scales. Construing class this way does not suggest that we overlook its explanatory capacity. Rather, this conceptualization of class reorients us toward the historical and embodied conditions of its very production. And, in fact, I argue that it is this inquiry into the very production of classes that endows the concept of class with explanatory analytic power – as opposed to taking the concept in its self-givenness as the transcendent constant of metaphysics that penetrates through phenomena to the real, which is precisely how 'the analytic primacy thesis' treats class.

Eisenstein also problematizes the compulsory insertion of intersectionality into the course syllabi at her institution, City University of New York. While she does "not want to be misunderstood as essentially trashing the concept [of intersectionality] or those who fought hard to gain acceptance for it" (Eisenstein, 2018: 257), in her view, the requirement of including intersectionality into the curriculum functions solely as a "lip service that does not add to our understanding of the social realities of class, race, and gender, not to mention the other required categories!" (Eisenstein, 2018: 257). To be sure, the mere incantation of 'categories of difference' indeed does not automatically produce a comprehensive account of the nature of embodied social relations. However, if we were to take the inclusion of intersectionality into syllabi not as an immediate production of knowledge, but as a politics and pedagogy of knowledge production, one could easily argue that intersectionality in the classroom might indeed help create the affective structure necessary for, as well as an entry point into, critical social analysis for those students who often feel that they "were never meant to survive" (Lorde, 1995: 31–32) inside and outside academia.

In other words, as I have previously argued, it is important to discern different uses of intersectionality and not to reduce them to one another. Eisenstein may be justified to argue that this institutionally required emphasis on intersectionality might sometimes turn into a "mantra, or checklist" (Eisenstein, 2018: 258), and "water down" (Eisenstein, 2018: 258) a thorough social analysis. However, as teachers in classrooms, I believe that it is our responsibility to engage in insurgent pedagogies to radicalize our students for a better world. We cannot know in advance what will move our students towards the very daunting and often life-long task of revolutionary social transformation. It is not enough to provide what we might think of as the best analysis because the individual (not individualistic) circumstances (material or not) of each student will, at the end, determine their response to our 'correct' analysis. Therefore, the pedagogical use the 'checklist' of intersectionality does not necessarily signify the impossibility of checking all boxes. Instead, I suggest that the longer the checklist the better it is because if we can convincingly demonstrate to our students that even checking a single box is sufficient to get oneself involved in the ongoing struggles for a better world much more actively. Afterall, only in these struggles can one move beyond the 'checklist' towards more nuanced accounts of social organization, as one learns how to swim in a pool not by it.

VII The Ideological Techniques of Bourgeois Management

Having registered her concerns with the institutionalization of intersectionality, Eisenstein's argument takes, to use a rather euphemistic adjective, an interesting turn – a turn from "pay[ing] tribute to [intersectionality], and point[ing] out that its usefulness as an intellectual and political intervention needs to be recognized as a political master stroke by Black women activists and intellectuals" (Eisenstein, 2018: 256) to arguing that "the *true* authors of 'intersectionality' were the small but powerful group of industrialists, who used racism and sexism as organizing principles" (Eisenstein, 2018: 258, my emphasis). According to Eisenstein, "capitalism manipulated and continues to manipulate the categories of race, gender, and sexuality, we are not inventing intersectionality but discovering it!" (Eisenstein, 2018: 259). Considering the historical examples of seventeenth century slavery and the 1930s-1940s textile industry in the U.S. South that Eisenstein mentions in her text, it is not difficult to understand why she should interpret the nature of the relationship between capitalism and the embodied relations of social organization as being one of manipulation. However, as I have previously explained, such formulations overstate the ideological aspect of these relations and entirely misses how they have been generalized as the categories of human praxis in our contemporary moment.

In other words, I argue that embodied social relations are not merely the ideological techniques of bourgeoise management, but are real relations and forms of consciousness through which human praxis is achieved. On the one hand, I agree with Eisenstein that "in a capitalist society, class is not at all the same kind of difference as are race or gender" (Eisenstein, 2018: 259), and above I have provided an account through which this difference can be explained. On the other hand, Eisenstein and I disagree when she argues that "the fundamental difference between owners of the means of production, and those who must sell their labor[-power], is the central cleavage in our societies, no matter how much this is obscured by media representations and indeed, by most mainstream academic literature" (Eisenstein, 2018: 259). Although it is not named as such, here 'media representations' and 'mainstream academic literature' evidently function as the obscuring apparatuses of the superstructure, and the products of this obscuring are gender and race. In fact, Eisenstein states in the very next sentence that "it is within the mode of production that relations of gender and race are, and have been, shaped, whether we are talking about 17th-century slavery in the Americas or 21st-century *maquiladores* on the U.S.–Mexican border" (Eisenstein, 2018: 259).

VIII The Concept of the Mode of Production

In the account I have provided above, the concept of 'mode of production' also figures as a central concept. However, Eisenstein and I treat the concept very differently. For Eisenstein, the mode of production operates as an indeterminate negative concept that is only capable of determining social relations in an *a priori* fashion. For instance, in the example she cites the capitalist mode of production over four centuries seems to have been an unchanging force of shaping gender and race to obscure class relations. However, such an indeterminate shaping neither explains the enormous change in productive forces, production relations, and the maturation of class relations during this period, nor provides an account of the lived realities of gender and race as embodied social relations. In other words, such a conceptualization of the mode of production becomes a metahypothesis "about putative hidden mechanisms which leave unexplained residua at the empirical level" (Sayer, 1977: 150), thus rendering Eisenstein's analysis of intersectionality into a re-writing of the base and superstructure metaphor. I, on the other hand, mobilize mode of production as a determinate positive concept, requiring an account of its continual making, and, at the same time, setting a field of existence for the actualization of the corporeal sensuous subjective human praxis as life. As such, mode of production dispenses with the base and superstructure metaphor altogether.

The mode of production, in Eisenstein's text, spatially functions as an envelope, containing and manipulating its contents to comply with its form. The spatial function of my use of the mode of production is of a horizon, setting the limits of the visible and sensible not because of an innate force that it possesses, but because of the specific coordination, configuration, and contradiction of the embodied sensuous subjective human praxis it collectively produces. To make the implicit explicit, in a use such as Eisenstein's, revolutionary social transformation occurs with the implosion of the present envelop for a future one. If the subjects of history cannot organize such a transformation, the contradiction of productive forces produces this change. My use however suggests that such a change does not require an implosive event – conscious or teleological – but is made in the everyday activities of actual human beings insofar as they are able to alter the subsumption of all aspects of their life by the imperatives of the capitalist economy through a constant remaking of their social relations.

Eisenstein concludes her contribution to the symposium with the following questions: "Is it possible to frame a Marxist analysis that has due regard for issues of gender, race, sexuality and so forth? And if so, how would we proceed?" (Eisenstein, 2018: 260). These questions do accurately represent the spirit of contemporary marxist-feminist theory and are certainly important to reckon with. However, it is also important to remind ourselves that we cannot pretend to be working outside the purview of any social and cultural identity, while indicting others who examine the theories and political practices grounded in embodied social relations such as race, gender, and sexuality as being within the boundaries of identity politics. A pretension of this sort runs the great danger of confining marxism into the bounds of the very identity politics that some of its practitioners condemn by rendering it irrelevant for women, people of colour, queers, trans folks and many more, and thereby asking *whose identity marxism is*. Therefore, for me, the question is less to do with having a 'due regard' for the categories of embodied social relations than having to demonstrate that marxism needs to be made to the measure of life, and it is certainly capable of being so. It is in this spirit that I have engaged with Eisenstein's text. With the same aim of examining the conceptual possibilities of producing a marxist theory of embodied social relations, I continue my engagement with Martha E. Gimenez's contribution to this important symposium.

IX   The Methodological Tension between the Phenomenology and Ontology of the Social

Martha E. Gimenez, who has been at the forefront of contemporary marxist-feminism for decades, begins her article, "Intersectionality: Marxist Critical Observations," by asking whether intersectionality is a theory or a method. Then, she provides her own response to the question: "At best, it is a descriptive approach which, through empirical research, can ascertain the relative contribution of the factors that interest the researcher (gender, ethnicity, national origin) to the problems or issues affecting the research subjects" (Gimenez, 2018: 261).Though Gimenez acknowledges the possible productive uses of this kind of description, in her estimation a methodological mobilization of intersectionality seems to be operationable through the construction of *a priori* theoretical categories by researchers. This assumption might be validated on anti-positivist grounds that researchers might have these categories in their minds as heuristic devices to facilitate the research in question. However, it does not follow that they should impose these theoretical categories on the lived experiences of their research subjects. In fact, the trademark of a 'good' researcher would be a constant critical vigilance practiced reflexively on their own conduct and their relationship with the participants. I would agree with this view and add that intersectionality qua method already operates on this anti-positivist ground.[10]

The construction of *a priori* theoretical categories points to an important methodological consideration. This is partly captured by Gimenez as she notes that these descriptions "assume that race/ethnicity, sexuality and other identities are always socially and economically relevant and are always intersecting and significant in their effects upon all women's lives. They apply to women in general, i.e., to all women, in all classes" (Gimenez, 2018: 262). It is true that in its quest of make the violence inflicted upon marginalized subjects visible and the due immediate legal protection actionable,[11] and to map the violent territories of power as a matrix of domination,[12] intersectionality operates through the presupposition that one can anticipate the appearance of difference prior to its very arrival. Therefore, intersectionality conceptually conforms the particular appearance to the universal categories constructed in an *a priori* fashion – as though, every category of embodied experience and social relations is built to be a Lego piece and every other difference can appear at any time and sit neatly on top of the previous category.

I suggest that a marxist account of embodied social relations in contemporary capitalist societies ought to be able to provide an account of the diremption between the actual appearance of these embodied social relations as the categories of human praxis and the existing categories through which social organization is effected. Put differently, an examination of the non-coincidence between the appearances of social differences and their categorization through the tension between the phenomenology and ontology of the social must be a part of such a marxist account. However, Gimenez's above approach to the construction and operation of analytical categories does not offer such an account. In this effort of thinking about embodied social relations through marxism, my conceptual approach differentiates itself both from other marxist approaches, and redeployments of intersectionality, as well as the post-structuralist accounts of subjectivity in the following manner:

1) Unlike other marxist accounts, I do not presume that all social differences are derived from class. Therefore, the task of the marxist critic, in my analysis, is not to demonstrate how, in an imputed social totality, these differences have a dialectical relationship with class. Rather, it is to show how class and other embodied social relations are morphologically inflected in their relationship to social reality and ideology.

---

10   See Hancock, 2007; and McCall, 2005.
11   See, Crenshaw, 1989; and Crenshaw, 1991.
12   See, Collins, 1990.

2) Contrary to the redeployments of intersectionality, which conceptually operate through prescribing a coincidence between the particular and the universal, I investigate the unceasing passage of the particular into the universal vis-à-vis embodied social relations. These passages – their facility and blockage – account for the generalization of embodied relations as the categories of life in my account.

3) A post-structuralist response to the assertion of coincidence between the particular and the universal might be to charge intersectionality with a logic of equivalency. Subsequently, such a response may be expected to pose an ontological alterity between the different categories of embodied social relations. As opposed to this tradition of thought, I suggest a propinquitous relationship of mutual limited intelligibility that hinges on the plasticity of these different relations as the conditions of the actualization of life through human praxis.

x   The Need for the Recovery of the Concept of Experience in Its Lived Sense

Having clarified the main tenets of my approach, I continue with Gimenez's thought-provoking critique of intersectionality. Gimenez argues that "everyone is located at the intersection of identities is a truism" (Gimenez, 2018: 262). Other contemporary marxist-feminists agree with Gimenez in arguing that "in actual experience of human life, social identities intersect all the time and all at once" (Mojab and Carpenter, 2019: 2). In fact, Shahrzad Mojab and Sara Carpenter assert that "we live in a perpetual intersecting mode" (Mojab and Carpenter, 2019: 2). I, on the contrary, suggest that such assertations, far from being a truism, or our perpetual mode of existence, need to be re-evaluated in terms of their epistemological validity. An uncritical and willing acceptance of these assertions commits at least two errors. First and foremost, by "misidentifying intersectionality" (Luft and Ward, 2009: 12) as a theory of subjectivity, these critics contribute to its "citational ubiquity" (Wiegman, 2012: 240) both in academia and beyond. Second and more importantly, by positing an epistemological transparency and trans-temporality to experience, these assertions can only conceive experience either as "the mimicry of the past" (Lefort, Lawlor, and Massey, 2010: 7) or "the fulguration of the future" (Lefort, Lawlor, and Massey, 2010: 7).

Against these truncated understandings of experience, I argue that in order to capture the tension between how embodied social relations are experienced and how they are socially organized, a marxist conceptualization of these social relations must recover experience in its lived sense. Only through examining this tension might we conceptualize the limitations of the existing categories of these social relations, thereby producing the knowledge for their social transformation. I suggest that the social philosopher Gillian Rose's rejection to craft an *apologia pro vita sua*[13] provides us with the glimpse of such a notion of experience. Maintaining the tension between the novelty of experience and traditional ways of describing it, Rose claims that:

> [i]f I knew who or what I were, I would not write; I write out of those moments of anguish which are nameless and I am able to write only where the tradition can offer me a discipline, a means, to articulate and explore that anguish … [I]t has been within the philosophical tradition … that I have found the resources for the exploration of this identity and lack of identity, this independence and dependence, this power and powerlessness. My difficulty is not addressed in any rejection of that tradition which would settle for only one side of my predicament: lack of identity, dependence, powerlessness, or any account of otherness which theorizes solely exclusion and control.
> ROSE, 2017: 9–10

Thus, I argue that accepting an always-already-all-at-once unity of the intersections of our being and trying to identify the primary unit of this unity merely helps position marxism as either superior, or inferior vis-à-vis intersectionality – rather than, facilitating the tasks of the production of revolutionary knowledge, as well as identifying the real limits of intersectionality.

XI Embodied Social Relations and the Levels of Analysis in Social Sciences

Continuing in the critical spirit that these tasks demand, I turn to what I take to be Gimenez's most important methodological critique of intersectionality. That is, the ideology of obscuring class. Gimenez argues that "[a] fundamental problem inherent in blind allegiance to the ideology of intersectionality is the neglect of the complexity of Marxist theory" (Gimenez, 2018: 263). Such neglect, according to her, manifests itself in the inability to "specify the level of analysis at which it is appropriate to consider class in conjunction with gender

---

13   A defense of one's life.

and race" (Gimenez, 2018: 263). Thus, Gimenez articulates a conceptual and methodological differentiation between "the abstract level of analysis of the theory of the capitalist mode of production ... and the historical level of analysis of social formations" (Gimenez, 2018: 263).

Mobilizing this difference at the level of the mode of production, Gimenez writes that "[w]hen examining class at the level of analysis of the capitalist mode of production, it would make no sense to take into account gender, race or other forms of oppression. Class is identity blind. Far from being an error, or a problem in need of correction, this 'blindness' indicates that the logic of class relations, exploitation and capital accumulation is indifferent to the actual individual characteristics of capitalists and workers" (Gimenez, 2018: 263–264). In order to make her point even more concrete and clearer, Gimenez tells us that no matter where the individual capitalist is from, they are equal in their ruthlessness with the white Western capitalist. Likewise, she asserts, although he might be paid more, the white male worker is equal in his exploitation with women workers and workers of colour because their surplus labour is extracted from all of them. On the other hand, at the level of social formations, Gimenez argues that the matter is to "acknowledge the historicity, i.e., the capitalist origins of the taken-for-granted identities, categories of analysis or 'axes of inequality' whose 'intersections' constitute the foundation of intersectionality" (Gimenez, 2018: 263). Although she argues that these categories are conducive to reification and function ideologically, Gimenez asks: "[a]t what level of capitalist development, and under what historically specific conditions is it possible to argue that women are oppressed 'as women'? What is the relationship between capitalist accumulation, slavery, the rise of racial ideology and the notion of race?" (Gimenez, 2018: 263).

As a metatheoretical issue, the discussion of levels of analysis in social sciences is an important one. Marxism is especially careful about this issue mainly because of Marx's own discussion of the 1857 Introduction to *Grundrisse* (Marx, 2005), a short text that has animated many debates within marxism and contributed to invaluable studies on Marx's method.[14] Much of these debates focus on the labour theory of value and its extrapolative relationship to a generalized method of dialectical social inquiry by way of examining how Marx traverses between different modalities of abstractions and, finally, via them arrives at the concrete. Despite the vast literature this discussion has generated, this scholarship has mostly remained within the bounds of political economy and

---

14   Consider the following: Ollman, 1977; Hall, 1974; Banaji, 1977; Sayer, 1979; Sayer, 1987; Murray, 1988; Smith, 1993; Ollman, 2003; and Carver, 1975.

its philosophy. Therefore, within this context, Gimenez's reminder of the discussion of levels of analysis is important and welcome insofar as it emphasizes the need to return to Marx's method in relation to the phenomena that intersectionality reveals.[15]

However, I argue that Gimenez's brief treatment of this discussion in relation to gender and race is not only inadequate, but also potentially forecloses such a re-turn that is not oblivious to its own historical conditions. The more charitable reading of Gimenez's argument regarding the capitalist mode of production as the abstract level of analysis suggests that although she may be right about the logical structure of capitalism, at this level, all one can tell is that capital necessitates constant extraction of surplus value for its own futurition. Note that in the previous sentence the subject is capital, not the capitalist, whose body remains fleshed, even though their soul belongs to capital. Therefore, the specific ways in which capital secures surplus are necessarily contingent upon and require a knowledge of a particular social formation consisting of social subjectivities and agencies. Thus, Gimenez's argument that class should not be considered in conjunction with gender and race would be in breach of her own analysis. Even in her own examples, the ruthless capitalist and the exploited workers are those with gender, nationality, ethnicity, and race, which necessarily put them in a particular historical and political relationship with one another.

For instance, the ruthlessness that is produced in the global South capitalist is a particular effect of a long history of capitalist colonialism and imperialism – not simply a 'personality trait' equally distributed to capitalists. Understanding the making of the comprador bourgeoisie, and of the metropole bourgeoisie, indeed require a different level of analysis. Although it is correct in its truth claim, the argument asserting the common ruthlessness of capitalists is not a valid abstraction, but a fallacy of thought. For the conceptual ground of this commonality lies not in the person, but in the relational processes of formation and spatialization of colonial and imperialist capitalism. Likewise, making a distinction between the degree and kind of exploitation when considering the exploitation of workers, and suggesting that independent of the degree of their

---

15 Marxist social theorist Himani Bannerji's engagement with Grundrisse and Marx's method is the most notable example of turning to class, race, and gender in their formative relations with one another. Bannerji's work is often dubbed as a 'co-constitutive approach' and misinterpreted as a part of the scholarship I take issue with here. However, as I demonstrate in Part II of this book, Bannerji's work offers a different account of these social relations from other marxist theorists discussed here and provides me with a resource for a return to subjective human praxis as its main contribution.

exploitation, workers are just as exploited is not an erudition emanating from the ability to separate levels of analysis, but a violent abstraction forced upon life that completely erases the lived experience as part of concept formation in social analyses. Before asserting an equality of exploitation, Gimenez's analysis needs to consider how the white male worker was, to begin with, produced as inhabiting those particular embodied categories.

I argue that the so-called blindness of class with an apodictic certainty of what it shall not see is not not-seeing-at-all, but not seeing this or that particular social relation. In other words, the capitalist mode of production might well be enunciated as an abstraction, but it is a determinate abstraction with many historical and social properties and dimensions. It is in referential relationship with previous modes of production and the social relations originated in them. Failing to recognize this referential relationality results in separating history from the social. Thus, in Gimenez's account, history becomes the metaphysical unfolding of capital as an ideal type. Consequently, a conceptual struggle to reconcile history with the social begins.

XII   Class Burdened with the Difficult Conceptual Task of Reconciling History with the Social

This struggle finds its most crisp articulations in Gimenez's discussion of class. Here class is burdened with the difficult task of reconciling history with the social. When belonging to the higher level of abstraction (i.e., mode of production, in Gimenez's scheme), class is expressed in a language of stratification: "Class location inflicts its burdens and opens possibilities to workers and capitalists alike; for both, it is a matter of economic survival" (Gimenez, 2018: 264). When on the lower level of abstraction (i.e., the level of social formation), "the aggregates of individuals sharing the same class location are divided in terms of a variety of criteria such as gender, race, national origin, citizenship status, sexual orientation, marital status, ethnicity, religion, etc." (Gimenez, 2018: 264). In Gimenez's analysis, this fall from the higher planes where classes exist in their pure categories (i.e., class locations determining the life possibilities of *workers* and *capitalists*) to the lower ones where classes turn into masses (i.e., 'aggregates of individuals') with reified ideological identities (e.g., race, gender, etc.) represents the political predicament of our contemporary society. Therefore, a class politics needs to unify these divided masses back into the totality of classes, and through their struggle a new mode of production (i.e., communism) becomes possible.

Even then, however, the problem of a conceptual struggle to reconcile history with the social that has sprung from the separation between levels of analysis remains in Gimenez's text. Unless one commits to an 'end of history' hypothesis, the reconciliation of history and the social cannot be assumed to have been achieved once and for all, even with a new mode of production in sight. Thus, the concept of class demands another language, other than the language of stratification. This need arises from a conceptual necessity, not merely from a desire to be acquitted from the hackneyed charges of economism. The charge of economism, or of being an economistic marxist, is rather tedious in the contemporary left political landscape. It often functions as a commissive, inciting the accused to prove that they are not ignorant of extra-economic social power dynamics in their political utterances. With the hope of defying such charges, contemporary marxist-feminist theorists often state their 'non-economistic' view of class in a procataleptic fashion. These statements customarily emphasize a distinction between class as a social relation and class as a thing, favor the former conception over the latter, and, finally, bestow the non-economistic version of class with an always-already socialized content without any specificity as to the nature of this socialization.

Opting for this socialized version of class might be argued to produce a better political strategy for movement building. However, far from solving the deeper conceptual problem of reconciling history with the social, such a conceptualizing merely emphasizes the gravity of the problem. For it recognizes the value of the categories of the social (race, gender, sexuality, etc. in this scheme) through the certifying validity of class which envelopes them for their inclusion in history. This conceptualization, therefore, I suggest, reproduces the base and superstructure analysis once more. If class is an economistic concept, as Gimenez's abstract level of analysis suggests, in a communist mode of production that abolishes relations of private property, class could no longer reconcile history and the social. Thus, the social world becomes unknowable, and freedom untenable. In this manner, any justification for the need for communism is self-contradictorily undermined.

This problem of reconciliation between history and the social imposes itself with such a force that a language of culture becomes a necessary supplement to the previous language of stratification in Gimenez's text. She writes that "[t]here is more to class, however, than exploitation; class is also a terrain where cultural patterns develop, where the members of the different classes are reproduced daily and generationally" (Gimenez, 2018: 265). This etymologically faithful[16] and analytically circular deployment of class as the cultivated soil in which classes are reproduced attempts to solve the problem of reconciling history with the social by reconceptualizing the social as the culture of class. In this quasi-transcendental structure, the social is reduced to culture, and culture to a product of class. In other words, class becomes the originary precondition that issues validity to culture, which, then, confers value on the categories of identity, which, then, ideologically organizes social formations. In positing class as the epistemological *a priori,* the analytic primacy of class is restored. Once again, it can explain culture and, therefore, ideological workings of a given social formation. However, class itself remains unexplained without referencing the very categories it issued to begin with. As a result, class's overcoming of the social via culture ironically results in the very unknowability of class itself.

Class, although itself in this analytic structure is the ground in which *ideological* social relations are (re-)produced, becomes knowable only in a level of analysis that operates on the *real* relations of production, i.e., the mode of production. Appealing to this level as its own precondition, the quasi-transcendental structure takes on a fully transcendental shape in which any attempt to reconcile history and the social becomes entirely untenable because a relative, or absolute identity between these two terms is epistemologically foreclosed. Caught in this foreclosure, which is an effect of a Simmelian understanding of *culture as value* and a Weberian understanding of *class as the stratification of life-chances on the market* subtending her text, Gimenez's theoretical and methodological insistence on distinguishing levels of analyses and other theoretical insights suddenly leave their place to appeal to politics. Although this conceptual impasse is not at all a consequence of Marx's thought, Gimenez summons a class politics to get out of this impasse.

With this sudden 'political' turn, Gimenez declares that "the main value of intersectionality is ideological, for it reinforces the divisions within the working class, pitting workers against each other, exacerbating sexism, racism, xenophobia, and nationalism" (Gimenez, 2018: 266). Because, in Gimenez's analysis, the epistemological standpoints of the mode of production and social formation are rendered incommensurable, the experiential categories of contemporary human praxis (i.e., embodied social relations) cannot possibly find room for themselves within this analytic structure. They can only be admitted as culturally derivative ideological categories. Consequently, political struggles addressing embodied social relations are understood to be "centered on the

---

16   For the relationship between culture and agriculture, see Williams, 2015: 49–54.

various individual characteristics that employers and communities and institutions use to exclude, oppress, stigmatize and economically exploit female and male workers, i.e., sexuality, gender, race, ethnicity, citizenship status, and so on" (Gimenez, 2018: 267). Conceptually speaking, it is rather mindboggling how 'sexuality, gender, race, ethnicity, citizenship and so on' can be 'individual characteristics,' unless we live in an entirely voluntaristic and ultimately solipsistic universe of our own individual making. Positing an alleged unity of class politics over an alleged division of identity politics, Gimenez's sociological reason bars any access to understanding the social and historical processes of the formation of these relations, thereby also ironically rendering any emancipatory and revolutionary political project untenable. To conclude, Gimenez's text transmogrifies these social relations into unknowable 'individual characteristics,' and class politics into a unified phantasmagoria fighting the divisions created by these unknowable individual characteristics.

XIII Mistaking Critical Marxist Epistemologies for a Sociology of Knowledge

Gimenez's contribution to the Symposium is followed by that of another well-known marxist-feminist, Barbara Foley. Foley's contribution also introduces a set of important questions about intersectionality. For instance, how embodied social relations and class correlate; whether they are "commensurable, or distinct" (Foley, 2018: 271); if they are "ontologically equivalent" (Foley, 2018: 271); and, perhaps most practically, "does one have to speak of them all at once in order to speak of them at all?" (Foley, 2018: 271). While these are important questions deserving thorough investigation, Foley does not unpack and address them with critical rigor. Instead, she falls back unto a well-worn distinction between oppression and exploitation. These constitute two elements of a structural analysis in which the systems of oppression ensure that the system of exploitation, which is the 'root cause' of social inequality, remains intact. I suggest that neither this distinction nor the very confutation of it provides us with any reliable knowledge necessary to elucidate either the nature of these social relations (i.e., class, race, gender, sexuality, etc.), or the relationship between them. In fact, the exchange between Foley and Ashley Bohrer that composed the 'On the Contrary' of the Fall 2019 issue of *New Labour Forum: A Journal of Ideas, Analysis and Debate* demonstrates that such a debate spotlighting this distinction merely results in mutual comradely charges of reductionism (Bohrer, 2019; Foley, 2019).

Instead of focusing on Foley's operationalization of the oppression versus exploitation dichotomy, I am interested in understanding Foley's overall evaluation of intersectionality that "its usefulness ends, and it becomes in fact a barrier when one begins to ask other kinds of questions about the reasons for inequality – that is, when one moves past the discourse of 'rights' and institutional policy, which presuppose the existence of capitalist social relations" (Foley, 2018: 271). For Foley, intersectionality can describe the ways in which the systems of oppression work, but cannot locate their root causes because, as a mode of analysis and redress, it is strictly "confined to the plane of bourgeois jurisprudence" (Foley, 2018: 270).[17] I suggest that Foley's critique, problematizing the scopic relationship between intersectionality and the law, is an important one to reckon with.[18] For it provides an opportunity to demonstrate how a general sociology of knowledge stands in for a critical marxist epistemology[19] in the course of Foley's intervention, which bears the subtitle 'a marxist critique.'

According to this line of critique, intersectionality could only be launched from within the scope of the law. As a result, not only does its analytic validity remain bound by this juridical field of vision, but also its very analytics are produced by the relations and discourses of ruling that set up this field of vision in the first place. Therefore, it is not unpredictable that this line of critique concludes, as Foley herself does, that intersectionality cannot provide us with an epistemological standpoint through which a critique of capitalist social relations in their totality may be levelled. Moreover, any such effort to use intersectionality to understand the broader social organization ends up uncritically reproducing the categories of race, gender, sexuality, etc. Thus, according to Foley, intersectionality cannot help us in a quest for finding the root causes of social inequality but is a symptomatic, conceptual mediation of "the ideological air that we breathe" (Foley, 2018: 274).

---

17   For a similar marxist critique that takes intersectionality to be a juridical intervention, see Aguilar, 2015.
18   Intersectionality has been subjected to similar critiques before. For instance, in *Object Lessons,* Wiegman conducts one of the most nuanced critique of intersectionality as being founded upon a "juridical imaginary" (Wiegman, 2012: 30). Also, it is important to note that Brittney Cooper convincingly responds to Wiegman's critique with clarity and rigour (Cooper, 2016).
19   For a social philosophical account of the difference between the sociology of knowledge and epistemology, see Israel, 1990. This article and other works of Israel constitute an interesting attempt to present a non-transcendental and non-quasi-transcendental account of the social in conversation with Jurgen Habermas and Karl Otto Apel.

Because intersectionality was most prominently mobilized in a court case to address the experiences of black women workers by Crenshaw, its validity is conveniently assumed to be exhausted by its legal context. Likewise, because the nature of its context necessitates individual redress, all its possible uses are, again, conveniently asserted to be individual-*ist-ic*. I suggest that Foley's critique of intersectionality as "confined to the plane of bourgeois jurisprudence" (Foley, 2018: 270) can only be made operationable within a general sociology of knowledge. This sociology of knowledge parses out heteroclite islands of knowledge and explores the bounds of these discrete planes in positive (e.g., knowledge production and encoding) and negative (e.g., knowledge retrieval and decoding) modalities of its methodological rules (Kaiser, 1998). I call this a general sociology of knowledge, as opposed to *mainstream*, because it forwards an applied critical epistemology, whose political character is variously determined by its practitioner and does not have to be conservative. For instance, in Foley's argument, the political import is clearly progressive, although this is achieved by epistemologically confining intersectionality into the realm of bourgeois jurisprudence in a dichotomous fashion. Thus, in Foley's argument, intersectionality becomes, or is rather rendered, at best a device for describing the organization of bourgeois jurisprudence, and at worst a 'barrier' if one mistakes this description for the explanation of capitalist social relations.

As a sociological object of investigation, bourgeois jurisprudence might be identified as a realm of knowledge system with its own rules and procedures. However, this distinct and identifiable sociological object of knowledge does not stand in isolation from other sociological objects of knowledge. Therefore, various approaches producing the knowledge of these objects cannot be assumed to have been confined within these objective realms that they themselves help discover. Arguing otherwise is to mistake critical marxist epistemologies for a general sociology of knowledge that produces a sophisticated series of correspondences between different social groups, ideologies, and institutions. It is such a confusion that leads Foley to declare intersectionality inadequate to the task of understanding capitalist social relations.

This declaration brings with it a wholesale rejection of gender, race, sexuality, and other embodied social relations as critical analytics through which we can analyze contemporary capitalist social organization. Foley makes a distinction between class as a subject position and as structural analytic unit of explanation. However, she chooses to outstrip the analytic powers of gender, race, sexuality and other embodied social relations and to fix them *merely* as subject positions. This analytical move rends the subjective and the objective from one another and reproduces a series of derivative dichotomies, such as the ideological and the real, the ideal and the material, the appearance and the essence. Having conceptually created these binary oppositions due to the above misapprehension, Foley then turns to mend these rended categories of embodied social relations by invoking Marx's authority under the auspices of "the explanatory superiority of a class analysis" (Foley, 2018: 272).

Here, too, Marx is summoned to solve a problem that Foley produced through replicating the antinomies of classical sociology. In this way, marxism is transformed to a mode of analysis that insist on not comprehending contemporary capitalist social organization by covering over any possibility of the knowability of embodied social relations as they appear and are lived. Through this kind of 'marxism,' Foley argues that "oppression ... is indeed multiple and intersecting, producing experiences of various kinds; but its causes are not multiple but singular" (Foley, 2018: 272). In other words, class exploitation is the singular cause of the multiple systems of oppression. Deriving all other embodied social relations and categories of experience from class, Foley, like the other symposiasts discussed above, reproduces the base and superstructure analysis. Moreover, through this derivation Foley's explanatory framework takes a quasi-transcendental form that sets up class as the condition of possibility of embodied social relations.

This quasi-transcendental framework, also, creates further problems in relation to the philosophy of history that it implies. All embodied social relations and experiences are traced through the unfolding of class as the unifying concept of this philosophy of history. Therefore, the history of embodied social relations and experiences themselves become coincident with the history of class societies and economic production. Such reductionism does not only fuel charges of teleology, but more importantly it both ontologizes differences that precede capitalist societies, such as sexual difference and kin-based differences, and stymies political imaginary and action for future classless societies. Put simply, the analytic inability to recognize how subjective human praxis is achieved through embodied social relations and fixing these relations as subject positions that are determined by class relations, does not result in establishing an internal relation between class, gender, race, and other embodied social relations. Rather, it further separates them in irreconcilable heteroclite islands away from the reach of critical marxist epistemologies, and only partially knowable through an autochthonous sociology of knowledge.

XIV   A Quasi-transcendental Framework of Explanation Premised upon a First Principle

In order to demonstrate how this quasi-transcendental structure of explanation and its attendant philosophy of history work in a more concrete and sociological register, let us turn to Foley's text again. Drawing on Eve Mitchell's critique of intersectionality (Mitchell, 2013), Foley argues that "categories for defining types of selfhood that are themselves the product of alienated labor end up being reified and, in the process, legitimated" (Foley, 2018: 272). Here, I shall not dwell on how the embodied social relations, which were already reduced to simply being 'subject positions' in the text, are now subjected to a further reduction, thereby becoming a psychologistic classification of 'categories for defining types of selfhood.' It suffices to note that this double reduction itself is a function of the explanatory structure at work in the text. Nor shall I dwell on the theoretical legerdemain of moving from alienation to reification, then, to legitimation, which creates an illusion of an explanation of how those 'categories for defining types of selfhood' are actually produced, without accounting for the relationship between these three concepts (viz., alienation, reification, and legitimation) that are often mistaken for one another.[20]

Instead, I argue that the real problem with this formulation lies in the relationship it establishes between alienated labour and embodied social relations. The argument that the "categories for defining types of selfhood that are themselves the product of alienated labor end up being reified and, in the process, legitimated" (Foley, 2018: 272) is predicated upon a prelapsarian state of unalienation – as though, in this hypothetical state of unalienation, embodied social relations and social formation ceases to exist, and in place of a society, an oasis springs forth. The urge to derive all embodied social relations from class exploitation replaces the analysis of a mode of production with an analysis of alienated labour, thereby leaving the whole structure of explanation wanting of a theory of the state, social forms of consciousness, and power.

More importantly, the implicit suggestion that with a revolutionary transition into communism as a classless social organization, gender, race, and

---

20   For an excellent discussion of how reification is used in many different ways in even seemingly similar schools of thought, see Rose, 2014. For an important recasting of the concept of reification and rich responses to this new conceptualization, see Honneth, 2008. *Reification*. For Butler's, Geuss', and Lear's responses to Honneth, see Butler, 2008; Geuss, 2008; and Lear 2008. For the exhaustive and classical accounts of alienation, see Mézsáros, 1970; Ollman, 1977. For detailed and important accounts of legitimation, see Beetham, 2013; and Habermas, 1975.

sexuality (among others) can be abolished is misleading. The question is not whether such an abolition is plausible. Rather, it is: how is such an abolition viable? I suggest that for such an abolition to be viable, the explanatory framework must be able to recognize: the pain and suffering caused by the power dynamics within these embodied social relations; the history, cultures, and consciousness of the struggles produced by those who suffered and fought; and the experience of how these embodied social relations are sedimented in individual spaces of immanence and the self. However, a quasi-transcendental framework of explanation premised upon a first principle cannot accommodate such recognition. Instead of recognition, it can best offer representation through empathy, sympathy, and friendship. Although these rarities are nothing to scoff at under capitalism, a program of abolishing gender, race, and sexuality (among others) based on these sentiments cannot go beyond formal bourgeois equality.

This lack of recognition shows up most clearly in Foley's discussion of the new social movements and her ultimate equation between the new social movements and intersectionality. Understanding the new social movements *only* as a 'retreat from class' through "pluralist coalitions around a range of non-class-based reform movements" (Foley, 2018: 274) reproduces and rigidifies both real and ideological binary oppositions. This rigidification bars any analysis investigating the relationship between class and embodied social relations that does not begin and end with its own methodological first principle. That is, how these movements represent and legitimate a reified collective subject to cover over their own alienated labour in favour of the ruling class. To be sure, "the retreat from class" (Wood, 1986) as Ellen Meiksins Wood expounds it, is a serious shortcoming of many contemporary social movements, but it is beside the point I make here. The point, however, is that Foley's framework of analysis allows only one kind of relationship between class and other embodied social relations due its methodological antinomies explained above.

To recapitulate, my critique has revealed the quasi-transcendental structure of Foley's analysis through an investigation of the ways in which a general sociology of knowledge stands in for a critical marxist epistemology in her critique of intersectionality. Furthermore, I have demonstrated that such sociological reason operates by conceptually creating binary oppositions that generate a very limited and one-sided understanding of class and other embodied social relations. A politics, which is predicated upon this understanding, is inadequate for a revolutionary transformation of society.

xv Marxism and the Non-identity of the Law and Life in Contemporary Capitalist Societies

Against this kind of contemporary marxist-feminism, the main tenets of which the above symposiast sketch in contradistinction to intersectionality, I argue that marxism does not have to be mobilized as a political accoutrement to a sociological reason with a quasi-transcendental structure of explanation. Such a marxism must refuse covering over embodied social relations through a first principle. And its philosophy of history must be commensurate with the ways in which people actualize their embodied human praxis. In fact, I suggest that only such a marxism is capable of adequately explaining the nature of embodied social relations under capitalism. As I have pointed out above, this marxism must be effected from the standpoint of "human society or social humanity" (Marx, 1845: n.p.) in which sensuousness is not a contemplative, abstract, and representational matter but is "practical activity" (Marx, 1845: n.p.) through which life is lived. Thus, in such a marxist account of embodied social relations, the problem of ideology does not belong to the individual's psychic processes of identification and disidentification – whether these processes are conceived in psychologistic or sociologistic fashion. Instead, it belongs to capitalist social organization that misrecognizes the economy as reality itself with the results of normalizing, naturalizing, and eternalizing the economic subsumption of life. Within such a society, people's social relations bear a twofold nature of being both ideological and real because this subsumption and the resistance to it comprises the social and its historicity. Therefore, in this account, positing any of these relations as stemming from the real material base, and others from various ideological superstructures, would be simply untenable. Any one of these embodied social relations, however, may be taken methodologically as entry points into this social organization because they are irreducible yet reversible hinges that open to the self, the other, and the world within the long enculturation of a common – albeit antagonistic – history, beyond the calculability of any matrix.

Confronted with intersectionality in the courtroom, this marxism, unlike that of Foley, does not resort to a general sociology of knowledge to declare the confinement of intersectionality into the realm of bourgeois jurisprudence. Instead, it asks whether intersectionality can provide us with the clues of the workings of a legal system that is external to people's everyday experiences, that is not identical with the actuality of people in our social organization. For it would be an important objective of this approach to understand the non-identity of the law and life in contemporary capitalist societies, and to reveal the nature of this non-identity and the ways in which it is experienced by people. In the critical marxist epistemology of this approach, bourgeois jurisprudence does not constitute a distinct plane. An intersectional analysis and description of bourgeois jurisprudence helps our approach trace the generalization of embodied social relations as the categories of subjective human life. For instance, we can ask the following set of questions:

1) How might the valuable knowledge, which is that the formal equality of bourgeois civil society is predicated upon the proletarian's freedom of unfreedom, itself perform certain conceptual and epistemological practices of power that obscure other important aspects of the same contemporary capitalist social organization?
2) Who is this said proletarian, and how are they constituted as a subject?
3) What breathes life into them, and how are they suffocated? As it must be evident, even if we have a robust theory of class exploitation, none of these questions could be adequately answered if we do not have an equally robust understanding of embodied social relations.

For an extraordinary concrete analysis capable of answering the above questions through a critical marxist epistemology, let us briefly turn to the antiracist feminist marxist historical sociologist Himani Bannerji's essay called "In the Matter of 'X': Building 'Race' into Sexual Harassment" (Bannerji, 1995). I argue that Bannerji's work and thought not only constitutes one of the essential resources for, but also exemplifies, the kind of marxism that we need for an adequate understanding of embodied social relations under capitalism. In this essay, Bannerji takes us back to the courtroom. Unlike Foley, Bannerji does not lock the door upon bourgeois jurisprudence but delivers the social out of bourgeois jurisprudence, thereby exhorting us to reconsider the non-identity between the law and life. "In the Matter of 'X'" is an analytic recounting and reflection upon a court case that Bannerji was involved in as an expert witness in 1992. This case was about a black woman's experience of sexual harassment in her workplace, "the industrial section of [a] multinational pharmaceutical company operating in Canada" (Bannerji, 1995: 156). The main question that necessitated Bannerji's expertise was: "How could we build that fact of blackness into the case so that we could say that racism was an integral part of the sexual harassment which she underwent?" (Bannerji, 1995: 121).

In this essay, Bannerji subjects the categories of 'woma(e)n,' 'black woma(e)n,' and 'sexual harassment' to a critical marxist epistemological scrutiny in order to reveal the very making of these categories in Canadian social organization. "Treat[ing] 'power' as a 'concrete' social form and relation with a specific history and locale" (Bannerji, 1995: 131), Bannerji's scrutiny moves in and through the areas of state formation, colonization, immigration regimes, labour markets, economic history, and class formation. Through this remarkable canvas,

Bannerji situates the sexual harassment that X was subjected to within the global structure of colonialist capitalism, showing the violently intimate webs of relations that connect Canada to the U.S., South Africa, Latin America, and the Third World. However, in sharp contrast to the other marxist-feminists I have so far discussed, in Bannerji's account, X never becomes an instantiation of the disinterested logic of capital. X is never lost in the grand scheme. And the racialized and gendered social relations that produce X's gruesome experience are not an effect of a first principle. X is not an incarnate ideology standing on two legs.

Neither does Bannerji take a representational approach to X and her experience. Her analysis is a thorough recognition of X's experience. Bannerji begins with X and does not use her experience as a skipping stone from the subjective to the objective. Even though it is given epistemic privilege, X's experience cannot constitute an epistemological ground for such a skipping. Because X's experience is not self-evident, it needs to be reconstructed. This methodological point cannot be overemphasized. It is precisely because Bannerji's philosophy of history does not derive embodied social relations from class as a unifying first principle, that both embodied social relations and class need to be explained as human praxes. Therefore, Bannerji begins with X in order to reconstruct her experience in history, the social, and life. Through this reconstruction, she arrives back at X and her experience. X is always present and central in Bannerji's text. X's experience is recognized and reckoned with, albeit not reconciled. X is real.

At the end of this long article, we realize that Bannerji leaves no room for any theoretical legerdemain. X is of course an alienated worker. However, her alienation is not the same as either the alienation of her white female co-workers, or the alienation of her (majority white) male co-workers who brought her to a violent nervous breakdown. The sexual harassment that she experiences also differs. It is replete with tropes of the racial violence of apartheid, slavery, and post-slavery. X's alienation is in a different configuration than that of her co-workers vis-à-vis one another, their labour union, and their employers. These different conditions and realities of alienation cannot be reconciled and sublated into a state of unalienation because, as Bannerji shows, embodied social relations are always part and parcel of alienation and unalienation. Just as those who occupy the present differently do not possess an identical remembrance of the past, the future does not hold the same for them either. Thus, any project for a revolutionary social transformation cannot bypass the question of embodied social relations and experiences either by erasing the self and the singularity of flesh through a historicist confinement to the bourgeois present, or by erasing them through an eternal universality conceived in the coincidence of the subject and object in history.

XVI   Supra-racial Epistemology of an Aleatory and Subjectless Conception of History

In what follows I examine whether Lise Vogel's marxist-feminism offers a conceptual and methodological contribution to an understanding of embodied social relations that avoids the pitfalls of sociological reason that I have identified in the analyses of other symposiasts. Like the other contributors discussed so far, Vogel is a noted marxist-feminist, whose works have been squarely canonized in the literature. Vogel's contribution, "Beyond Intersectionality," opens with the following prefatory paragraph:

> In this paper I examine the genealogy of 'intersectionality.' More specifically, I look at the history of the conceptualization of 'diversity' as consisting of the interaction of multiple 'categories of social difference,' for example race, class, gender, etc. 'Intersectionality' turns out to be only one of several attractive yet flawed concepts deployed over the past 80-plus years to represent such social heterogeneity. I conclude with some suggestions for developing a more adequate approach to conceptualizing 'diversity'.
>
> VOGEL, 2018: 275–276

This paragraph displays the fulcra of Vogel's text: its presuppositions, its operant logic of equivalency, and its assertations. However, my engagement with Vogel's contribution does not enlarge upon these fulcra and reveal how they structure the text. Nonetheless, I briefly note them here because they illuminate the background as I focus on Vogel's approach to embodied social relations. First, it is important to register that Vogel uses genealogy and history interchangeably.[21] This conflation merits attention because it displays the tension between Vogel's aleatory history and apodictic politics.[22] Second,

---

21   Strictly speaking, contrary to Vogel's claim, this contribution constitutes neither a genealogy nor a history of intersectionality.

22   For the difference between genealogy and history, see Foucault, 1984; 76–100. In this important article, Foucault engages with Nietzsche's three modalities of history in order to elucidate his own new method of genealogy. According to Foucault, "The first is parodic, directed against reality, and opposes the theme of history as reminiscence or recognition; the second is dissociative, directed against identity, and opposes history given

I discern another important set of conflation between the uses of intersectionality, diversity, categories of social difference, and social heterogeneity.[23] This conflation is not a simple result of the allure of thesaurus; rather, it is both a corollary of Vogel's understanding of history and builds upon it. Vogel's failure to differentiate between these concepts and terms does not allow her to have room for relations of power and domination in her analysis of embodied social relations.[24] Consequently, race, for instance, for Vogel becomes more "problematic" (Vogel, 2018: 284) than gender and class. Third, Vogel asserts that intersectionality is "one of several attractive yet flawed concepts deployed over the past 80-plus years to represent such social heterogeneity" (Vogel,

---

as continuity or representative of a tradition; the third is sacrificial, directed against truth, and opposes history as knowledge. They imply a use of history that severs its connection to memory, its metaphysical and anthropological model, and constructs a countermemory – a transformation of history into a totally different form of time" (Foucault, 1984: 93) . For Foucault, "[g]enealogy is gray, meticulous, and patiently documentary. It operates on a field of entangled and confused parchments, on documents that have been scratched over and recopied many times" (Foucault, 1984: 76). However, it is important to remember that Foucault's grey is opposed to that of Hegel, according to whom "[w]hen philosophy paints its grey in grey, one form of life has become old, and by means of grey it cannot be rejuvenated, but only known. The owl of Minerva takes its flight only when the shades of night are gathering" (Hegel, 1991: 23). It is this readiness to reckon with history as a formative process where the real, the ideal, the substance, and the subject are in constant mutual movement of formation and deformation in civil society that characterizes Hegel's philosophy of history. Out of these different philosophies of history, of Foucault (via Nietzsche) and Hegel, comes the irreducible difference between genealogy and history. For the most formidable critique of Foucault's methodology, see Rose, 1984: 171–207.

23 This conflation is not new and has been thoroughly and convincingly critiqued by scholars of intersectionality. For instance, against such conflations, Rachel E. Luft and Jane Ward states unequivocally that "intersectionality is not diversity nor an intellectual version of diversity management" (Luft and Ward, 2009: 14). Examining the institutionalization of intersectionality, they argue that "diversity initiatives do not meet [the] definition of intersectional justice if they are dependent on, and accountable to, institutions rather than grassroots movements" (Luft and Ward, 2009: 14). Another important critique of this conflation is that of Vivian May. She argues that "[e]quating intersectionality with diversity or description is more than simply reductive: it can actively buttress the logics of domination" (May, 2015: 149).

24 For a superb analysis of diversity in relation to difference and heterogeneity, see Bannerji, 2000. Focusing on "the degeneration of powered difference into diversity" (Bannerji, 2000: 32) Bannerji shows how diversity is divorced from class and used by the politics of liberalism as the "semiological basis" (Bannerji, 2000: 33) of identity's "sovereign mark" (Bannerji, 2000: 33). Juxtaposing Vogel's contribution with Bannerji's article is instructive for every critical sociologist to see how even well-intentioned texts with 'good' politics can be ideological in their methodological approach to the questions of embodied social relations.

2018: 276). Considering how easily it follows the first two points, this assertation hardly comes as a surprise. However, it is important to note this point because the assertation exhibits how, for Vogel, social heterogeneity is neutral and naturalized. The concepts that aim to comprehend this heterogeneity are uniformly flawed, despite the historical changes of the past eight decades. It is as though embodied social relations, understood as categories of difference by Vogel, belong not to history but elsewhere, thereby rendering flawed any attempt to understand them in history.

After the prefatory paragraph, Vogel lays out, what she takes to be, "the standard account" (Vogel, 2018: 276) of intersectionality, and then corrects this account with "the historical record" (Vogel, 2018: 278). Vogel objects to the historical representation of second-wave feminism as being "a monolithic white middle-class phenomenon that ignored race and class" (Vogel, 2018: 277). Vogel calls this a myth that is produced by the standard account.[25] According to this account, Vogel writes, "[o]nly in the 1980s, the myth continues, when black women entered the academy and forcefully challenged white-dominated feminism, did things change" (Vogel, 2018: 277), and Black women's "hard-fought leadership under the banner of 'intersectionality' was at last able to break with the errors of so-called white feminism" (Vogel, 2018: 277). In Vogel's estimation, this standard account, which she also calls the "'white feminism' paradigm" (Vogel, 2018: 277), flattens the complex history of feminism in the U.S. by rendering other histories of feminism invisible.

Vogel attempts to correct this standard account by turning to the historical record. She argues that decades before the 1980s, "[m]any socialist feminists argued that three systems (or dimensions of difference, or whatever) – race, class, and gender – interact in peoples' lives, whether or not they are aware of it" (Vogel, 2018: 278). Furthermore, according to Vogel, "[b]y assuming that the various dimensions of the race / class / gender framework are comparable, even equivalent, socialist–feminists were making a political statement that was important at the time: namely, that no one element of the trilogy could be put forth as prior" (Vogel, 2018: 278). Citing her own political trajectory as an example, Vogel suggests that the reason socialist-feminists were already using "race / gender / class thinking" (Vogel, 2018: 278) was that they already participated in the "civil rights / black liberation and antiwar movements" (Vogel, 2018: 278). Therefore, she concludes that "race / class / gender thinking did not originate in the activities of black feminist scholars during the 1980s. Rather, it

---

25   In order to show the salience of this standard account, Vogel cites the Wikipedia entry on intersectionality, presumably thinking that Wikipedia represents the academic and activist common-sense of our time.

emerged alongside the women's and other social movements of the 1960s and early 70s" (Vogel, 2018: 278).

The spirit in which Vogel interrogates how a dominant representation of the history of feminism is produced is, of course, a plausible one. For it bears important implications in regard to both knowledge production and the politics of knowledge production.[26] However, Vogel's staging of this interrogation is so arrestingly equivocal that it creates many conceptual problems. If, for instance, race, gender, and class analytics are so commonly and advisedly used in socialist feminist theorizing, their nature ought to be explicated in a way that makes it clear whether they are understood as a 'system' (if so, of what, and what kind?), or as 'dimensions of difference' (then, what is the relationship between these dimensions both in relation to this difference and its hegemonic others?), or simply as 'whatever' (read as: an expression of perplexity and a feeling of dismissiveness in the face of complex social organization, an indication of the indeterminacy of that social organization).

Vogel's interchangeable use of these three different analytical and affective terms gives the impression that perhaps, race, gender and class were not adequately worked out in the 'correct' history she provides. Likewise, Vogel's corrective account itself suggests that race, gender, and class were not conceptualized in relation with each other, but they were rather ditransitive representations of political isomorphisms produced in the course of socialist feminists' participation in different social movements. In other words, what Vogel's rather sketchy alternative account may be able to register is that race, gender, and class as units of analysis and praxis existed before the 1980s. However, her contention that these were already well developed relationally by the socialist-feminists of the 1960s and 70s is not substantiated enough to constitute a correction to, what Vogel calls, the standard account.

Vogel's 'correction' continues with the hypothesis that "the race / class / gender conceptualization that became popular in the 1960s derived from a century-old tradition, transmitted in the lived experience and activism of African American women" (Vogel, 2018: 280) including "Maria Miller Stewart,

---

26 The most important aspect of Vogel's historical interrogation of the standard account is her brief mention of the relationship between women's liberation and the Communist Party USA (CPUSA). This discussion is hardly registered in the literature for various reasons, chief among them being the role of the cold war. For a thorough historical study of this discussion, see Weigand, 2001. For an intellectual and political biography of the Black woman communist leader Claudia Jones and her experiences in the CPUSA and CPGB (the Communist Party of Great Britain), see Davies, 2007. For a brief account of CPUSA's treatment of the woman question as it relates to both gender and race, see Ferguson, 2020.

Sojourner Truth, Anna Julia Cooper, Mary Church Terrell, [and] Pauli Murray" (Vogel, 2018: 280). After informing her reader that "the race / class / gender analytical framework seemed familiar, and immediately available to me [Vogel]. It was not something I [Vogel] had to think deeply about, much less invent" (Vogel, 2018: 281) because she had left-wing parents, Vogel indicts Black feminists for missing "an opportunity to root their contribution more deeply in the historical context of black women's lives" (Vogel, 2018: 281). This argument is rather astonishing because it is incorrect through and through. The above Black women thinkers and activists (and many more) are not merely "cited by intersectionality writers as interesting but unconnected forerunners" (Vogel, 2018: 280). In fact, their thought and contributions are rigorously researched and analyzed in the literature.[27] Moreover, this literature, unlike Vogel, is careful in recognizing the different strands and rich history of Black feminisms, rather than assuming intersectionality and Black feminism are one and the same thing that cannot afford any differentiation.[28]

I argue that Vogel's attempt to fend off 'the white feminism paradigm' fails in not discussing the role of whiteness (not as an essence, but as a social relation of power and domination) and white supremacy at all. The historical record Vogel brings in to correct the standard account confuses matters further as it functions as a way of suppressing a necessary analysis of the relationship between knowledge production and systematic racism. Vogel seems to assume that her invocation of former generations and traditions of Black women thinkers and activists, and the authority she borrows from this citational practice, is enough to dispense with the white feminism paradigm. In Vogel's contribution, it is very difficult to ascertain the specific ways in which she and her fellow socialist feminists of the 1960s 'derived' their race, gender, class analysis from Black women's lives and activism.

In this way, Vogel's 'correction' enfolds race into a racially blind category of 'socialist-feminists,' while at the same barring the subjects subjected to racism out of this construction. At no point is the reader given an indication of whether this group is predominantly white or not, or how whiteness and white supremacy might have operated in this group. On the contrary, the reader is given the impression that this group is not epistemologically marked by their racialization, without any explication of how this supra-racial epistemology might have been achieved. In short, Vogel's 'correction' treats race as a unit of structuralist analysis that can be gleaned from an other's experience, while the

---

27 For instance, see Cooper, 2017; and May, 2007.
28 For instance, see Hancock, 2016; and Nash, 2019.

self of this other who is founded and confounded by this experience is kept external to this analysis. Although, as I demonstrate later, this approach to race in particular, and to other embodied relations in general, is more than inadequate on ontological and epistemological grounds, it is entirely compatible with Vogel's aleatory and subjectless conception of history.

XVII   Marxist-Feminist Aporetic of Description versus Explanation

Assuming to have corrected the historical account, Vogel moves onto theoretical observations and suggestions in relation to intersectionality. Vogel argues that intersectionality and the previous 'race / gender/ class approach' are "primarily descriptive. That is, they provide a conceptual framework for describing and investigating 'diversity,' but by themselves they do not explain anything. Strictly speaking, then, they are imprecise, and some would argue against using them" (Vogel, 2018: 282). However, because they might be useful "as consciousness-raising mechanisms" (Vogel, 2018: 282) for the uninitiated, Vogel does not wish to be "the person chastising these activists for using an incorrect concept" (Vogel, 2018: 282).

Instead of focusing on Vogel's rather condescending and dismissive approach towards people who work hard to make a difference in real people's real lives, I turn to the analytic distinction between description and explanation, which is a common theme among the symposiasts discussed thus far. The political corollary of this analytic distinction is easily discernible in the pedagogical moments of the contributions that comprise the symposium. The symposiasts refer to students and activists with the anticipation and encouragement that in the fullness of time, upon the completion of the novice phase of their political consciousness in which intersectionality is mobilized as a device for description, these students and activists should gradually settle into a marxist-feminist worldview, which does not merely describe the everyday experiences of oppression and domination, but explains the social totality as a whole, thereby providing a full comprehension.

I argue that the analytic distinction between description and explanation that Vogel draws on is yet another example of the aporias encountered in contemporary marxist-feminism. Furthermore, this aporia, like the others that I have discussed above (viz., mode of production vs. social formation; culture vs. class; bourgeois jurisprudence vs. capitalist society), results from the unchecked epistemological and ontological assumptions entrenched in the antinomies of classical sociological reason influenced, not by Marx, but by Kantian and Neo-Kantian traditions in sociology.[29] Moreover, once again, as is the case with the earlier examples, marxism *qua* politics is summoned to take us out of the aporia that it had no hand in producing to begin with. To be sure, a marxist politics, with its ethos and pathos sedimented through a long history of peoples' struggles, is more than capable of achieving this emergency rescue. However, such a marxist politics made to the measure of this summoning rigidifies marxism. Here, marxism cannot exercise a self-reflexive reckoning with its own thought and action. For the aporia it is summoned to resolve belongs not to its own contradictions, but to a sociological reason that is antithetical to Marx's method of understanding the social life and the world.

As a result of this rigidification, politics can no longer be the social mediation of understanding and action, but rather becomes a forceful covering over of this necessary gap between the two, which makes neither interpreting nor changing the world possible. Marx's 11th thesis on Feuerbach is often read as a call for action: "The philosophers have only interpreted the world, in various ways; the point is to change it" (Marx, 1845: n.p.). It is indeed profoundly, but not merely, so. Read in the context – and as the consequence and culmination – of ten preceding theses, the 11th thesis demands an epistemological engagement with itself.[30] I argue that such an engagement with the 11th thesis requires a threefold consideration which deliberates both the identity and non-identity of interpretation and change, as well as a speculative proposition that emerges out of the tension between the identity and non-identity of interpretation and change. I suggest that it is a lack of this kind of consideration that marks the feminist -marxist symposiasts' engagement with intersectionality. And this is precisely why, in contemporary marxist social theory,

---

29 Although, it is not the focus of the book, this problematic might be also explored through other sociological traditions, notably symbolic interactionism. Herbert George Blumer's rendering of symbolic interactionism is important in this respect. Influenced by George Herbert Mead and John Dewey, Blumer makes a distinction between definitive and sensitizing concepts in sociology and social theory. Blumer's differentiation resonates with the description versus explanation paradigm with which I take issue here. For Blumer's discussion of concepts in relation to methodology in sociology, see Blumer, 1986 (especially, chapters seven through ten).

30 For an excellent epistemological engagement with the 11th thesis, see Patnaik, 2019. For Adolfo Sánchez Vázquez's most original engagement with the *Theses* in their entirety, see Gandler, 2007: 127–153. As I am unable to read Spanish, instead of engaging with Sánchez Vázquez's own work, I am gratefully relying on Gandler's work in English. Also, even though I disagree with it in important respects, for Derrida's recently translated thought-provoking discussion of the *Theses* in relation to Kant, Althusser, and Heidegger, see Derrida, 2019.

the pitfalls of sociological reason cannot be avoided. Thus, before returning to Vogel, I embark upon a detailed threefold consideration upon the *Theses*.

XVIII 10+1 Theses on Feuerbach

Let us begin with the most conventional consideration about the 11th thesis, according to which interpretation and change are two different predicative expressions of enacting within and upon the social world. Here, interpretation is considered to have a contemplative relationship to life, autonomous from the social world it inhabits. This passive stance, however grandiose its philosophical proclamations might be, is an effect of the mental-versus-manual division of labour. Therefore, it provides those who fall into the mental side this division of labour, the interpreters (philosophers), with two epistemological possibilities: a delusionary metaphysics[31] that mistakes its interpretive schemes for the tendencies by which the social world unfolds; or a recognition of and reckoning with the very alienation from the social world that finds its expression in this delusionary metaphysics. For those who fall into the manual side of this division of labour, effecting a transformative change in the social world becomes an imperative, as they do not have the weight of a grand interpretive scheme standing between themselves and their alienation. And, of course, those philosophers who have the possibility of recognizing and reckoning with their own alienation can join to fight the change the social world, but they must forego their metaphysics to be able to do so because *merely* interpreting is no longer compatible with change.

While this first consideration of the 11th thesis is important and generally agreed upon, it ought not to cover over a second consideration that helps to build the full epistemological import of the *Theses*. Here, I suggest, considering the mutual identity between interpretation and change. After all, the above

---

31 Metaphysics – not unsimilar to idealism, materialism, and ontology – is a rather freely and vaguely used epithet in marxist and non-marxist social theory. Often, it is difficult to understand what is exactly meant by its use, other than having a sense that the word is meant as a sophisticated affront. Here, in the context of the *Theses*, I use the term as a complex system of interpretive scheme comprising ontological, epistemological, and methodological suppositions and presuppositions about the nature of the social world. Properly speaking, however, I consider metaphysics to be an essential part of any philosophy. For an important working out of the idea of 'marxist metaphysics' in relation to Ernst Bloch's philosophy, see Hudson, 1982. For an intriguing contemporary defense of metaphysics, see Avanessian, 2020. For an impressive survey of how the idea of metaphysics is dealt with by a number of political philosophers, see Flynn, 1992.

division of labour does not divide the social world into the realms of activity and passivity. Rather, it designates a social organization in which forms of activity and passivity exist in both sides of the division of labour. Each act of interpretation changes the world. For interpretation, by definition a highly mediated social activity, cannot be a solipsistic affair even when it is *merely* contemplative. However, it must be submitted that the change I refer here is not only of a revolutionary order.

On the one hand, revolutionary change requires a fissure within the existing social formation, or, rather, a recognition of such fracturation already occurring in society and the co-ordination and organization of this social fracturation into a political configuration capable of representing the general will within that society. It is at this particular intersection of recognition, co-ordination, and organization that *praxis* becomes a key term of identity between interpretation and change. However, even this term does not capture the full epistemological import of the *Theses*, which will become clear below in the third consideration of the 11th thesis.

On the other hand, non-revolutionary change saturates the sedimentation of existing social formation, beyond the reproduction and repetition of a static *status quo*. Each reactionary, liberal, or reformist interpretation of the social world bestirs and foments the centrifugal force of social action that organizes the miscibility and immiscibility of embodied social relations along the class axis of that society, which, then as a temporal consequence, comprises the sedimentation of that very social formation in history. Therefore, at any given moment of this process of sedimentation, interpretation takes on a constitutive role in its retrospective deployment, and a regulative role in its projective deployment. In other words, in the case of non-revolutionary change too, the identity between interpretation and change is discernable.[32]

A student, although not a follower, of German Idealism, Marx was abundantly aware of the identity between interpretation and change that I have explicated above.[33] Assuming otherwise would be to read the 11th thesis as an enthymematic aphorism, severed from the other ten theses throughout which Marx examines the relationship between materialism and idealism in

---

32 Understood from the vantage point of this identity implicit in the 11th thesis, it should be clear that Hegel's often confounding antimetabole "what is rational is real, and what is real is rational" is not an eminent manifestation of his compromised, right-wing politics. Quite the contrary, it is the most succinct formulation of a philosophy of history that exhibits profound sociological insight in its understanding of social change and the formation of society.

33 On this connection, see Rockmore, 1980.

a most fascinatingly evocative and associative manner in relation to the figure of Feuerbach who represents both the good and the bad within the tradition. Then, how might we engage with the 11th thesis in a way that would attend both to the non-identity and to the identity between interpretation and change, and resist the aphoristic allure of the thesis that often prevents further reflections on the *Theses*?

I argue that one example of such an engagement would be presented by approaching the 11th thesis with an epistemological curiosity that arises out of the tension between the non-identity and the identity between interpretation and change. I, therefore, carry out this third consideration of the thesis through such an epistemological inquiry. Having attended both to the non-identity and the identity above, it must be now clear that the 11th thesis, as opposed to providing a clear answer, poses an important question on the nature of the relationship between interpretation and change. Simply put, the question is this: what kind of interpretation results in what kind of change?[34] Needless to remind that by interpretation what is meant is not some fanciful construal of one's environment; rather, it is an act of understanding through the use of concepts, and, thus, it is a matter of knowledge. The kind of change meant by the thesis is communist revolutionary change. Therefore, the above question ultimately could be rephrased as: what kind of understanding and concepts can perpend a change capable of effecting freedom?

Let us, then, elucidate this question with the aid of the 8th thesis on Feuerbach,[35] which reads as follows: "All social life is essentially practical. All mysteries which lead theory to mysticism find their rational solution in human practice and in the comprehension of this practice" (Marx, 1845; n.p.). The social is a highly mediated expression of collective human practice that defies any totality of vision. As a result, many everyday social phenomena appear to us, rightly, as a mystery. Mysterious phenomena need not to be mystical. However, class societies have a particular inability to recognize the difference

---

34 The chiasmatic ordering of this question (i.e., what kind of change results in what kind of interpretation?) is also important, especially in relation to ideology. However, it is not the immediate focus of the *Theses* – partly because it is rather obvious that any change transforming the nature of taken for granted events in a given society will result in novel interpretations of the newly changed society, and chiefly because there was a sore need of revolutionary social change and no shortage of interpretation in Marx's time (much like ours). In that context of plentifulness of interpretation and scarcity of desired change, questioning the relationship between interpretation and change was of utmost importance (as it is in our context). Therefore, the question emerges in not this chiasmatic form, but in the form stated above.

35 For an interpretation of this thesis in relation to Kant and Fichte, see Rockmore, 2018: 110.

between mystery and mysticism. In fact, the more advanced they become, the more susceptible they are to this inability because the social division of labour grows more elaborate in severing human practice from its comprehension as two discrete realms of the social world with various subsets. This paradoxical prerogative, the *explanation of mystery as mysticism,* owes its condition of possibility to this severance, and its proliferation to the structures of exploitation and domination of that society. Depending on their place in these structures, those who specialize in comprehension produce the content of these mysticisms – ideological versions of religion and philosophy, among others. Such mysticisms, often operating through an idea of totality, might be convincing for many, but they cannot effect the rational solution that is a communist revolutionary change.[36]

At the end of this threefold consideration, we can now return to the 11th thesis as an epistemological question advising caution in our concept formation and methods of understanding social relations. It is social relations that are at stake here because, according to Marx, "[s]ociety does not consist of individuals, but expresses the sum of interrelations, the relations within which these individuals stand" (Marx, 2005: 265). However, Marx does not give a categorical answer to the question he poses precisely because social relations, the forms they take, and the force and excess of these relations are always in process and polyvalent. Thus, any social inquiry striving towards an understanding of social relations needs to be self-reflexive about its concept formation and methods if it is committed to contribute to a revolutionary change in society: What kind of concepts and methods help us recognize human practice and their contemporary predicament, and understand this practice and predicament without generating new content for mysticism, even if of a utopian kind?

---

36 There is absolutely no *reason* why here Marx should be tediously charged with 'rationalism' which is seen as responsible for both modernism and its atrocious results (through various deployments of 'instrumental rationality'). The intensification and immiseration of the majority of the globe can be rationally ended in a communist society which is capable of cultivating and accommodating real (not formal) freedom. The actual shape of this communism depends on how and what we understand our problems to be. For the most accurate understanding of these, we must use our reason and reconsider our concepts. To abandon reason is rather flattering. To me, judging by the situation that the world is in, it seems we do not seem to have any spare reason to abandon. One must also remember the urgency of reasoning when we still have some reasonable time before reason ceases to be of any help with an advent of barbarism. For an excellent philosophical exposition of the futility and danger of abandoning reason, even for the sake of a better ethics, see Rose, 1996.

XIX The Non-coincidence of Experience and Explanation

In light of this question and threefold consideration, let us re-examine Vogel's separation between description and explanation, and her *explanation* of the relationship between class, gender, and race. I argue that the separation between description and explanation – a separation explicit in Vogel, and implicit in the other symposiasts – marks the inability to recognize human practice. This inability counterposes human practice to its comprehension, thereby leaving the former bereft of the latter. To put it differently, in this separation, the experience of human practice cannot be registered as lived, but is to be reconstructed afterwards according to that which is deemed as its explanation. Such separation, therefore, renders lived experience impossible. For a rigid coincidence between experience and explanation is imposed; and, for the value of experience is validated by its explanation.

As a result, an exposition of experience becomes possible only within a quasi-transcendental structure which issues the explanation in the first place. If it is registered at all, the non-coincidence of experience and explanation – those provinces of experience which are not already anticipated by explanation – functions as the description of a phenomenal manifestation through which a novel frontier of the explanation is discovered. The malleability of experience evinces the power of explanation; and the comprehension of human practice becomes the fetters of the recognition of human practice, as opposed to being its chaperone in its journey towards freedom.

It is important to note that my objection does not lie in a naïve belief that experience ought to be conceived as an unconstructed and unconstrained locale of epistemology. Rather, it is to do with recognizing the non-coincidence of experience and explanation on its own terms. Only in such recognition can the subject reckon with the preliminary and provisional nature of comprehension in the fullness of a phenomenological exposition. Here, the subject comes to bear witness to their own movement of (self-)comprehension: how does the plasticity of their experience require a reconsideration of a previous explanation in their (self-)formation? For no new frontier of experience is devoid of an other's history, simply waiting to be engulfed in an explanation issued prior to any movement of experience. It is in these collective encounters that the political resides. The subject no longer traverses back and forth between the fully formed stages of mutually exclusive description and explanation. The coincidence between experience and explanation is no longer necessary to ensure the stability of these stages. Instead, in this alternative non-transcendental structure of knowledge, "the coincidence of the changing of circumstances and of human activity or self-changing can be conceived and rationally understood only as *revolutionary practice*" (Marx, 1845: n.p., emphasis in original).[37]

However, in Vogel's framework, the separation between description and explanation forces the subject's self-consciousness – the mode in which revolutionary practice is necessarily carried out – into either being a continual misrecognition, or an objectified consciousness. Experience provides the self-consciousness of the subject with the description of their everyday life, which, in this framework, by definition, generates a lesser degree of knowledge.[38] Therefore, any reliance on the epistemic privilege of the subject as the knower of their own life situation would lead self-consciousness to misrecognition. This is so not because experience, *qua* experience, is endowed with absolute knowledge, but because the framework of analysis imposes a prohibition upon self-consciousness, which is therefore not free to engage with its own experience to assess its limits for itself, among other reasons, to evaluate the validity of the description of their everyday life. It can only engage with its experience as misrecognition without knowing how this misrecognition itself is attained.

As a result, everyday life is pushed out of history as the locus of social inquiry, even though the subject themself is situated in this locus. Instead of this lived space, a theoretical, Euclidian space of explanation becomes the locus of social inquiry in which the subject's everyday experience is transmogrified into an object of knowledge. Here, the experience of the subject is explained beyond its description. Even if the self-consciousness of the subject is allowed here, it encounters itself as an objectified consciousness whose contents are ordered and examined according to the rules of a Procrustean method that fits the singularity of her experience into a universality discovered by the explanation.

---

37 This is the second half of the Third Thesis on Feuerbach, where Marx famously discusses the need to educate the educators. The separation of human practice from its comprehension "divide society into two parts, one of which is superior to society" (Marx, 1845: n.p.). To overcome this divide and educate the educators, a subject who is conscious of the movement of their own experience is the necessary condition of history. However, such a subject cannot be expected to come into being through a political evolution from description to explanation, as Vogel seems to hope. This subject and their experience exist as a part of the unfolding and making of history.

38 It is difficult not to suspect another Kantian influence in Vogel's separation of description and explanation. According to Kant, "in regard to the objective content of our cognition in general, we may think the following *degrees*, in accordance with which cognition can, in this respect, be graded: 1) to represent, 2) to perceive, 3) to be acquainted, 4) to cognize, 5) to understand, 6) to conceive, and 7) to comprehend" (Kant, 1992: 569–570). It is important to seriously consider this connection; however, such a consideration would take this conversation elsewhere, and, therefore, for the present argument's sake, it will have to suffice to direct the reader's attention to this connection.

Once again, the problem here is not that singularity ought not to be connected to any universality. It is rather that the passage between singularity and universality is presented as a *fait accompli*, therefore not open to the examination of self-consciousness as a moment of its journey. Self-consciousness is left bereft of any way of knowing the coincidence and non-coincidence between their own experience of human practice and its comprehension, as well as possible results of these coincidences and non-coincidences that help chart their way in their making of history. Thus, alienation becomes their fate, and self-emancipation a fantasy.

xx Marxist-Feminist Inscription of the Binary of the Idiographic versus the Nomothetic

It must now be unsurprising to discover that Vogel's and other symposiast's separation between description and explanation, which *prima facie* appears as only common sense and unproblematic, is in fact a most peculiar blend of the binaries of the idiographic versus the nomothetic – an important and problematic Neo-Kantian inheritance in sociology[39] – and the base and the superstructure. For Vogel, the everyday experiences of embodied social relations are non-repeatable yet describable singular occurrences in need of explanation by a concept capable of interlacing them into its framework of explanation. This concept is class, and the framework of explanation is the capitalist mode of production. Therefore, I argue that for Vogel intersectionality fulfills an idiographic function, whereas marxism fulfills a nomothetic one.[40] Strictly

---

39   For the history of this opposition within the Southwest School of Neo-Kantianism and its influence on sociology, see Oakes, 1988. For the relationship between the Marburg School and the Southwest School of Neo-Kantianism, and their influence on Durkheim, Weber, and Simmel, see Rose, 1981: 1–48. For a consideration of the epistemological problems this opposition poses and some attempt to remedy them through the social thought of Schmoller, Weber, and Adorno, see Strohmayer, 1997.

40   By this argument, I do not mean that Vogel and other symposiast are conscious and purposeful in constructing this prescription of functions. Rather that, their concept formation is an uncritical one, and that they do not self-reflexively analyze the conceptual unconscious and practices of their theoretical and political arguments. Examining and discovering the ways in which the epistemological problems of the opposition between the nomothetic and the idiographic is a well-established methodological procedure in critical social thought. For the examples that are in this same spirit, see how the following articles respectively discern this opposition in Soviet Marxism (especially in relation to 'Asiatic mode of production' and 'historical Orientalism' discussions) and in Latin American debates on development (especially, in relation to the binary of core and periphery, and the dependency school): Foursov, 1997; and Grosfoguel, 1997. And, for the

speaking, however, even this prescription of functions is inaccurate because, in effect, intersectionality, too, is nomothetic. However, the difference is that in intersectionality there appears to be a continuation between the idiographic and the nomothetic because both functions use the same epithets (i.e., race, gender, sexuality, etc.) for their concepts, although the work and formation of these concepts in their respective functions are radically different from one another. In the case of the marxism of Vogel and other symposiasts, however, there is no homophonic illusion because they use a different concept (i.e., class) for the nomothetic function of their explanatory framework.

Identifying this opposition does not mean that embodied social relations are wholly outside of the purview of Vogel's marxism. Rather, it means that the way and extent in which they can be accommodated within such marxism depends on their nomothetization by class, thereby generating structuralist understandings of embodied social relations.[41] Put differently, the aspects of these embodied relations that can be demonstrated to have a logically necessary relationship with class can indeed be added to the fray. This can be easily seen in the unequivocal identification of the symposiasts as marxist-feminists. However, those experiences of these embodied relations that do not have a logical relationship of necessity with class (i.e., non-coincident excesses of embodied social relations) can be captured by idiographic descriptions that represent the evil ornaments of the capitalist mode of production as ideology.

This separation of description and explanation does not only rehearse the notorious epistemological problems produced by the idiographic and nomothetic distinction. It also has important consequences for the base and superstructure metaphor. It recalibrates and refines this metaphor. As those aspects of embodied social relations with a logically necessary relationship to class are nomothetized and rendered structurally to fit into the broader

---

history of this opposition in U.S. sociology, see Kim, 1997. As the founding director of the Fernand Braudel Center, Immanuel Wallerstein, in his introduction to this remarkable special issue, states that "there is no question that this (methodo-)logical debate – or call it if you will an epistemological or philosophical debate – has been central to the history of the social sciences in the last 125 years at least," and continues that "we must go beyond this debate. We must, in the classic phrase, sublate it" (Wallerstein, 1997: 277–78). With the kind of marxism I advocate in this book, I hope to contribute to this effort.

41 It is important to note that this is why the problem of structural-functionalism in marxist-feminist should not be understood only as a problem of exposition and presentation. In other words, this serious problem cannot be overcome with discursive and rhetorical strategies in a new theoretical presentation. It must be reckoned with in terms of concept formation. This problem has been most powerfully and instructively critiqued by Himani Bannerji in "But Who Speaks for Us?" (Bannerji, 1995).

system of explanation (i.e., capitalist mode of production), the argument that they wholly belong to the superstructure and are, therefore, epiphenomenal to primary class relations becomes void. For they are now part and parcel of the base. However, interpreting this advance as the overcoming of the base and superstructure and as arriving at a concrete unity and a genuine identity between class and other embodied social relations would be an act of gross misconstrual for two reasons:

1) Those embodied social relations that do not have a relationship of logical necessity with class (in the case of Vogel, race is an example of this) are still understood as the ideological manifestation of the institutions and relations of the superstructure.
2) The lived aspects of those embodied social relations having a relationship of logical necessity with class that resist nomothetization are also banished to the realm of the superstructure and ideology. As a result, the structural aspects subsume the lived aspects of these relations, thereby making human practice *and* its comprehension severely limited.

XXI Why 'Race' Cannot Be Accommodated within a Marxist-Feminist Analysis as an Embodied Social Relation?

Let us now see how this methodological and epistemological problem shows up in Vogel's analysis of the relationship between class, gender, and race. First of all, Vogel suggests that we discard "the assumption that the various dimensions of difference – for example, race, class, and gender – are comparable" (Vogel, 2018: 282) because only after such jettisoning can we "break out of the tight little circle of supposedly similar categories" (Vogel, 2018: 282). This suggestion registers as contradictory at first, considering she has spent two thirds of her contribution hoping to convince the reader that the problem of whiteness in socialist feminism was only a myth by providing examples of how her own work and that of others always considered class, gender, and race as "comparable phenomena, and of equal weight or importance" (Vogel, 2018: 278). However, my focus here is not to evaluate the consequences of this contradiction for the alternative historical account Vogel produces. For my methodological and epistemological focus, this suggestion does not constitute a contradiction. It is entirely consonant with Vogel's and other symposiasts' analyses.

Having put forward her suggestion, Vogel draws on Gimenez's and Victor Wallis' work in order to argue that "it is becoming possible, even acceptable, to recognize class as key while at the same time incorporating analyses of other factors" (Vogel, 2018: 283). This second movement of analysis completes the impetus of the first by separating and privileging the nomothetic function of class over the idiographic function of embodied social relations. The third movement of the analysis, as ought to be predictable now, is to demonstrate how "'class' and 'gender' have materialist foundations and an intimate link to one another" (Vogel, 2018: 284) because "capitalism depends on the labor power of human beings" (Vogel, 2018: 284). According to Vogel, "[t]o the extent that biological processes contribute to the reproduction of labor power, 'gender' intersects with 'class'" (Vogel, 2018: 285).[42] As a result, for Vogel, "'class' and 'gender' can be analyzed in the abstract, forming part of the system of capitalist accumulation understood at the theoretical level" (Vogel, 2018: 285). In other words, not the everyday lived experiences of gender, but the structural aspects of gender are deemed admissible in Vogel's analysis. The fourth, and the final, movement represents the crescendo of Vogel's analysis. Here, not having a 'materialist foundation' and 'an intimate link' to class, race falls from Vogel's analysis and she declares that "'[r]ace' has always struck [her] as the most problematic of the elements in the so-called trilogy" (Vogel, 2018: 284). For Vogel, race becomes ideological, even though she is careful to add a rejoinder to her diagnosis: "[t]o say that 'race' is ideological does not mean that it isn't real –indeed, powerfully real, as historians have demonstrated and as we in the United States experience every day" (Vogel, 2018: 285). As a result, according to Vogel, we can take the idiographic description of race and racial violence non-white people experience in their everyday lives as the horror and terror of societies where white supremacy reigns. However, we cannot *explain* it within Vogel's analysis and would have to conclude that "'race' stands apart – more real and at least as damaging in our daily lives, I [Vogel] think – than either class or gender" (Vogel, 2018: 285).[43]

---

42 Vogel ends this sentence with "but is not logically necessary to it" (Vogel, 2018: 285). The 'logical necessity' mentioned here is considered in terms of its temporal and spatial reach – in the sense of always and everywhere needed as a precondition. However, the logical necessity I mention above is, in strictly formal sense, neither time nor space bound.
43 It is important to note that Vogel's analysis does not to provide alternatives to the following assumptions; in fact, it seems to reinforce them: the working class is gendered as male; women are white; and race is the inexplicable, irrational, unintended consequence of the social formation in the capitalist mode of production.

XXII Conclusion

To conclude, in this part of *Grounding Critique*, I forward the following conclusions by critiquing some of the leading contemporary marxist-feminist theorists' critiques of intersectionality:

1) Within contemporary marxist-feminist social theory, it is conceptually and methodologically impossible to account for the relational formation of human practice and its comprehension, which constitute embodied social relations.
2) Contrary to the ardent political claims of contemporary marxist-feminist theorists, the production of this impossibility does not share anything with Marx's thought. Rather, it results from the unacknowledged presence and influence of the antinomies of classical sociological reason in the methods and epistemologies of contemporary marxist-feminism.
3) Thus, contemporary marxist-feminism cannot be argued to offer a robust marxist understanding of embodied social relations under capitalism. However, an examination of their conceptual and methodological practices that produce this analytical inability must be considered as imperative, instructive, and invaluable for future marxist efforts to study embodied social relations.

In the next part of this book, I turn to social reproduction theory, whose claim to be a unitary social theory of exploitation and oppression has recently created considerable analytical and political excitement. I investigate concept formation and methodology in social reproduction theory with the same aim of evaluating whether this recent theoretical enterprise might be able to provide a marxist account of embodied social relations under capitalism. I carry out this examination through a critique of the relationship between social reproduction theory and intersectionality – as the former has been fashioned as a marxist-feminist alternative to the latter.

PART II

Embodied Social Relations in Social Reproduction Theory

∴

1 Introduction

In order to clarify concept formation concerning embodied social relations under capitalism that is operative in contemporary marxist social thought, Part I of *Grounding Critique* has performed a methodological close reading of contemporary marxist-feminist critiques of intersectionality. With the same aim of examining how contemporary marxist social theory conceptualizes embodied social relations, Part II critiques 'Social Reproduction Theory' by problematizing its relationship to intersectionality. I suggest that these discrete bodies of knowledge discussed in Part I and II constitute two different moments of contemporary marxist social theory – the negative and the positive, respectively. By the negative, I refer to that mode of critique which does not systematize the elements of its critique, but confines itself to assessing the fundaments, presuppositions, and truth claims of that which is under scrutiny. By the positive, I refer to that mode of critique which systematizes the findings of its assessment into a theoretically ordered alternative framework.

It is important to mention, however, that both the negative and positive moments of critique cannot be reducible to criticism in the sense of faultfinding for its own sake. For critique always involves the labour of thought to delineate the very possibility of rational thinking and its limitations. Accordingly, then, Part I of this book conducts a critique of the negative moment because the theorists discussed produce a critique of intersectionality without offering an ordered alternative. And Part II undertakes a critique of the positive moment because social reproduction theory is fashioned to be a marxist-feminist alternative to intersectionality with a definite claim of constructing a novel social theory. Put differently, while Part I of this book is a critique of critique, Part II is a critique of metacritique.[1]

The methodological principle followed in Part II remains the same as Part I: a close reading that reveals concept formation in contemporary marxist social theory, which examines embodied social relations and their relationships to one another and class. However, this methodological identity across Part I and II, on which the analytical coherence of this book is built, is not a mere deployment of a dogmatic scheme or procedure that is inattentive to the

---

1 For important discussions of critique, metacritique, and postcritique in relation to the methodological close reading I sustain throughout this book, see Anker and Felski, 2017; Butler, 2004; Fassin, 2017; Gasché, 2007; and Zembylas, 2022.

phenomena under consideration (i.e., embodied social relations) and to the different ways of studying them (i.e., the negative and positive moments of critique).[2] Conceived in this dogmatic manner, such a methodological identity may perhaps account for a (school of) thought. Yet, it cannot undertake the labour of thinking, thereby becoming subject to the theoretical rigidification and political incapacity it aims to discern in the first place. To avoid this serious pitfall, I effectuate the methodological identity in this book speculatively through a phenomenological approach.

Therefore, in *Grounding Critique*, I refrain from issuing validity for any secure ontological claim by elaborating on some conclusion that has already been reached, which is the customary function of methodology in quasi-transcendental and transcendental social theories. Instead, I treat the multiple attempts and negotiations to reconcile embodied social relations with one another and class as being part and parcel of the very historical conditions that generate the concept formation I examine throughout Part I and II. Put differently, the research presented here does not simply uncover the inadequacies of the contemporary marxist social theories examined in terms of their concept formations and, consequently, dismiss those theories *tout court*. Instead, and more importantly, my methodological aim is to recover those inadequacies as objects of knowledge in each of their different manifestations as indicative of and phenomenal to the social fracturation of political subjectivities in contemporary capitalist societies.

Therefore, while in Part I my methodology has required a close reading and tracking of concept formations in individual marxist-feminist texts critiquing intersectionality, in this part it demands a focus on the very making of a particular feminist concept (i.e., social reproduction) into a theory (i.e., social reproduction theory). In Part II, I demonstrate that this theory functions as a metacritique with secure ontological and political claims to solving the impasses of intersectionality by syntactic and formalistic reordering of the relationship between and among embodied social relations and class. As a result, the identity and continuity across Part I and II are to be found less in the exact and fixed methodological procedures than in the phenomenological

---

2 My methodological deliberations here are influenced by the exchange between Theodor Adorno and Lucien Goldmann, which took place at the Second International Colloquium on "Sociologie de la Littérature," with a special theme of "Critique sociologique et critique psychanalytique" in Royaumont, Dec. 10–12, 1966, which is reproduced in Goldmann, 1977: 129–145. For Goldmann's other influential essays on method, see Goldmann, 1980.

unfolding of the methodological focus on concept formations and their historicity in the theoretical approaches under scrutiny.[3]

Thus, Part II of this book examines the ways in which social reproduction theory establishes itself as a marxist-feminist alternative to intersectionality. Taking this claim seriously, and in its own terms, I treat social reproduction theory as a social theory that offers an account of the social and society through the relationship between embodied social relations and class, as opposed to being a feminist political economy that exercises varying degrees of epistemic reflexivity in relation to its social context.[4] Therefore, in this part of the book, I thematize, problematize, and clarify social reproduction theory's relationship to intersectionality, and investigate the consequences of this relationship in terms of methodology, concept formation, and the selection and articulation of social problems, which constitute the three main pillars of any critical social theory.

11 What Is the Relationship between Social Reproduction Theory and Intersectionality?

Tithi Bhattacharya's 2017 edited collection *Social Reproduction Theory: Remapping Class, Recentering Oppression* is declared to be "presenting a more sophisticated alternative to intersectionality"[5] on the book's main information webpage by its publisher Pluto Press. This claim should not be taken as a mere advertisement designed to increase the life-chances of the volume in the ever-expanding market of academic publications. Indeed, intersectionality consistently appears as a bar, gauge, reference, and measure in the various evaluations of social reproduction theory. However, as I demonstrate in the

---

3   To be sure, the identity and continuity mentioned here is of methodological variety. Other sets of identities and continuities between Part I and Part II are easily found when considered in terms of the contents and themes of these respective parts. However, as I go onto discuss, various thinkers in these two parts treat these contents and themes differently despite their unanimous identification with both marxism and feminism. Privileging the methodological identity and continuity over the contents and themes is particularly productive in the face of such unanimous identifications, especially also considering that I deeply share those identifications.
4   As will become apparent in the course of Part II, the latter designation would have been perhaps a more productive and a defensible position for the proponents of social reproduction theory.
5   "Social Reproduction Theory," *Pluto Press*, accessed 24.05.2023, https://www.plutobooks.com/9780745399881/social-reproduction-theory/.

following paragraphs, there has yet to be a general agreement as to the nature of the actual relationship between intersectionality and social reproduction theory. Therefore, here I investigate the existing ways in which this relationship is conceptualized in the literature by the critics and commentators of social reproduction theory. Then, I ascertain the nature of this relationship by examining the texts of the leading proponents of social reproduction theory.

The renowned British marxist sociologist Colin Barker assesses that "Social Reproduction Theory, as illustrated by this excellent collection [Bhattacharya's volume], is both a heady brew, and a very productive line of thought. Its starting point involves a critique of the one book which might stand in for a 'bible' in Marxism: the three volumes of Marx's *Capital*" (Barker, no year: n.p.). Concurring with social reproduction theory's foundational argument that Marx did not adequately discuss the reproduction of labour-power, Barker engages in a rather dreary homophonic paronomasia[6] by announcing that "the 'holy' work [*Capital*], it turns out, is very holey" (Barker, no year: n.p.). According to Barker, there has been two strategies to fill in the gaps existing in marxism. One is to look outside marxism; the other is "to protect the *unitary* status of Marxist theory" (Barker, no year: n.p., emphasis in original). The former strategy, according to Barker, includes intersectionality which adds "racism and other forms of inequality" (Barker, no year: n.p.) to gender domination to "provide a more complete set of categories and notions to grasp the character of modern society" (Barker, no year: n.p.). Barker argues that the latter strategy, of which social reproduction theory is representative, seeks "to 'deepen', 'expand', 'supplement', 'broaden' or 'stretch' the language of Marxism by 'going beyond' *Capital*" (Barker, no year: n.p.). In sum, Barker methodologically counterposes intersectionality and social reproduction theory as two alternative and competing strategies that address the same gaps in our understanding of the social world.[7]

---

6 Also known as pun.
7 It must be noted that Barker's counterpositioning is itself in need of clarification. In footnote number two of his text, Barker suggests that the first strategy, of which intersectionality is representative, is also related to E.P. Thompson's proposal to "turning to 'history' to provide the categories that the narrow discipline of 'political economy' (into whose maw he [Thompson] thought Marx himself had been sucked) could not provide" (Barker, no year: n.p.). The relationship that Barker establishes between Thompson and intersectionality indicates the limitations of the conceptual criteria he uses to delineate the works he considers to be inside or outside marxism. It is also important to ask whether the gaps Barker identifies in marxism are 'linguistic' in nature because it seems that, according to Barker, social reproduction theory can address them by stretching "the language of Marxism" (Barker, no year: n.p.).

Contrary to Barker's conclusion that social reproduction theory and intersectionality are diametrically opposed in their relationship to marxism and that social reproduction theory consolidates marxism's unitary scientific status, Joshua Depaolis argues that Bhattacharya's volume "is neither Marxist in the sense of adhering to the conceptual categories of Marx's critique of political economy as a point of departure, nor a theory in the sense of an internally consistent conceptual object constructed in order to grasp the variegation of the real object and differentiate the essential and the inherent from the contingent" (Depaolis, 2018: n.p.).[8] Depaolis arrives at this judgement about social reproduction theory partly because of its relationship to intersectionality in his review of the edited volume for one of the main sites of contemporary marxist knowledge dissemination, *Marx & Philosophy Review of Books*. According to Depaolis, intersectionality is "an umbrella term for struggles for substantive equality of rights in the bourgeois democratic order" (Depaolis, 2018: n.p.). To justify his view Depaolis turns to Lise Vogel's foreword to the edited volume. According to Vogel, the contributors of the volume "argue that it is possible to embrace social reproduction theory without discarding the strengths of intersectionality thinking, especially its ability to develop nuanced descriptive and historical accounts of various 'categories of social difference'" (Vogel, 2017: XI).

Drawing on Vogel's approval of the productive togetherness of intersectionality and social reproduction theory,[9] Depaolis concludes that social reproduction theory begins "from an acknowledgement of the 'strengths of intersectionality theory [sic.]'" (Depaolis, 2018: n.p.). Depaolis interprets this

---

8 It should be noted that Depaolis works with a very restricted and problematic notion of theory here. This notion of theory is oblivious to its own historicity. Especially considering Depaolis' monopolistic emphasis on what counts as marxism, it is rather necessary to remember the historical evolution of 'theory.' With the violent historical ascendency of colonial bourgeois rationalism and its attendant capital accumulation oriented instrumental rationality, theory has come to signify the schemata of general principles explaining the nomological regularities in the structure of the world. Aiming at sempiternal replicability and universal applicability, this conception of theory has produced positivist models of explanation and prediction such as hypothetico-deductive and deductive-nomological. To ensure its scientificity and validity, these models operate with strict rules and procedures of conduct by conjoining privileged axiomatic propositions and required observations and experiments. For a detailed discussion of this evolution, see: Olson, 1993; Nowak, 1976; and Benton, 2014.

9 Vogel registers her approval of this agenda by noting that "this strikes me [Vogel] as a promising direction in which to go" (Vogel, 2017: XI). As the section on Vogel in Part I of this book attests, this is rather puzzling given that a year later she produces an article with a diametrically opposed conclusion regarding intersectionality, especially considering the fact that this foreword and that article share chunks of text in verbatim.

departure point as a "deferential nod to bourgeois-reformist social thought" (Depaolis, 2018: n.p.). In his estimation, this nod and the "severe crime of omission" (Depaolis, 2018: n.p.) that Marx is charged with for not investigating the (re)production of labour-power substitute "the radicality of Marx's critique for an essentialist and conventionally bourgeois view of gender relations" (Depaolis, 2018: n.p.). Subsequently, Depaolis argues that social reproduction theory merely constitutes "a diffuse attack on oppressive power relations" (Depaolis, 2018: n.p.), rather than a "serious Marxist analysis of the democratic struggle for women's emancipation in relation to the proletarian struggle to abolish capitalist relations of production" (Depaolis, 2018: n.p.).

Although neither Barker nor Depaolis discuss what qualifies a text as 'marxist' or not in any serious conceptual capacity, what is at stake in their assessments is social reproduction theory's relationship to marxism: Does social reproduction theory constitute an advancement within marxism, or does it instantiate a retreat from marxism? Intersectionality simply functions as the sagittal plane on which this relationship between marxism and social reproduction theory is ascertained. The reference and comparison to intersectionality, in Barker's and Depaolis' assessments, does not pose or answer the following questions: How does social reproduction theory conceptualize embodied social relations under contemporary capitalism and analyze their relationships with one another? Does social reproduction theory conceptualize class, gender, and race to be the same kind of social relations, or does it consider class a social relation that encompasses gender and race? What, according to social reproduction theory, is the relationship between gender, race, and other embodied social relations, are they analogically derived from one another, and what is the nature of the relationship between and among them? Instead of contemplating these questions, which help us better understand embodied social relations under contemporary class societies, Barker's and Depaolis' evaluations of social reproduction theory render intersectionality as an extrinsic plane of locomotion away or towards marxism, thereby missing an opportunity for a more productive theoretical engagement.

III Social Reproduction Theory's Ambiguous and Inadequately Self-Reflexive Relationship to Intersectionality

In other treatments of social reproduction theory, too, intersectionality remains as a constant reference point. Not all critics and commentators, however, use intersectionality in the manner of Barker and Depaolis, as a third term through which social reproduction theory's relationship to marxism is determined.

Some critics and commentators, including both those who critique the main tenets of social reproduction theory and those who find themselves in general agreement with them, focus directly on the relationship between social reproduction theory and intersectionality, without a triadic meaning structure in place.

For instance, Marina Vishmidt and Zöe Sutherland argue that "contemporary social reproduction theory aims to produce a more materialist intersectionality" (Vishmidt and Sutherland, 2020: 146–147). According to them, social reproduction theory is a materialist intersectionality "that would not only anchor gender, but also racialization, and other categories of subordination, within a thinking of 'totality', and generate a form of politics that would take the imbrication of all these into account, albeit not as independent variables or the contingent outcomes of multiple interacting systems of oppression" (Vishmidt and Sutherland, 2020: 147). Anna Carastathis and Myrto Tsilimpounidi, on the other hand, forward that social reproduction theory is "a Marxist answer to the theoretical and political contestations surrounding intersectionality" (Carastathis and Tsilimpounidi 2020: 12), which, according to the authors, is "a theoretical framework originating in Black feminist thought, which has become the predominant way of theorizing the mutual constitution of systems of oppression that are falsely constructed as mutually exclusive in single-axis analyses and monistic politics" (Carastathis and Tsilimpounidi 2020: 12). A third view, which is different from both social reproduction theory as a 'more materialist' intersectionality and as a marxist response to intersectionality, is that of Alessandra Mezzadri. Citing David McNally's critique of intersectionality (McNally, 2017), which she finds "rather selective" (Mezzadri, 2019: 34), Mezzadri maintains that social reproduction theory is "overly adversarial towards other theorisations moved by compatible intellectual and political concerns" (Mezzadri, 2019: 34), such as intersectionality. Instead of this adversarial approach, Mezzadri suggests cultivating "productive ways in which Marxism and Intersectionality approaches may articulate and complement each another" (Mezzadri, 2019: 40, footnote 7).[10] Although the thinkers mentioned in this paragraph unite in cultivating a more critical approach to social reproduction theory, it is apparent that they do not agree on the specific relationship between intersectionality and social reproduction theory. Nor do they problematize this relationship by discussing the different kind and place of materialisms within the concept formation of these two bodies

---

10   Here Mezzadri finds Bohrer's work as an important step, see Bohrer, 2019.

of knowledge, or by investigating the epistemological preconditions of a partnership between them.

Of those critics and commentators who display a general agreement with social reproduction theory, the renowned marxist-feminist scholar Rosemary Hennessy argues that social reproduction theory provides the basis for "an approach [that] offers a historical and materialist analysis of the reproduction of gender and race as historically specific ideologies that the metaphor of intersectionality fails to offer" (Hennessy, 2020: 4).[11] Nicole Leach's assessment is similar to that of Hennessey. For Leach, social reproduction theory as unitary marxist theory challenges "the ahistorical bent of certain feminisms" (Leach, 2016: 113), such as intersectionality and dual-systems theories, which "repeat[s] ... base/superstructure separation through a disarticulation of the social into separate spheres" (Leach, 2016: 112). Perhaps, one of the most interesting claims with regard to the relationship between social reproduction theory and intersectionality is issued by Cinzia Arruzza. According to Arruzza, "as a consequence ... of the delay in the articulation of the concept of social reproduction, the standard form of explanation of the relationship between gender, race, and capitalism became that of the distinction between systems of oppression, their 'relative autonomy,' their 'reciprocal articulation or intersection,' or their 'consubstantiality'" (Arruzza, 2016: 27). This rather extraordinary claim amounts to arguing that intersectionality has merely served as an inadequate placeholder until the dilatory advent of "a unitary theory of social reproduction" (Arruzza, 2016: 28), which is capable of solving the dilemmas and impasses that intersectionality has introduced.[12]

The above discussion of the reception of social reproduction theory is helpful in establishing the fact that social reproduction theory is a contemporary response to the ascendancy and salience of intersectionality. While some commentators assert which one of the two bodies of knowledge fares better

---

11 Here it is crucial to note that while it is clear that Hennessey analytically favours social reproduction theory, it is not as clear whether according to her: a) gender and race are merely historically specific ideologies – as though, they are not more than a social form of consciousness and do not have an actual everyday existence as power relations; b) social reproduction theory explains the reproduction of gender and race; and c) intersectionality has ever claimed to produce 'a historical and materialist analysis of the reproduction of gender and race as historically specific ideologies.' I suggest that these questions are important because they direct us to the often-unexplained ground for the comparison between intersectionality and social reproduction theory.

12 Evaluating the validity of Arruzza's claim in relation to the history of social thought lies outside the remit of this section. Suffice it to note that I find this claim to be ahistorical and untenable.

at developing a comprehensive theoretical framework to understand the relationship between class, gender, and race, none of them examine and explain the nature of the relationship between intersectionality and social reproduction theory. Neither do they examine the way in which social reproduction theory conceptualizes class, gender, and race as social relations through its relationship to intersectionality. However, it is important to note that, in my view, this problem does not fully reside in the analyses of the above critics and commentators; rather, it is a function of social reproduction theory's ambiguous and inadequately self-reflexive relationship to intersectionality.

IV Social Reproduction Theory as a Marxist-Feminist Alternative to Intersectionality

I, thus, argue that any rigorous assessment and critique of social reproduction theory demands that its relationship to intersectionality be clarified. For the knowledge claims of social reproduction theory are oriented towards the field of social inquiry and problem set by intersectionality in the first instance. Put differently, social reproduction theory does not conceptually explain how its initial focus on the relationship between class and gender is expanded into a focus on race other embodied social relations of power. Instead, it simply finds these relations in the knowledge production efforts of intersectional feminists as they conceptualized and mobilized them. Having found them through intersectionality, social reproduction theory turns its analytical attention to these relations, as well as their relationship with one another, in order to produce a theoretically coherent account of systems of social oppression. In other words, aiming at producing a marxist-feminist alternative to intersectionality, social reproduction theory transfigures its scientific status into a total social theory, as opposed to merely reanimating the focus on the concept of social reproduction in feminist political economy analyses.

This expansion in the scientific status of social reproduction theory does not come as a result of a series of self-reflexive reckonings with the methodological, epistemological, and ontological frameworks of earlier social reproduction and feminist political economy analyses.[13] Rather, it is fashioned as

---

13 In fact, I suggest this is why, in their search for origins social reproduction theorists isolate and emphasize the work of Lise Vogel, which is not only not among the first to come to mind when one thinks of the vibrant socialist feminist scholarship and domestic labour debates of the 1970s, but is also much less associated with any particular tendency within these debates (i.e., the dominant Italian, German, and Canadian schools), thereby not

an alternative to intersectionality, an external analytical framework, in a non-dialogical manner by being hoisted upon Vogel's *Marxism and The Oppression of Women*, a work whose thirty year hiatus is explained away as a mere result of the popular ascendence of post-structural and postmodern feminisms, yet another set of external analytical frameworks (Ferguson and McNally, 2013: XVII–XL). What is, therefore, at stake with this expansion into the realms of social theory is that the social problem that this theory is supposed to identify and investigate is simply inherited, implicit, and incondite. Therefore, this dilemma of the lack of articulation and selection of a social problem undermines social reproduction theory's status as a social theory from the outset because a self-reflexive determination of a social problem that coheres with consistent concept formation and investigative method constitutes the formal and operative validity of any social theory.[14]

Thus, the crucial tasks of this part of *Grounding Critique* are the examination of if and how social reproduction theory articulates and selects the social problem it treats. To guide this examination, I pose the following set of questions:

1. Does social reproduction theory explain how the analytic and conceptual focus passes from the question of *women's relationship to capitalism as a social group*, which was the main organizing social problem for feminist political economy, to the question of *the relationship between class, gender, and race under capitalism*?
2. What kinds of changes in concept formation does this passage require, and what are the ontological, epistemological, and methodological consequences of such a passage?

---

having become overdetermined in the range of interpretations it might offer. It is interesting to note that *Historical Materialism*'s guest editors of the special issue on social reproduction list Vogel along with Eli Zaretsky and Wally Seccombe in their categorizations of marxist-feminism, whereas the above-mentioned schools are all lumped together in the same category (Ferguson, LeBaron, Dimitrakaki, and Farris, 2016: 27). Vogel, as the only woman in her category, emerges from this classification as the originator of social reproduction theory. I suggest that if any of the above schools were to be chosen as the originator of this framework, there would be more conceptual labour needed to justify the shift from gender-class analytics to race and other embodied social relations because of the well-established epistemological practices of these schools.

14   To be sure, what social theory is and what it is composed of are not easy questions and have been the subject of volumes of important monographs, of which the following have been the most influential on my thinking regarding the subject: Benton, 2014; Eisenstadt and Curelaru, 1976;. Levine, 1995; Martindale, 2013; Stark, 2013; Sztompka, 2013; and Warren, 2008.

3. How is the focus on a collective subject (i.e., women) replaced by a focus on a singular social relation (i.e., gender), and how does this new focus on the particular social relation of gender multiply into other social relations (i.e., race, sexuality, etc.)?
4. Does social reproduction theory account for the problematization of a unitary collective subject in relation to other social relations of oppression within its own conceptual and historical formation? Or does it simply inherit this problematization from other feminisms, and, if so, what kind of conceptual reckoning does it perform regarding the theoretical presuppositions of these feminisms?
5. Put summarily, how does social reproduction theory understand and expound the concepts of subject (collective and singular), subjectivity, social relations, society, and the social both individually and in relation to one another?

With these questions in mind, below I investigate and clarify the relationship between social reproduction theory and intersectionality by turning to the foundational texts that are written by social reproduction theory's chief proponents.

v Social Reproduction Theory's 'Methodology' and Its Articulation and Selection of Social Problems

The guest editors of *Historical Materialism*'s special issue on social reproduction[15] trace the beginnings of social reproduction theory to "the work carried on at Historical Materialism conferences – especially since the 2011 launch of a Marxist-Feminist stream of panels" (Ferguson et al., 2016: 28). They argue that both these stream of panels and their special issue were inspired by the twofold challenge with which marxism-feminism "as a whole" (Ferguson et al., 2016: 28) struggled: 1) "to reconcile its limited terms of reference – the binary concepts of class and gender – with the multi-faceted complexity of real-world relations and political struggles" (Ferguson et al., 2016: 27), and 2) "the ways in which racial oppression intersects with gendered forms of domination and class exploitation" (Ferguson et al., 2016: 27).[16] I suggest that this twofold

---

15   Sue Ferguson, Genevieve LeBaron, Angeliki Dimitrakaki, and Sara Farris.
16   I draw attention to the editors' usage of the verb "intersect" not only to note the difficulty of expression to explain the relationship between different forms of embodied social relations, but also to highlight the irony this expression offers in their text considering the critique of intersectionality launched therein.

challenge belongs more to the editors' construction of marxist-feminism than the actual history of marxist-feminism itself. The editors understand 'marxist-feminism' to consist of the following currents:

> (i): At the beginning of the twentieth century, Kollontai, following Frederick Engels's method, if not his conclusions, saw *private property and marriage* as the pivotal institutions whose existence signalled and entrenched women's secondary status within the burgeoning capitalist social order. (ii): Building on the conceptualisation of the household as the key site of women's oppression, in the 1960s and 1970s the writings and political activism of Margaret Benston, Peggy Morton, Selma James, Mariarosa Dalla Costa, Maria Mies, Silvia Federici and others emphasised the role played by women's *domestic labour* therein. Domestic labour, they pointed out, produces labour-power, which in turn produces capitalist value. (iii): Finding such formulations overly structural and mechanistic, some Marxist-Feminists – most notably, Michèle Barrett and Mary McIntosh – retained a focus on the private family but turned to Althusserian ideas about the *relative autonomy of ideology* to explain the apparently anachronistic co-existence of patriarchal and capitalist systems. (iv): And lastly, Lise Vogel, Eli Zaretsky, Wally Seccombe (to name a few early contributors) developed the *social-reproduction* perspective, which highlighted and examined the logic of the contradictory but necessary internal/external relationship between gendered and economic productive relations. Various theorists have defined the concept of social reproduction differently, but broadly it encompasses the activities associated with the maintenance and reproduction of peoples' lives on a daily and intergenerational basis.
>
> FERGUSON ET AL., 2016: 27–28.

I argue that this reconstruction of marxist-feminism consisting wholly of 'white' scholars is not only factually incorrect, but also profoundly at odds with one of the main goals of the special issue, which is to account for race, racialization, and racism within a social reproduction theory framework. I suggest that if the editors had a more accurate list of marxist-feminists – one that included, to name but a few, Angela Davis, Audre Lorde, June Jordon, Himani Bannerji, Claudia Jones, Hazel Carby, Michelle Wallace, Pratibha Parmar, and Swasti Mitter – their project of addressing social problems of race and sexuality would actually have a chance of organically developing within marxist-feminism. I would be remiss if I did not note that some of the thinkers in the above list I provide admittedly focus more on 'race' than 'gender.' However, if the majority of thinkers who only focus on 'gender' in the editors' list could be thought of as integral to understanding 'race,' I cannot think of a valid rationale as to why those thinkers who focus on 'race' cannot be drawn upon to understand 'gender.'

However, insisting on this inaccurate, incomplete, and white genealogy of marxist-feminism, the editors continue to argue that "[s]ocial-Reproduction (Marxist-) Feminism, or SRF, stands out as a promising approach for grasping some of the complexities that have eluded it and the other strands in the past" (Ferguson et al., 2016: 28) (i.e., those strands that focus on: the social relations of private property and matrimony; the household division of labour and domestic labour; and the ideological autonomy of gendered social relations as the main cause of women's oppression under capitalism). The editors attribute the eluding of "race, sexuality, colonialism and other constitutive social relations" (Ferguson et al., 2016: 30) to working "from within a binary [sic] class-and-gender framework" (Ferguson et al., 2016: 28). Although the editors accept this shortcoming has also afflicted "the first generation of SRF theorists" (Ferguson et al., 2016: 28), they argue that "the methodology they [SRF theorists] developed has encouraged others to extend and deepen the theoretical range of SRF approaches" (Ferguson et al., 2016: 28).

While the above claim concerning the methodology of social reproduction feminism might have the appearance of validity, the soundness of this claim remains to be demonstrated. Such a demonstration ought to involve a discussion of concept formation, investigative method, and the articulation and selection of the social problem addressed. More concretely, and in this particular instance, it requires a thorough explication of the methodology of social reproduction feminism; the reasons the previous generations of social reproduction theorists eluded the above social relations in their explanatory frameworks; and the ways in which this methodology recognizes and congrues with other social relations. However, nowhere do the editors engage with any aspect of such a demonstration.

In fact, the editors' introduction references 'methodology' only once when they suggest that the methodology of social reproduction feminism is capable of accommodating the need of going beyond a gender-class analytics and bringing "constitutive social relations" (Ferguson et al., 2016: 30) into the framework of analysis. In addition to the unelaborated nature of this 'methodology,' the editors also leave unanswered the crucial question: what are these social relations constitutive of? Instead of a response, they offer a list in which 'race,' 'sexuality,' and 'colonialism' are juxtaposed as the examples of these 'constitutive social relations.' In the absence of a discussion of the similitude of these concepts in terms of their ontology, composition, and function, this list fails to explain why and in what specific fashion these relations ought to be integrated into the promoted methodology. Moreover, as the editors diagnose the separation of these 'constitutive social relations' from gender-class analytics as "Marxist-Feminism's greatest weakness" (Ferguson et al., 2016: 30), their failure – to account for the relationship between these relations, and of what they are constitutive – indicates that social reproduction theory, too, must have a self-reflexive explanation of its articulation and selection of social problems in relation to its methodology.

To be sure, the editors' failure to attend to these crucial queries might be attributed to the genre constraints of writing an introduction, as well as to the challenges of multi-authored academic knowledge production. It certainly does not evince any impossibility of attending to these questions within the social reproduction theory enterprise. Rather, it intensifies the need for doing so. It instills an analytical curiosity and attention to find the moments focusing on concept formation, investigative methods, and the articulation and selection of social problems in different texts under scrutiny. It also helps craft the working hypothesis that the accumulation of the lack of these moments points to the mere importation of the above 'constitutive social relations' into social reproduction theory from intersectionality to redress the 'greatest weakness of marxist-feminism.' Thus, in the remainder of Part II, I conduct an examination of the presence and absence of these moments in other fundamental texts in relation to the conceptual, social, and political consequences of this working hypothesis for social reproduction theory.

VI 'Race,' Racialization, and Experience in Social Reproduction Feminism

Susan Ferguson's article titled "Canadian Contributions to Social Reproduction Feminism, Race and Embodied Labor" (Ferguson, 2008) constitutes one of most important resources of social reproduction theory. Ferguson has been at the forefront of promoting social reproduction feminism and theory for two decades. I argue that this article richly deserves an analytical engagement through a methodological close reading because it contains classical arguments regarding the need for developing social reproduction feminism as a unitary social theory. In this article, Ferguson argues that early attempts to produce a marxist anti-racist feminism failed because of the structuralist mobilization of economic reductionism in social reproduction feminism. While at first glance it is not entirely clear how, in terms of their concept formation, these early attempts tried to produce an 'anti-racist' marxist-feminism, later in the course of article it becomes evident that these attempts refer to early (Canadian) social reproduction feminisms exemplified in the works of, *inter alia*, Meg Luxton, Bonnie Fox, Pat Armstrong, Hugh Armstrong, Martha MacDonald, Patricia Connelly, Wally Seccombe, Angela Miles, Margaret Benston, and D.W. Livingstone (Ferguson, 2008).

According to Ferguson, although "the postmodern turn and cultural feminism pushed SRF [social reproduction feminism] to the margins of Canadian feminist discourse, its most serious theoretical challenge came not from a Foucauldian, but from an anti-racist socialist feminist, Himani Bannerji" (Ferguson, 2008: 44).[17] Ferguson, in fact, borrows the charge of structuralism and economic reductionism against early iterations of social reproduction feminism from Bannerji's work. However, it must be noted that Ferguson's and Bannerji's uses of structuralism are different from one another, and this difference remains unexplored and unacknowledged in Ferguson's article. While 'structuralism' features frequently and saliently in Ferguson's text, the term operates as a generalized *bête noire* whose specificities, as well as the ontological and epistemological consequences of these specificities, are not explicated. Instead, 'structuralism' for Ferguson seems merely to constitute a semiotic formalism at the level of linguistic expression.

Bannerji, on the other hand, counterposes structuralism as an interpretative framework to Marx's method as delineated in *the German Ideology*, thereby specifically showing how the 'marxism' of social reproduction feminism shares much less with Marx's method than with structuralist reproductions of Marx's 'theory' (Bannerji, 1995).[18] A crucial effect of this unacknowledged difference is made manifest in these authors' respective conclusions concerning the future of social reproduction theory. According to Ferguson, "Bannerji holds little hope for redeeming SRF [social reproduction feminism] from the stranglehold of structuralism and reductionism. But her pessimism may be unwarranted as it overlooks the potential explanatory power of SRF's foundational concepts" (Ferguson, 2008: 48).

Bannerji conducts her anti-racist feminist marxist critique of socialist-feminist political economy at the level of concept formation by insisting that concepts cannot be simply transposed from one framework in which they are operationalized to another without changing their constitutional properties.

---

17   *Pace* Ferguson, it is important to note that Bannerji's critique does not address 'social reproduction feminism' *per se*. Rather, she critiques socialist-feminism, and this critique may be said to have implications for social reproduction traditions. It is also crucial to mention that Bannerji does not identify herself as a 'socialist-feminist.'
18   In particular, see p. 81–89, and p. 34–38.

However, I argue that Ferguson mistakes this critique for an individual psychological attitude of 'redemptive hope' and 'unwarranted pessimism.' This mistaking results in Ferguson's abandoning a crucial methodological investigation of concept formation in social reproduction feminism in favour of demonstrating the accommodative capacity of the 'concept' of labour used in the "more recent work in the paradigm" (Ferguson, 2008: 48) of social reproduction feminism. Here, it is imperative to clarify that a study of 'concept formation' entails a thorough engagement with the methodology of social sciences as that which mediates social ontology and epistemology in rendering them actionable in the course of social investigation. Such an approach, therefore, differs from that of Ferguson, who proceeds by providing definitions of the concept of labour, as mobilized in the paradigm of social reproduction, and scans the contents in their givenness.

Ferguson espouses this approach in order to argue that "with its expansive definition of labor and its comprehensive focus on the full spectrum of practical activity" (Ferguson, 2008: 42) social reproduction feminism "is uniquely positioned to accommodate such complexity [of racialization] without forfeiting attentiveness to social relations of class and/or capitalism" (Ferguson, 2008: 42). In the course of Ferguson's argument, in other words, the failure of earlier social reproduction feminism in relation to explaining race and racialization is severed from the methodological limitations of their theory and reduced to a mere need for a more capacious definition of labour. This separation and reduction bypass the need for expounding social reproduction feminism's conceptual inability to produce an adequate explanation of the embodied social relation of race and processes of racialization, which also requires an investigation as to why these relations and processes constitute a social problem for social reproduction theory in the first place. Instead, this shortcoming is merely pointed out by acknowledging, but not engaging with, Bannerji's conceptual critique; then, it is thematically incorporated by importing multiple social relations from intersectionality as social problems to be addressed.

Ferguson, in this article, understands intersectionality to be a "comprehensive materialist approach" (Ferguson, 2008: 43), which insists that "any given social moment embodies a historically specific nexus of institutionalized relations of class, race, gender, etc." (Ferguson, 2008: 43). According to Ferguson, "intersectionality overcomes many of the weaknesses associated with early Marxist feminism" (Ferguson, 2008: 43), the chief of which is the lack of an understanding of race and racialization. Within this context, Ferguson envisions social reproduction feminism's role as "provid[ing] intersectional analyses with a methodology that brings 'both capitalism and class back into the discussion'" (Ferguson, 2008: 42). Therefore, Ferguson leaves the initiation of the embodied social relationship of race and the processes of racialization into the framework of social reproduction feminism and theory unexplained – both at the levels of concept formation and at the selection and articulation of social problems.

Thus, in lieu of a self-reflexive conceptual reckoning, the relationship between social reproduction theory and intersectionality is reduced to one of contiguous externality within the field of feminist knowledge production. This relationship makes an advantage-disadvantage, or pros-and-cons, assessment between theoretical frameworks without examining their constitutive propositions and presuppositions. For instance, according to Ferguson, "intersectionality overcomes many of the weaknesses associated with early Marxist feminism" (Ferguson, 2008: 43) because it "has the decided merit of exploring subjectivities, of focusing analysis on people's lives, not just abstract categories of race, gender and class" (Ferguson, 2008: 43). This often-repeated claim is one of the main imports of Ferguson's text. Ferguson argues that by "identifying nexuses of oppression and probing their inner workings" (Ferguson, 2008: 55), intersectionality "has the advantage of 'starting from experience'" (Ferguson, 2008: 55), which constitutes "a clear advance on structuralist political economy" (Ferguson, 2008: 55). Recognizing this perceived strength of intersectionality, Ferguson strives for "a revised and expanded SRF framework [that] conceptualizes those intersectional nexuses as products of labor – of creative activity undertaken to reproduce ourselves" (Ferguson, 2008: 55). Ferguson believes that this new framework renders "real and systemic connections between the endlessly varied struggles of the oppressed ... apparent" (Ferguson, 2008: 55) in a planetary scope: those between, "for instance, a childcare worker strike in Vancouver, the struggle to protect schooling for girls in Kabul, and the environmental movement against mega-dams along India's River Narmada" (Ferguson, 2008: 55).

I argue that Ferguson's text attempts to display a certain plausible semantic, syntactic, and political clarity, and is of great importance on account of being one of the earliest examples of linking the social reproduction tradition with intersectionality. However, it does not clarify the relationship between social reproduction theory and intersectionality. Rather, it functions as a non-performative conceit,[19] one that assumes the successful integration of embodied social relations of race and others simply by mentioning the need

---

19 My use of the term, 'non-performative,' is borrowed from Sara Ahmed's work. For different iterations and details of Ahmed's thinking on the subject see Ahmed, 2004; Ahmed, 2006; and Ahmed, 2016.

for including them into social reproduction feminisms. To be concrete, the text sets up structuralism and reductionism as the encumbrances responsible for the early social reproduction analyses' indifference to and exclusion of race and other embodied social relations. Then, it continues to argue that intersectionality is able to offer an analysis of these social relations because it begins its account with experience.[20] Ferguson's text ends by forwarding an improved framework for social reproduction analyses that treats the intersections of embodied social relations as products of labour, thereby presuming to supplant intersectionality and explain the capitalist social totality.

This unfolding of Ferguson's argument, I contend, is possible due to the following set of conceptual omission, equivocation, and slippage:

1) Ferguson suggests that structuralism and structuralist analyses cannot accommodate experience. But, she does not explore this suggestion in any conceptual capacity, thereby unwittingly contributing to the misapprehension that a mention of 'experience' suffices to dispel structuralism and its limitations in social scientific analyses.

2) The equivocation between an epistemological ordering of experience and lived experience itself, which prevents a rigorous examination of the possibilities of dialogue between social reproduction theory and intersectionality.

3) Throughout the text, the slippages between the concepts of 'experience,' 'identity,' 'consciousness,' and 'subjectivity' effect an appearance of achieving an analytical unity of the concepts that were omitted from the earlier social reproduction analyses. This appearance subsequently undergirds the claim of the new 'revised and expanded' version of social reproduction analysis of being able to explain the capitalist social totality.

---

20 As I demonstrate below, Ferguson does not explain in analytical terms what it means to begin one's analysis with experience because her text does not involve a consideration of what experience is and how it is produced, beyond presuming that experience merely is an interpretation of an event in social and ideological terms. I have also noted above the same use of gender and race in Hennessy's evaluation of social reproduction theory in relation to intersectionality.

VII Vacillating between Supplementing and Supplanting Intersectionality

I suggest that the consequences of these conceptual problems manifest themselves most clearly in Ferguson's contradictory treatment of intersectionality and in her analysis of race. One of the main limitations of intersectionality, according to Ferguson, is that "the most such analyses can do is highlight similarities and differences amongst discrete instances of oppression, and explain those oppressions in terms of contingent economic and cultural forces (state policies, policing practices, or the culture of whiteness, for example)" (Ferguson, 2008: 55). However, earlier in the same article, she argues that the chief merit of intersectionality is that it "shifts the goal of analysis away from isolating and ranking particular forms of oppression, and toward interrogating the manner in which they reinforce and/or contradict one another in and through people's lived experiences" (Ferguson, 2008: 43). This evident contradiction between intersectionality's having a discrete, isolated conceptualizing of oppression and, at the same time, moving away from an isolated analysis towards relationality and connectivity between different forms of oppression results in a dramatic shift regarding Ferguson's view of the relationship between intersectionality and social reproduction feminism.

In the beginning of her article, Ferguson maintains that social reproduction feminism may methodologically supplement intersectionality.[21] However, once we reach the end of the same article, she holds that intersectionality ought to be supplanted by social reproduction feminism. I argue that this ambivalent and contradictory relationship to intersectionality that Ferguson's text displays is crucial to note because it is, perhaps, the earliest example of trying to transfigure socialist feminist political economy into a marxist social theory by overcoming intersectionality. Ferguson's attempt also contains the kernel of all future social reproduction theory efforts to this end. However, as I have shown above, neither positive nor negative receptions of social reproduction theory have been of any avail in illuminating its relationship to intersectionality in terms of concept formation, as well as the consequences of this relationship in terms of the social scientific validity of social reproduction theory. In fact, this ambivalence and contradiction remains unresolved and unexplored to this day in the literature.

---

21   I note that Ferguson does not elaborate upon the nature of this methodology that may be capable of supplementing intersectionality. In fact, the meaning of 'methodology' in the text remains entirely unclarified.

In this context, the embodied social relation of race and processes of racialization occupy a singular position.[22] As I have detailed, the contact between intersectionality and social reproduction theory has been initiated by and premised on the later generations of social reproductions theorists' acknowledgement that the former generations assumed a mere gender-class analytic. Any future of this theoretical enterprise, moreover, has been understood to be conditional upon its being able to respond to the critics who have pointed out the severe defects of leaving race and racialization out of social analyses. However, instead of inaugurating the necessary conceptual work in tandem with an articulation of why race and racialization constitute a social problem to grapple with, the acceptance of these criticisms has moved social reproduction theorists towards admitting the superiority of intersectionality on account of its deeming race and racialization integral to social analyses. This admission has then provided the opportunity for the appearance of the inclusion of race and racialization into social reproduction frameworks. I argue that this external importation of a social problem, circumventing the level of concept formation, cannot be integrated in a framework that has not explored the possibilities of the newly identified social problem, and, therefore, necessarily harkens back to its former conceptual contours, leaving the novelty of this social problem at the level of empirical variety.

Ferguson's article is exemplary in this respect. Discontented with the intersectional analysis of race, Ferguson actually offers an alternative social reproduction account of race and racialization. I argue that Ferguson's account is valuable in demonstrating the difficulty for social reproduction theory to become a social theory. The substance of Ferguson's argument is that "it is not just what we do to reproduce society, but where we do it that counts in an imperial capitalist world" (Ferguson, 2008: 42). In so arguing, Ferguson emphasizes spatial aspects of social reproductive labour. She contends that "the location of our laboring bodies as well as their biophysical attributes are crucially important in determining how individuals and groups take part in the process of social reproduction" (Ferguson, 2008: 51). Therefore, according to Ferguson, "people become racialized insofar as they are associated (by skin color, cultural identity, language or accent) with other socio-geographic

---

22   Although, 'sexuality' is customarily added to the list of social relations to be included in social reproduction analyses, the necessary work undertaken to achieve this has not yet been at the forefront of social reproduction theory. To be sure, there exists a certain relationship between queer- and trans- marxisms and social reproduction theory, but a robust analysis of this relationship that requires a careful historical and theoretical delineation that goes much beyond the remit of my present focus.

spaces" (Ferguson, 2008: 51). Putting it differently, she states that "while people are necessarily 'territorialized' by matter of their birth (we are all born and live somewhere), they are only racialized as a function of how their location figures in the broader socio-geo-political ordering of capitalism" (Ferguson, 2008: 52, emphasis in original).

To be sure, Ferguson's account of race and racialization begs a number of serious questions. Admittedly, she is well aware of the inadequacies this account. In effect, throughout her account, Ferguson offers a set of caveats (Ferguson, 2008: 51–54) that, in my estimation, amounts to undoing the theoretical import of her own claims. However, here my objective is not to conduct an assessment of the validity of Ferguson's account of race and racialization. Rather, it is to demonstrate the consequences of a non-conceptual external importation of a social problem into an existing framework of inquiry.

Ferguson has previously identified the strengths of intersectionality over earlier social reproduction analyses. These were the following: 1) beginning from experience, 2) exploring subjectivities, and 3) avoiding the use of gender, class, and race as abstract categories. She has then argued, contra Bannerji, that transposing these intersectional advances into social reproduction feminism eliminates the chief shortcomings of this tradition (i.e., structuralism and reductionism), thereby revising and expanding the framework for future utility. Ferguson intends her account of race and racialization to exemplify such a revised and expanded version of social reproduction feminism. Ferguson's account may be said to be materialist. For it is centered on the labouring body. However, as Marx himself would have argued, this materialism is a defective one because it is unable to accommodate the active side of its own formation.[23] In Ferguson's account, this labouring body becomes racialized only due to the spatialization of 'biophysical differentiation'[24] in 'the broader

---

23 See the First *Thesis on Feuerbach*: "The chief defect of all hitherto existing materialism – that of Feuerbach included – is that the thing, reality, sensuousness, is conceived only in the form of the *object or of contemplation*, but not as *sensuous human activity, practice*, not subjectively. Hence, in contradistinction to materialism, the *active* side was developed abstractly by idealism – which, of course, does not know real, sensuous activity as such. Feuerbach wants sensuous objects, really distinct from the thought objects, but he does not conceive human activity itself as *objective* activity ... Hence he does not grasp the significance of 'revolutionary,' of 'practical-critical,' activity" (Marx, 1845: n.p.).

24 It is crucial to note that gender, sex, sexuality, and ability do have aspects that may be considered as 'biophysical differentiation.' Furthermore, they too are necessarily spatialized. However, it is interesting that in Ferguson's analysis only race seems to be subject to spatialized biophysical differentiation. What is more interesting that Ferguson appears to consider 'cultural identity,' 'language,' and 'accent' to be biophysical attributes. I suggest that this not only points to a universalization and naturalization of gender and other

socio-geo-political ordering of capitalism.' It is in this manner that Ferguson believes that her account offers an analysis of the "totality of social relations" (Ferguson, 2008: 56).

Contrary to her intention, however, Ferguson's account reverts back to the structuralist-functionalism that Ferguson identifies in earlier social reproduction analyses and hopes to surpass in the first place. I argue that this account treats race as an abstract category that is the outcome of the spatial organization of global capitalism. The experience of racialization, and racialized subjectivities are, at best, derived from this spatial organization. In fact, the concept of lived experience does not feature in Ferguson's analysis at all, and, as opposed to beginning from experience, the only viable notion of experience appears at the end of her account, even then only as an index of that which has happened to a labouring body. The question of this body's becoming a subject – as well as the subjectivity of this subject – cannot be posed as an object of knowledge in this framework; rather, it remains assumed. Furthermore, this 'race as spatialization' approach produces a homogenous binary conceptualization of race, which cannot account for the different forms of racialization in a relational modality. For instance, it cannot explain the power relationship between racialized and racializing subjects that is reproduced through everyday practices of power. Conflating otherization with racialization, Ferguson strips off the specificity of the power relations that animate race as an embodied social relation. Finally, the connection between gender, class, and race remains conceptually and analytically unclarified.

Having identified the shortcomings of this account, it is important to keep in mind that Ferguson's text represents one of the earliest attempts to transfigure socialist-feminist political economy into a total social theory. In a more recent blog piece, which aims to popularize social reproduction theory, Ferguson repeats her earlier claims with a clearer reference to intersectionality:

> What began as a theorisation of the relationship between gender and class is being recalibrated by a new generation of SRF theorists and activists. More recent work grapples with how not just gender, but also race, colonialism, sexuality and other oppressions are implicated in the necessary but contradictory relationship SRF identifies as a defining feature of capitalist societies. This may sound a lot like some articulations of Intersectionality Feminism. And indeed, certain key Black Feminist and

---

social relations above, but also to a lack of conceptualization of the differences between different social relations within the social reproduction tradition.

Intersectionality Feminist insights into the co-constitution of social relations inspire and inform this new thinking in SRF. SRF, however, moves beyond some of the theoretical quandaries of that approach.

FERGUSON, 2017: n.p.

In the remainder of this part of *Grounding Critique*, I analyze whether or not more recent texts in social reproduction theory address the important limitations I identified above, and offer any robust theoretical and conceptual solutions to these dilemmas (viz., how 'race, colonialism, sexuality and other oppressions' are integrated into the previous gender-class analysis and analytics; what conceptual work this integration requires and the consequences it produces; and what precise relationship this integration establishes among these 'oppressions').

VIII   Inauguration of Socialist-Feminist Political Economy as a Unitary Social Theory

Susan Ferguson and David McNally's "Capital, Labour-Power, and Gender-Relations: Introduction to the *Historical Materialism* Edition of *Marxism and the Oppression of Women*" (Ferguson and McNally, 2013) represents an important turning point in the revitalization of social reproduction theory. In this introduction, Ferguson and McNally firmly canonize Lise Vogel's conceptualization of social reproduction. Following this republication, thirty years after its first emergence in 1983, Vogel's book becomes the ground on which social reproduction theory is built. I suggest that this moment represents social reproduction theory's break from the tradition of socialist-feminist political economy. This moment also inaugurates social reproduction theory's attempt at transmogrifying itself into a 'unitary' social theory of exploitation and oppression.[25]

The last section of Ferguson and McNally's introduction discusses the future directions of social reproduction theory as "a fully integrative account of the co-constituting relations of class, gender, sexuality, and race" (Ferguson and McNally, 2013: XXXVI) with reference to intersectionality. I suggest that this particular choice for the future of the theory that the authors make is not arbitrary but fully consonant with the pattern of social reproduction theory's

---

25   I examine this canonization and Vogel's indubitable influence on social reproduction theory in the following section.

continual reference to intersectionality I have discerned so far. In fact, it constitutes a part of this pattern, thereby reminding us – once again – that an accurate understanding and formulation of social reproduction theory cannot be achieved without clarifying its relationship to intersectionality.

Ferguson and McNally's understanding of intersectionality, in this introduction, builds upon Ferguson's previous analysis of the subject from five years earlier, which I have examined above. For instance, Ferguson and McNally also maintain that intersectionality displays "an abiding materialist orientation" (Ferguson and McNally, 2013: XXXV). And, similarly, they argue that the main strength of intersectionality is its ability "to elucidate the interrelations among distinct dimensions of social experience and the institutions and practices that shape them" (Ferguson and McNally, 2013: XXXV). Ferguson and McNally's critique of intersectionality, like that of Ferguson, rely on Johanna Brenner's critique (Brenner, 2000) according to which "much work in this tradition [i.e., intersectionality] limits itself to describing and explaining the dynamics of specific social *locations*, exploring how a particular location shapes experience and identity, while often failing to ask how those locations are produced and sustained in and through a system of social power" (Ferguson and McNally, 2013: XXXVI, emphasis in original). Hence, Ferguson and McNally continue their critique by arguing that intersectionality under-theorizes "the social *relations* of domination (of a racialized, patriarchal capitalism)" (Ferguson and McNally, 2013: XXXVI, emphasis in original). The authors surmise that the reason for this under-theorization is the deployment of "the spatial metaphor of intersection" (Ferguson and McNally, 2013: XXXVI) which orients intersectionality towards an analytic field of vision in which "each mode of domination [appears] as a distinct vector of power, which then crosses paths with (intersects) others" (Ferguson and McNally, 2013: XXXVI). Ferguson and McNally conclude that "by taking each power-vector as independently given in the first instance (prior to the intersection), this approach struggles to grasp the co-constitution of each social relation in and through other relations of power" (Ferguson and McNally, 2013: XXXVI).[26]

This understanding and critique of intersectionality, for Ferguson and McNally, illuminates the road that social reproduction theory must take to become a unitary theory of exploitation and oppression. According to Ferguson and McNally, such a unitary theory provides "a conceptual map of the real in all its complex and contradictory processes of becoming" (Ferguson

---

26 It is important to note that Ferguson and McNally do not offer any textual evidence to substantiate this conclusion.

and McNally, 2013: XL) by focusing on "the ongoing production and reproduction of the social totality" (Ferguson and McNally, 2013: XL). The successes and failures of intersectionality, for the authors, point to the veritable necessity of "a truly integrative theory of capitalism and its multiple oppressions" (Ferguson and McNally, 2013: XXXVI). It is at this point that Vogel's work is pronounced to be indispensable to the creation of such a unitary social theory. According to Ferguson and McNally, Vogel's work extends Marx's "great innovation" (Ferguson and McNally, 2013: XL) of revealing "the great secret to understanding the totalising processes of capital" (Ferguson and McNally, 2013: XL) by grasping the "specifically female reproductive activities in working-class households" (Ferguson and McNally, 2013: XL) within the processes of "the production and reproduction of labour-power" (Ferguson and McNally, 2013: XL) even though Vogel does not provide an explanation how her theoretical 'innovation' may be of help to better understand other embodied social relations and their relationship to class.

Ferguson and McNally's critique of intersectionality and, subsequent, charting of a new map for social reproduction theory, *prima facie*, seem plausible. However, as I demonstrate below, the authors' critique is predicated on a conceptually faulty relegation of 'experience' into the empirical, and that this critique conceptually does not warrant the direction that Ferguson and McNally chart for social reproduction theory, notwithstanding the political desirability of this direction. Therefore, this text merely rehearses the dilemmas that were introduced in Ferguson's earlier article, but does not overcome them, even though it represents the inauguration of the knowledge production efforts to transmogrify socialist-feminist political economy into a unitary social theory.

IX   One-Sidedness of Experience in Social Reproduction Theory

Ferguson and McNally assert that "intersectionality has inspired significant empirical work documenting how oppression is lived in non-compartmentalised and often contradictory ways" (Ferguson and McNally, 2013: XXXVI). According to the authors, "this empirical orientation has been both its strength and its weakness" (Ferguson and McNally, 2013: XXXVI). Since Ferguson and McNally do not offer any textual evidence or reference to support their assertions, it is rather difficult to assess the validity of these assertions. However, it is clear that the authors do not use the phrases 'empirical work' and 'empirical orientation' with respect to the established meanings of these terms in the social sciences as referring to social inquiry that is the outcome of data and observation driven methodologies and hermeneutics.[27] Neither do they use these terms in the sense of 'empiricism,' thereby referring to the epistemological position that the scientifically valid and solid knowledge can be only derived from sensory experience.[28] Rather, Ferguson and McNally use these terms merely as "drawing attention to the *experience* of oppression" (Ferguson and McNally, 2013: XXXVI, emphasis in original). The strength of the 'empirical orientation' of intersectionality, according to the authors, is to reinsert "people, human agents, into the analysis of history and social life" (Ferguson and McNally, 2013: XXXVI). Ferguson and McNally argue that this very strength also constitutes the weakness of intersectionality. While social locations explain the production of experiences in intersectionality, the production of these locations is not explained. As noted above, they attribute this weakness to the use of the metaphor of intersections, although they do not clarify how the conceptual status and analytical capacity of experience may be possibly constituted by the mobilization of this metaphor.[29]

I argue that Ferguson and McNally, in their analysis, relegate and reduce experience to the empirical in the sense that which what one undergoes, encounters, and is subsequently affected by. Through this relegation and reduction, the authors substitute experience with existence. What is actually recognized in their account is not the experience of, but the empirical existence of oppression. Therefore, not unlike Ferguson's earlier account, Ferguson and McNally's introduction too only engages with and enlarges upon this passive side of experience as an index and reservoir of events and occurrences.

---

27 Any reference work attests this common meaning of 'empirical.' For example, see Bruce and Yearley, 2006; Johnson, 2000; Marshall, 2004; and Ritzer, 2007.

28 For the diversity of empiricisms, see Benton and Craib, 2011; and Cassirer, 2020.

29 I find myself unconvinced by Ferguson and McNally's critique and reading of intersectionality for the simple reason that, in my estimation, intersectionality does not explain people's experience through an analysis of social locations. On the contrary, it reveals how the existing social locations in their singularity do not allow an understanding of social experiences and identities, especially those that are rendered invisible because they do not squarely occupy any single axis of oppression. Intersectionality makes use of its metaphor in order to shed light on the omitted existences of these subjects in the institutional organization of the social world. In other words, intersectionality aims to lay bare the specific ways in which social relations of power systematically produce institutional categories that legitimate, mostly by way of liberal bourgeoise jurisprudence, the oppression, violence, and death inflicted on the bodies that are not safely ensconced in those institutional categories with sanctioned access to various forms of redress. For me, this aspect of intersectionality has been clear from one of its earliest articulations in Crenshaw, 1989. For my own phenomenological and methodological critique and questions about intersectionality, see Part I of this book.

In so doing, this analysis reads intersectionality as registering *the fact and type of experience* regarding multiple systems of oppression. And, consequently, it argues that intersectionality offers a rich 'empirical' catalogue of the *effects* of these systems. Determining Ferguson and McNally's reading of intersectionality, this one-sided understanding of experience is generative of conceptual aporias for the future direction of social reproduction theory.[30] To begin with, the inability to grasp the active side of experience[31] reduces the analytical capacity of experience to an optional extra in the study of the social organization of systematic oppression, as though the subject's experiences of oppression and the systems of oppression may be conceptually separated. And, concomitantly, it restricts the epistemic constitution of social subjects in 'the analysis of history and social life,' as though human beings may be deemed as opting in and out of the making of history and the social organization of life.[32]

Instead of developing the active side of experience in their concept formation, these shortcomings lead Ferguson and McNally simply to adapt Brenner's binary operationalization of social locations and social relations. As a result of this adaptation, social locations are not conceptualized as historical sedimentations and congealment of social relations that are subject to ongoing processes of legitimation, delegitimization, change, and transformation. I argue that this uncritical adaptation, the first instance of which was displayed in Ferguson's earlier text, results in a threefold movement in the formation of contemporary social reproduction theory: first, an ontological entrenchment of a quasi-transcendental, or metacritical structure of unity; second, an

---

30 In the following section, I demonstrate that these conceptual aporias are underwritten by the antinomies of classical sociological reason that I have examined in great detail in Part 1 of this book, especially that of description versus understanding, and the nomothetic versus the idiographic.

31 By this, I specifically mean the constitutive aspects of social relations, as opposed to the regulative aspects that are captured by the passive side of experience. Put summarily, the active side of experience conceptually orients us toward the praxial and epistemic social interactions in the everyday life of individual and collective subjects that make society possible in concordant and discordant fashions.

32 It might be argued that these limitations are inherent in and pertain to intersectionality, not to the social thought of Ferguson and McNally. The authors, however, do not dispute the conceptualization of experience in intersectionality. Furthermore, not only do they highlight and engage with the passive side of this conceptualization, but they also recognize it as a great advance over many marxist-feminism, including pre-Vogel social reproduction approaches. I argue that this mobilization of experience is entirely consistent within social reproduction theory, as Ferguson's use of the concept in her earlier article and that of the guest editors of *Historical Materialism* attest. I have examined both these views in the preceding subsections.

epistemological deployment of a unitarian phraseology; and, third, a resultant methodological circuit in which all social phenomena to be investigated, irrespective of their specificity, are conjugated into the metacritical structure by the use of unitarian phraseology. Some widely used examples of this unitarian phraseology include, but are not limited to, the following: 'the social totality in all its diversity,' 'co-(re)production,' 'co-determination,' 'co-constitution,' 'unity of difference,' 'differentiated-yet-unified,' 'diverse-yet-unified,' 'distinct-yet-merging,' 'messy-yet-unified,' 'differentiated-yet-shared,' 'diverse unity,' 'complexly differentiated yet nonetheless unified,' 'complex yet unitary social process,' 'contradictory yet constitutive,' 'unifying without suppressing.'[33]

x   The Values, Facts, and Factuality of Oppression in the Quasi-transcendental Structure of Social Reproduction Theory

This threefold movement emerging out of social reproduction theory's efforts to clarify its relationship to intersectionality finds its most mature and sophisticated articulations in the flagship publication of this recent theoretical enterprise, *Social Reproduction Theory: Remapping Class, Recentering Oppression* (Bhattacharya, 2017). As the subtitle of the edited volume suggests, social reproduction theory is concerned with the relationship between class and oppression. I argue that social reproduction theory recalibrates its conceptualization of embodied social relations through its relationship to intersectionality. In her introduction to the edited volume, Tithi Bhattacharya begins her exposition by asserting that social reproduction theory "treats questions of oppression (gender, race, sexuality) in distinctly nonfunctionalist ways precisely because oppression is theorized as structurally relational to, and hence shaped by, capitalist production rather than on the margins of analysis or as add-ons to a deeper and more vital economic process" (Bhattacharya, 2017: 3).

I suggest that this assertion has a procataleptic structure in anticipating the repetition of and wishing to circumvent Bannerji's critique of the structural-functionalism of socialist-feminist political economy. As I have shown earlier, this challenge was recognized first in Ferguson's foundational article, which in my periodization represents the conception of social reproduction theory. Since then, it has become a classical challenge that every key text hoping to develop social reproduction theory attempts to implicitly or explicitly address.

---

33   I generated this sample set from the following sources: Ferguson and McNally, 2013; Ferguson, 2016; McNally and Ferguson, 2015; Bhattacharya, 2017; and McNally, 2017.

For instance, it was further taken up in Ferguson and McNally's introduction, which represents the nascence of social reproduction theory. Like these fundamental texts, Bhattacharya's introduction to the flagship volume, which represents the maturity of social reproduction theory, attempts to demonstrate that a non-structuralist-functionalist articulation of this theory is possible. In fact, this trend of trying to reckon with Bannerji's critique still continues. One of the most recent texts that provides a self-conscious historiography of social reproduction also attempts to rise to this challenge (Bhattacharya, Farris, and Ferguson, 2022).

However, rather than addressing Bannerji's critique of structuralism and functionalism, Bhattacharya's above claim about social reproduction theory serves the function of 'the self-fulfilling prophecy.' To be sure, here I use this term not in its pejorative everyday sense, but in its original sociological meaning. Coining the term, the sociologist Robert K. Merton writes that "the self-fulfilling prophecy is … a false definition of the situation evoking a new behavior which makes the originally false conception come true. The specious validity of the self-fulfilling prophecy perpetuates a reign of error. For the prophet will cite the actual course of events as proof that he was right from the very beginning … Such are the perversities of social logic" (Merton, 1948: 194–195). In explaining the definitional criteria of this logic of social knowledge production, Merton further argues that those who engage in this practice "experience these beliefs [generated by the self-fulfilling prophecy], not as prejudices, not as prejudgments but as irresistible products of their own observation. 'The facts of the case' permit them no other conclusion" (Merton, 1948: 195). Michael Biggs adds another defining criterion to the self-fulfilling prophecy, which is that "the actors within the process – or at least some of them – fail to understand how their own belief has helped to construct that reality; because their belief is eventually validated, they assume that it was true at the outset" (Biggs, 2016: 295).

I argue that Bhattacharya's decree about social reproduction theory fully satisfies both Merton's initial and Biggs' subsequent definitional criteria of self-fulfilling prophecies. Thus, it becomes a self-fulling prophecy in relation to the internal structure of social reproduction theory's knowledge claims and their external reception. Bhattacharya produces this social logic by consigning functionalism to the relational positioning of the elements of the social problem under scrutiny, thereby substituting the real place of functionalism in the selection and articulation process of the problem of embodied social relations. Thus, instead of investigating functionalism at the level of concept formation and in terms of its ontological, epistemological, and methodological presuppositions in the making of social reproduction theory itself, Bhattacharya renders these presuppositions into the very procedure and definition of 'nonfunctionalism.' Thus, I argue that this self-fulfilling prophecy about social reproduction theory's 'distinct non-functionalism' is the particular effect of its quasi-transcendental, or metacritical, structure operating within the field of the politics of knowledge production. Through this effect, Bhattacharya definitively separates social reproduction theory from the tradition of socialist-feminist political economy and, thus, absolves the theory of the shortcomings of this earlier tradition by the mere force of this separation, rather than through the conceptual labour this task necessitates.

Having decreed the *a priori* 'nonfunctionalism' of social reproduction theory in regards to the 'questions of oppression,' Bhattacharya notes that social reproduction theorists recognize their work "as furthering the theoretical conversation with this existing body of scholarship [the recent literature on oppression] in two kinds of ways: (a) as a conversation between Marxism and the study of specific oppressions such as gender and race, and (b) as developing a richer way of understanding how Marxism, as a body of thought, can address the relationship between theory and empirical studies of oppression [i.e., intersectionality]" (Bhattacharya, 2017: 4). One of the most important objectives of social reproduction theorists, in Bhattacharya's opinion, is to adequately "express the complications of an *abstract level* of analysis where we forge our conceptual equipment, and a *concrete level* of analysis, i.e., the historical reality where we apply those tools" (Bhattacharya, 2017: 3, emphasis in original). It is evident that Bhattacharya operates within the binaries of the 'theory' and the 'empirical,' 'levels of analyses,' the 'abstract' and the 'concrete,' 'modes of production' and 'social formations.' In Part I of *Grounding Critique*, I have already examined in detail the presuppositions and consequences of these binaries in relation to the antinomies of sociological reason. Therefore, it suffices merely to register that Bhattacharya's thought, too, shares the limitations I have expounded earlier. The chief analytical limitation of these binaries is to severely limit the very knowability of the social world and, hence, the possibilities of its transformation.

Rather than rehearsing these conceptual consequences, my intent here is to establish that intersectionality provides the conditions for the possibility of social reproduction theory as an alternative social theory. Out of this conversation with intersectionality, to which Bhattacharya refers, social reproduction theory emerges as having acquired a social problem (i.e., race and racialization) and as having shed its former structuralism and functionalism. To be sure, knowledge production in social sciences may be said to advance in and through dialogical processes. However, I argue that in treating and representing this conversation as a *fait accompli*, the formation of the social problem of race and racialization as an object of knowledge remains unexplained and unelaborated within social reproduction theory. The social problem of race and racialization is considered as given, a social fact. Therefore, social reproduction theory, on the one hand, accepts that the empirical existence of race and the power that this embodied social relation exerts might be examined in competing frameworks of analysis, such as intersectionality. On the other, it argues that the very facticity – that is, how it has become a social fact in the first place – of the social problem can be only accounted as an effect of the quasi-transcendental structure of unity into which the imported problem is inserted. In other words, social reproduction theory cannot explain the social problem it tackles in relation to concept formation because it imports the problem from intersectionality, but, nonetheless, paradoxically maintains that only itself is capable of explaining the facticity of the problem.

I further submit that this rendering of social problems, and of the embodied social relations of which they are composed, into social facts within the quasi-transcendental structure of the theory is responsible for the self-certitude of social reproduction theorists with regards to their definitive overcoming of functionalism. As I show shortly, it is true that contemporary social reproduction theory treats the social structures of oppression differently from the way its predecessors treated them. However, the truth of these different treatments cannot be necessarily interpreted in methodological terms as solving the shortcomings of the prior treatment. In earlier social reproduction analyses of socialist-feminist political economy, social structures of oppression and their effects are rended into the objective and the subjective. The internal workings of the objective part are explained by the political-economic structures of capitalist society, whereas the subjective part is explained by the (semi-)autonomous ideological structures that conceptualize the social relations of oppression as cultural values. As a result, analyses within the early social reproduction tradition create two contiguous internalities externally connected to one another in the last instance, through the functions of the base and superstructure. This brings us back to the issue of Bannerji's earlier challenge, which is a constant reference point in social reproduction analyses. Bannerji critiques this dilemma and concludes thus:

> Without a materialist and historical view of consciousness, without a theory of a *conscious* and transformative relation between labour, self and society, the notion of self or subjectivity remains unconnected to social organization or history in any formative and fundamental sense. The 'feminist' component of marxist feminism is an uncritical adoption of an essentialist or idealist subjectivist position, just as much as the 'marxist'

> component is an objective idealism. In present-day socialist feminism this dilemma is silenced rather than resolved.
>
> BANNERJI, 1995: 80–81

I argue that the shift in social reproduction theory's analytic construction of oppression, which unquestioningly transforms cultural values to social facts, does not address any of the substantive issues that Bannerji raises. This shift from values to facts represents a well-rehearsed reversal in the application of classical sociological reason.[34] With this reversal, the structures of oppression, as well as the experiences of which they are generative, become moored within the explanatory framework of the theory as its constitutive parts. Therefore, the explanation of the multiple systems of oppression no longer requires and refers to an outside that is external to social reproduction theory. Instead, the modality of their explanation is rendered to be internally referring to the imputed totality within the organistic whole of social reproduction theory. This new analytic configuration, however, does not clarify the selection and articulation of social problems as objects of knowledge, as well as concept formation in social reproduction theory, any more than the earlier instantiations of social reproduction analyses. Thus, I submit that social reproduction theory does not further a marxist project of examining embodied social relations under the contemporary organization of capitalist societies because its conceptual operations still remain within the antinomies of classical sociological reason, much like the works of the theorists discussed in Part I of this book.

XI Social Reproduction Theory as Sublated Intersectionality

The new analytic configuration of social reproduction theory is borne out of the double need for supplementing the racial oblivion and supplanting the functionalism of earlier social reproduction analyses of socialist-feminist political economy by importing race and racialization as a social problem from intersectionality. And this new analytic configuration further develops by shifting from the cultural value paradigm to the social fact paradigm in the treatment of social problems. It finally becomes animated and actionable through subsuming all embodied social relations into the unitarian quasi-transcendental structure of social reproduction theory. Thus, as a result, social reproduction

---

34   For a detailed superb examination of this reversal in relationship to the aporias of neo-Kantianism, see Gillian Rose, 1981.

theory may be argued as having come into being *qua* itself. Having been fully formed, social reproduction theory revisits intersectionality. This time, however, it does so from the standpoint of this newly configured analytic.

For instance, acknowledging social reproduction theory's genetic relationship to intersectionality, David McNally writes that "social reproduction theory, which grew out of historical materialist analyses of gender relations, is being renovated in part as a response to critical challenges from intersectionality and antiracism" (McNally, 2017: 94). Then, he continues to argue that "a dialectically revitalized social reproduction theory – one that rises to the critical challenges posed by intersectional analysis – offers the most promising perspective for those interested in an historical materialist theory of multiple oppressions within capitalist society" (McNally, 2017: 94). Similarly, in a recent handbook entry, Tithi Bhattacharya, Sara R. Farris, and Sue Ferguson admit that the engagement with intersectionality "made it possible for SR [social reproduction] feminism to grapple with racial and other forms of oppression attending an increasingly globalized neoliberal capitalism and its authoritarian state" (Bhattacharya, Farris, and Ferguson, 2022: 58–59). Then, they, too, continue to argue that "the most compelling insights and commitments of intersectionality feminism have since been critically appropriated in the more recent renewal of SR feminism" (Bhattacharya, Farris, and Ferguson, 2022: 58). I argue that this convergent insistence by the chief contemporary proponents of social reproduction theory on the dialectical overcoming, or sublation, of intersectionality by 'retaining and repositioning its critical insights'[35] represents the final stage of transfiguration of social reproduction theory into a total social theory.

In other words, the uncritical importation of race and racialization and other relations of oppression as social problems without the necessary conceptual labour, finally, shows up as a form of analytical hyper-vigilance in relation to intersectionality. The sublation of intersectionality into a unitarian whole becomes the necessary condition for the internal consistency of social reproduction theory *qua* metacritique.[36] Therefore, in what follows it

---

35 See McNally, 2017: 95; and Bhattacharya, 2017: 17.
36 It is imperative to note that the unitarian emphasis in Lise Vogel's work is wholly absent. As a matter of fact, Vogel herself is rather surprised to find that the subtitle of her book has been granted a powerful new lease on life. She writes that "Social Reproduction Theory is said to offer a 'unitary' perspective on the question of women's oppression. The word 'unitary' appears only in the book's subtitle (*Toward a Unitary Theory*); it is completely absent from the text. Nonetheless, colleagues feel very strongly that 'unitary' is a meaningful characteristic of Social Reproduction Theory. They cling to it, I [Vogel] suspect, for two reasons. First, it marks a definitive rejection of the dual-systems theorizing that dominated even socialist–feminist thinking for so long. And second, it promises a theoretically

is crucial to examine how this sublation of intersectionality into social reproduction theory is reasoned, accomplished, and represented. More importantly, this examination must seek to answer the question of whether the dialectical overcoming of intersectionality by social reproduction constitutes an advancement towards understanding embodied social relations, as well as their relationships with one another, under the contemporary organization of capitalist social formations.

Social reproduction theory asks "whether intersectionality is an adequate tool, or the science we need, to expose the hidden phenomena that shape our apprehension of reality and whether such a theory can explain the relationship between the diverse 'real' elements that form a unified 'concentration of many determinations'" (Bhattacharya, 2017: 16). I argue that one must resist interpreting this question as merely rhetorical, requiring a categorical 'nay' with an immediate rejoinder that 'but, aye, social reproduction theory is.' In fact, the way in which this question is posed reveals the scientific self-validity of social reproduction theory, the standpoint from which it judges intersectionality, and the disjuncture between the apprehension and comprehension of lifeworld, experience, and social existence that it cannot bridge. In contrast to their earlier interlocution at the level of classed social organization and power relations of oppressions, social reproduction theory's revisitation of intersectionality now takes place on a metaphysical plane and is framed in ontological terms. It is only at this level that an appearance of sublation is possible because the standpoint of an imputed totality, whose analytic expression is social reproduction theory, affords a gracious acceptance of the findings of intersectionality as surface phenomena, while at the same time searching for its deep meaning and cause within the social whole that totality represents.

Strictly speaking, however, here any claim for such a sublation, in the sense of a dialectical overcoming, is untenable. For such a sublation requires all moments of the exchange between socialist-feminist political economy, intersectionality, and social reproduction theory to take place on the same ontological plane. Otherwise, the substantively different constitutive knowledge claims regarding the nature and reality of society, as understood by these separate schools, could not be adequately scrutinized. Also, in order for this sublation to be tenable, there would have to be a temporal requirement of explication, examining the moment in which the sublated position is discovered, along

---

unified solution" (Vogel, 2018: 283–284, emphasis in original). I argue that the reason for this difference between Vogel and social reproduction theorists is that Vogel's work was a contribution to socialist-feminist political economy, whereas social reproduction theory desires to fashion itself as a social theory.

with an account of how the moment of its discovery relates to the present as part of an ever-changing unfolding process. In the absence of any explication addressing these requirements, only an appearance of sublation could be sustained, not a valid and sound argument about sublation proper. Therefore, the analytical operation that social reproduction theory engages in might be better described as synthesis, subsumption, or appropriation. Here, however, I limit my task to an examination of the particularly contradictory concept formation that social reproduction theory displays in relation to its theoretical claims, which demands that I take these claims of sublation on their own terms, rather than evaluating their validity and performing a correction on them. Therefore, I continue to analyze the arguments of the main social reproduction theorists.

According to McNally, "the great accomplishment of intersectionality theory was to expand the framework of discussion – initially to race, gender, and class, and more recently to other relations of oppression, such as those of sexuality and ability" (McNally, 2017: 108). This expansion is understood to be accomplished through "the rich empirical work done by scholars of intersectionality" (Bhattacharya, 2017: 16).[37] Despite the acknowledgement of this laudable expansion and empirical work, the chief contemporary progenitors of social reproduction theory believe that "intersectional analyses bear deep theoretical flaws" (McNally, 2017: 95). These flaws are, in Bhattacharya's estimation, due to intersectionality's representational and constitutive properties and propositions: "intersectionality theory ... shows us a world where race, gender, and other oppressions 'intersect,' thereby producing a reality that is latticed" (Bhattacharya, 2017: 17).

From the point of view of the philosophy of social sciences, and according to the rigours of social theorization that takes concept formation seriously, it is expected that this situating of the 'flaws' of intersectionality in the metaphysical plane of the reality of the world ought to be followed by an ontological reconstruction of the intersectional position because intersectionality itself does not articulate its knowledge claims on this plane. Therefore, any critique should first elucidate that which it negates on the commensurate plane to the one on which the critique itself is conducted, so that the positive postulations of the critique may be validated with reference to that which is negated. However, instead of such a conceptual engagement, Bhattacharya merely compounds the metaphor of intersections with that of lattices in order

---

37 It is important to note that as in the other social reproduction theorists' use, here, too, the use of the term 'empirical' is unclear. Neither is there a reference to these 'rich empirical works,' nor is there any discussion of how 'empirical' is conceptualized and operationalized.

to assert that intersectionality apprehends reality as "a sum total of different parts" (Bhattacharya, 2017: 17). She, then, warns her reader by noting that "at first glance this 'whole,' as an aggregate of different parts, may appear to be the same as the Hegelian-Marxist concept of totality" (Bhattacharya, 2017: 17). Bhattacharya does not explain her own understanding of these two different conceptualizations; rather, with the help of a question, she implies that while the former "tells us [that] race and gender intersect like two streets, then surely they are two separate streets, each with its own specificities" (Bhattacharya, 2017: 17), the latter provides the "the *logic* of their intersection" (Bhattacharya, 2017: 17, emphasis in original).

Having thus charged intersectionality with explanatory inadequacy and gestured towards a framework into which intersectionality may be sublated, Bhattacharya concludes by "suggest[ing] that the insights or conclusions of intersectional theorists actually contradict their methodology" (Bhattacharya, 2017: 17) because "instead of race and gender being separate systems of oppression or even separate oppressions with only externally related trajectories, the findings of Black feminist scholars show how race and gender are actually co-constitutive" (Bhattacharya, 2017: 17). Once again repeating that "intersectionality theory's methodology belies its own findings" (Bhattacharya, 2017: 17), Bhattacharya refers to McNally's contribution in the edited volume to show "how SRT offers us a way to 'retain and reposition' the insights of intersectionality, yet reject its theoretical premise of an aggregative reality" (Bhattacharya, 2017: 17).

XII   Metaphorizing Concepts, Criticizing Metaphors

Bhattacharya's account of the dialectical overcoming of intersectionality is marked by important conceptual and theoretical problems that are emblematic of social reproduction theory. I argue that Bhattacharya's focus on how intersectionality and social reproduction theory consider the nature of reality, on which the question of sublation hangs, lacks a self-reflexive delineation of its ontological premises. In the absence of this conceptual groundwork and deployed as is, this acute focus has but a forceful rhetorical effect of creating an impression that the social problems intersectionality tackles are better explained by social reproduction theory. In other words, the dialectical overcoming of intersectionality by social reproduction theory is not only desirable, but also accomplished. Approached analytically, I argue that it becomes evident that Bhattacharya's focus is generative of arbitrary conceptual imputations and conclusions.

To begin with, Bhattacharya's imputation that intersectionality's mode of apprehension of reality as 'a sum total of different parts' begs the following question: Does intersectionality's focus on the ways in which systems of social oppression constitute – better still, intend to constitute, or can constitute – an ontology of the social? A response to this question in the negative suggests that a sublative relationship between the two frameworks is not conceptually warranted.[38] An affirmative response, on the other hand, demands that social reproduction theory explicate its own conception of the social and society in relation to that of intersectionality. Instead of producing such an explication, Bhattacharya simply concludes that the imputed intersectional ontology cannot accommodate the critical insights of its own main framework, thereby arguing for the importation of these insights from the discommoding ontology of intersectionality to the commodious totality of social reproduction theory.

I argue that social reproduction theory's customary strategy of critiquing intersectionality by ontologizing, politicizing, and metaphorizing concepts cannot produce reliable knowledge in social sciences because the conclusions, such as the one above, that are drawn through this procedure are not analytically necessary, and are therefore invalid. Bhattacharya's metaphorizing of lattice structures and assigning the 'sum total of different parts' to them as these structures' necessary mode of apprehension of reality, I suggest, demonstrates the serious shortcomings of this strategy of criticism. Because social reproduction theory often employs this strategy of criticism and because the ontological and political meanings of the claims of this strategy are merely taken for granted, below I examine the shortcoming of ontologizing, politicizing, and metaphorizing concepts through Bhattacharya's claim that intersectionality operates within a lattice structure.

First of all, it ought to be noted that even if Bhattacharya's claim were correct, a lattice structure of explanation cannot be argued to be predicated on a singular ontology because lattice structures by themselves are "not essential to an ontology, but it is an important guide to knowledge acquisition" (Sowa, 1999: 307). The relationship of necessity does not exist between lattices and ontology. Such a relationship does, however, exist between lattices and mereology, or the study of the parthood. This is so because lattices and lattice structures comprise a method of conceptualizing and ordering the relationship between parts and wholes, as well as between less and more complex systems.

Contrary to what Bhattacharya suggests, lattice structures do not merely denote ontologically enclosed externality between parts and wholes. Rather,

---

38   This would be consonant with my opinion on the subject.

lattice structures may be employed organistically to study internal relations,[39] especially when distinctness and relatedness cannot be comprehended independent of one another in a formational integrity. For "our understanding of the elements of the crystal's structure [i.e. lattice] cannot come about by observing single molecules, but rather by noting their relationships in the structure as a whole" (Tasić, 2001: 101). In fact, many critical sociologists, social theorists, and philosophers of social science use lattice structures to explain the relationship between individuals and society without falling into either sociologism or psychologism (Wight, 2006). In these studies, let alone being necessarily tethered to a reductionist ontology, lattice structures are deployed to elaborate "an 'ontological hiatus' between society and people" (Wight, 2006: 49), while at the same time "maintain[ing] material and ideational elements in one coherent account" (Wight, 2006: 48). Thus, I contend that social reproduction theory's insistence on the mechanistic-atomistic-extrinsic trinitarian imputation unto intersectionality, which constitutes the condition for its own possibility as a sublated unitarian social theory,[40] cannot be conceptually justified.

I further suggest that in critiquing the metaphors of intersections and lattices, the proponents of social reproduction theory frequently perform a reductionist conflation and correspondence between ontological and political positions. For instance, I agree with Bhattacharya's statement that "[t]he understanding of totality as an organic whole rather than an aggregate of parts is important precisely because it has real material implications for how we must choose to act upon that world" (Bhattacharya, 2017: 17). Yet, as I have shown, this statement becomes conceptually meaningless if it is used to issue an apodictic correspondence between understanding the internal relations of the "struggles against racism and sexism" (Bhattacharya, 2017: 17) and the

---

39   It ought to be noted that both Bhattacharya and McNally seem to be under the mistaken impression that organic internal relations can only be adequately examined within social reproduction theory.

40   Even the notion of unity itself, which is the ultimate goal of social reproduction theory, may be conceptualized in lattice structures. For instance, in course of a phenomenological discussion of the tropistic, intentional, and mediated dimensions of unity, Hiroshi Kojima writes: "These [phenomenological dimensions of unity] are not only hierarchically related to each other, but also interwoven like a movable semi-lattice. *Tropistic* unity is accompanied by no consciousness or solely by consciousness of results and not of process (e.g., the control of muscles during walking). It founds other unities from inside. *Intentional* unity is accompanied by consciousness or is easily brought to consciousness (e.g., emotion, perception, or imagination). It involves particular tropistic unities as substructures within itself and is determined by them while controlling them. Here the 'I' (ego) emerges as an intentional subject that is never completely objectified, because the 'I' is deeply rooted in the tropistic dimension" (Kojima, 1997: 370, emphases in original).

organistic model of totality – as though these internal relations cannot be conceptualized in any other way, but only through this correspondence. As a result, the conclusive suggestion that "a praxis-predicated philosophy such as Marxism" (Bhattacharya, 2017: 17) in the service of understanding embodied social relations may be best exemplified by social reproduction theory cannot be validated conceptually.

It is, therefore, important to remember that such correspondences are not accepted by all marxists. Indeed, there have been marxist philosophers, such as Kojin Karatani, who made productive uses of lattice structures to investigate the political subjectivities of individuals who "are living in plural dimensions of social relations" (Karatani, 2005: 305), as well as to analyze political movements that "take up the existential dimension that cannot be reduced to the previous movements centered on the relation of production and/or class relation" (Karatani, 2005: 305). Recognizing that a sublation among these different existential dimensions of social relations cannot be treated as a theoretical *fait accompli*, Karatani forwards that "if the counter movement against capital and state does not itself embody the principles that go beyond them, there is no way for it to sublate them in the future" (Karatani, 2005: 306). To this end, Karatani argues in favour of a political organizational model that takes the form of "a semi-lattice system that loosely synthesizes the multidimensionality, acknowledging the independence of each dimension and therefore acknowledging an individual's belonging to multidimensions" (Karatani, 2005: 306). For Karatani, "only here is the moment that individuals can become subjects. Association is finally the form based on individuals' subjectivity. In the organization of the semi-lattice structure … the multidimensional social relation that is beyond individuals' will and conditions individuals' beings is never abstracted" (Karatani, 2005: 306).

XIII (Hegelian-Marxist) Totality in Social Reproduction Theory?

Having shown that Bhattacharya's social-reproduction-theory-based imputation of intersectional ontology, and the conclusions she derives from this ontology (viz., externality, disunity, and contrariety to marxism) are arbitrary and conceptually invalid, I turn to the fact that the 'Hegelian-Marxist concept of totality' to which intersectional ontology is contrasted remains unelaborated in Bhattacharya's and other social reproduction theorists' texts. Thus, I forward that in social reproduction theory, neither that which is to be sublated (i.e., intersectional ontology) nor that into which is to be sublated (i.e., social reproduction theory's understanding of the Hegelian-Marxist concept of totality) possesses any conceptual clarity. However, both are presented with the strongest certitude so as to effect an impression that sublation is not merely argued for, but has already been realized. The 'Hegelian-Marxist' text Bhattacharya refers to is Georg Lukács' *History and Class Consciousness: Studies in Marxist Dialectics*. Yet, her engagement with Lukács' text is limited to a citational performance whereby Bhattacharya, without contextualizing, quotes a sentence from Lukács. Although this quotation makes it seem like both Bhattacharya and Lukács are concerned with the same object of analysis, the reality is far from this to be the case. In fact, Lukács, in that part of his text, conducts a philosophical critique of Kantian and neo-Kantian thought concerning the dilemma that modern bourgeois rationalism universalizes rational categories as the constitutive principle of cognition, while at the same time leaving the regulative principle of this faculty couched in the irrationalism of the thing-in-itself.[41] This discussion, as must be clear, does not provide an immediate and self-evident social science guideline for the study of social relations, formations, and systems of oppression; rather, it requires an explication of how it could be of use to study them. However, Bhattacharya does not provide such an explication.

In any case, as is well-known, four years prior to his passing, Lukács himself admits that while, in *History and Class Consciousness*, he has reinstated the concept of totality in marxist philosophy as a response to the scientistic vulgarization of marxism, his "efforts resulted in a – Hegelian – distortion, in which I [Lukács] put the totality in the centre of the system" (Lukács, 1971: xx). He continues to state, in an exemplary act of philosophical self-reflexivity and candour,[42] that this over-emphasis on the category of totality intensified a methodological paradox "by the fact that the totality was seen as the conceptual embodiment of the revolutionary principle in science: '[t]he primacy of the category of totality is the bearer of the revolutionary principle in science'" (Lukács, 1971: XXI). I argue it is, in fact, through this distorted understanding of totality that social reproduction theory repeats the above conflation between

---

41 See the Part II, "The Antinomies of Bourgeois Thought," of Lukács' essay "Reification and the Consciousness of Proletariat," in Lukács, 1971.

42 This self-critique ought not to be confused with those of 1929 and 1949, which were driven by Lukács' concern for self-preservation in the face of Stalinist violence and purges. Lukács' reconsideration I quote here comes from the famous 1967 Preface to *History and Class Consciousness*, fourteen years after Stalin's death. On the relationship between Lukács and Stalinism, see Löwy, 1975. Recently, Daniel Andrés López argued that Lukács' latest self-critique was not justified (López, 2019). While this is an intriguing exercise in thought, I agree with Lukács himself, especially considering his unfinished trilogy, the *Ontology of Social Being*.

ontology and politics again and again. At the conceptual level, this supposed 'Hegelian-Marxist' totality is merely reduced to a commonplace to mean that *"everything* is *socially* mediated" (Ferguson, 2016: 54, emphasis in original) by social reproduction theory. Accordingly, social reproduction theory is argued to have sublated intersectionality's empirical findings by transplanting them into their place in totality, thereby showing that the conditions for possibility of effecting a revolutionary outcome is accomplished in theory.

XIV   Severing Methodology from the Rest of the Theoretical Framework in Social Reproduction Theory

In addition to revealing social reproduction theory's conceptually untenable occupation with sublating intersectionality by way of ontologizing metaphors, battling them, and drawing political conclusions from them, Bhattacharya's text also crystallizes another problem. This is the colloquial employment of 'methodology' at the expense of observing any principle of theoretical consistency and coherence. The cardinal import of Bhattacharya's critique of intersectionality is the problem of intersectional methodology. As she puts it twice: "the insights or conclusions of intersectional theorists actually contradict their methodology" (Bhattacharya, 2017: 17) and "intersectionality theory's methodology belies its own findings" (Bhattacharya, 2017: 17). I suggest that the semantic clarity of these propositions obscures their conceptual meaning; therefore, they ought to be read and analyzed closely. Importantly, in the course of her critique, Bhattacharya does not explain what her understanding of intersectional methodology is, beyond that, according to her, the metaphor of intersections suggests "race and gender [as] being separate systems of oppression or even separate oppressions with only externally related trajectories" (Bhattacharya, 2017: 17). More importantly, Bhattacharya seems to argue that methodology has no bearing upon the knowledge produced within a given theoretical framework. It is rather puzzling to think that "the findings of Black feminist scholars [should be able to] show how race and gender are actually co-constitutive" (Bhattacharya, 2017: 17) with a mistaken methodology, theoretical premise, and understanding of reality that need to be rejected altogether.

One, then, must ask the following set of questions:
1) According to social reproduction theory, how, in spite of such methodological, theoretical, and ontological misconceptions, does intersectionality reach 'conclusions,' 'findings,' and 'insights' that are true and valid?

2) What are the epistemological criteria that social reproduction theory uses to evaluate and affirm the validity of these 'conclusions,' 'findings,' and 'insights?'
3) Why does social reproduction theory decide to 'retain and reposition' these 'conclusions,' 'findings,' and 'insights' that spring from such flawed misconceptions within its framework, instead of simply discarding them and reconceptualizing them from the standpoint of their own methodological, theoretical, and ontological principles?
4) How, in the face of such serious misconceptions, does social reproduction theory justify the necessity of this sublation?

However, as I have shown, because social reproduction theory is not a self-reflexive body of knowledge in terms of its own concept formation, it does not entertain any of the above questions in the consideration of its relationship to intersectionality. Consequently, it does not offer any analytically satisfactory response to these questions.

I argue that this cleaving off of methodology from the rest of the theoretical framework and from ontology is possible because of social reproduction theory's relegation of experience to empirical findings and, relatedly, because its claim to be a total social theory has been predicated upon the uncritical importation of the social problem of race and racialization from intersectionality. Social reproduction theory's acceptance of intersectionality's 'conclusions,' 'findings,' and 'insights' – that is, the co-constitutive relationship between race and gender (and, presumably, other social power relations subjected to systematic oppression)[43] – comes about through a gesture of epistemic deference, rather than through a conceptually rigorous analysis. As I have shown earlier, because social reproduction theory reduces lived experience to the empirical, as indexical accoutrements of the subject and subjectivity, social reproduction theorists readily accept what "Black feminist scholars" (Bhattacharya, 2017: 17) have to say about their experiences as a particular group of racialized subjects.

---

43   It is important note that Ferguson and McNally in their introduction to the *Historical Materialism* edition of Lise Vogel's *Marxism and the Oppression of Women*, "Capital, Labour-Power, and Gender-Relations," argued that intersectionality "struggles to grasp the co-constitution of each social relation in and through other relations of power" (Ferguson and McNally, 2013: XXXVI). However, two years after, they changed their view and accepted that intersectionality claims that "distinct oppressions are co-constitutive" (McNally and Ferguson, 2015: n.p). While they have never explained what theoretical shift in their thinking has resulted in this important change, they have since maintained the view that intersectionality understands social relations of power as co-constitutive of one another in their key single-authored contributions to social reproduction theory, such as Ferguson, 2016; and McNally, 2017.

However, because social reproduction theory does not recognize experience as a concept integral to social science research, social reproduction theorists can also easily strip off the ontological, theoretical, and methodological procedures through which 'Black feminist scholars' make sense of their experience, thereby resulting in an erasure of their identities as scholars.[44] Put differently, the conceptual shortcomings of social reproduction theory ends up producing results opposite to what the initial gesture of epistemic deference implies. Rehearsing the description versus explanation dichotomy of the marxist-feminists I have critiqued in Part I, social reproduction theory suggests that while intersectional scholars provide accounts of their experiences of the *body*, social reproduction theorists explain and analyze these experiences correctly, thereby doing the work of the *mind*.

XV   Co-constitutivity in Social Reproduction Theory

Because my discussion in *Grounding Critique* focuses on concept formation, I simply note the above as a problematic consequence of social reproduction theory's knowledge production practices in terms of the politics of knowledge production. And I continue to analyze social reproduction theory's acceptance of intersectionality's co-constitutivity thesis within the context of the supposed sublation between these two bodies of knowledge. I argue that this acceptance merely registers that the co-constitution thesis is deemed correct and pronounces its retention within the new theory into which it is sublated. Thus, it absolves social reproduction theory of the necessity of explaining the nature of this co-constitution. As a result, while forcefully arguing for a unitarian account of systems of exploitation and oppression through co-constitutivity, social reproduction theorists never explain what co-constitution might actually mean. The only sustained argumentation for co-constitutivity exists when social reproduction theorists argue against what they take to be 'the separate ontologies of oppressions' in intersectionality, which as I have shown above, is a conceptually unsound arbitrary conclusion.

---

44   It is imperative to note the slippage between 'Black feminist scholars' and intersectionality in Bhattacharya's use. While it is of course essential to emphasize that intersectionality springs out of the long tradition of Black feminisms, it is also important to remember that not all Black feminists are intersectional scholars. To be sure, however, this slippage is not a simple accident of linguistic expression; rather, a consequence of the conceptual universe of social reproduction theory.

For instance, Bhattacharya argues against "race and gender being separate systems of oppression or even separate oppressions with only externally related trajectories" (Bhattacharya, 2017: 17). Similarly, McNally writes that "[t]he distinct parts of a social whole are thus *internally* related; they mediate each other and in so doing constitute each other. And things (or relations) that are intermediated and co-constituting are not ontologically separate, even if they have properties that differentiate them and constitute a relative distinctiveness" (McNally, 2017: 104–105). Emphasizing, thus, that "[t]hese relations do not need to be brought into intersection because each is already inside the other, co-constituting one another to their very core" (McNally, 2017: 107), McNally moves onto offering an alternative metaphor: "Rather than standing at intersections, we stand in the river of life, where multiple creeks and streams have converged into a complex, pulsating system" (McNally, 2017: 107).

To be sure, this new fluid metaphor is much more poetic than that of prosaic intersections. However, as far as concept formation is concerned, the problem remains unilluminated. Social reproduction theory refutes intersectionality only to validate its conclusions. Perhaps the most charitable interpretation one could suggest is that, from the standpoint of social reproduction theory, intersectionality's conceptualization of co-constitution is static, whereas their own is dynamic. Even this distinction, however, does not explain what the dynamic conceptualization of co-constitution entails in analytical terms. For such an explication, I suggest, needs to consider the following set of questions:

1) Is the presumed co-constitution between race and gender genetic, historical, or existential?
2) How does a relationship of 'mediation' between embodied social relations produce their own 'constitution?'
3) Do they enter the relationship of mediation as themselves? If so, whence does their ipseity come; if not, *as what* they partake in this relationship?
4) If one accepts "race and racialization – and ultimately with sexuality and ability – as constitutive dimensions of class and gender" (McNally and Ferguson, 2015: n.p.), how does one explain the reason of their distinctiveness as different 'dimensions?' And does it simply follow that these dimensions are 'parts' while class or gender is the 'whole?'
5) If not, how does one explain the transitivity between parts and wholes?

I argue that social reproduction theory cannot consider these questions conceptually. Social reproduction theorists consequently and necessarily appropriate and abrogate the epistemic authority of intersectional scholars by nominally retaining 'co-constitution.' This retention of the social problem of race and racialization is given the impression of being seamlessly integrated into the social reproduction framework.

Therefore, I contend that what has been introduced by social reproduction theory as the dialectical overcoming of intersectionality is, in fact, an act of epistemic justification. This act aims to provide the conditions for possibility of social reproduction theory becoming a unitarian theory of exploitation and oppression, thereby satisfying the principle of internal theoretical coherence. In other words, the retention and repositioning of the critical insights of intersectionality within social reproduction theory does not produce a better conceptual framework for the explanation of embodied social relations. Battling metaphors and drawing arbitrary conclusions from an imputed intersectional ontology, this retention and repositioning generates a quasi-transcendental structure of analysis that issues validation for its theoretical arguments through political claims and justifies its politics through a theoretical discourse. One must be warned, moreover, that this move does not represent the dialectical union of theory and practice, that long-promised and much-yearned-for praxis.[45] On the contrary, this move constitutes a diremption between theory and practice by establishing a predetermined functionalist correspondence between them, and thereby depriving both theory and practice from the possibility of operating in an open system where they can encounter one another, in mutual effect, to self-reflexively respond to societal changes within the unfolding of history.

XVI 'Additive Method,' Anti-additivity, and Social Reproduction Theory

David McNally's contribution to the flagship social reproduction theory volume is exemplary with respect to displaying this quasi-transcendental structure most crisply and sophisticatedly. In the contemporary "intellectual renaissance of historical materialism in the context of new anticapitalist struggles" (McNally, 2017: 111), according to McNally, "it is not surprising that Marxist-inspired social reproduction theory has similarly resurged as a response to crucial aporias in intersectionality approaches, while also drawing upon critical insights about multiple forms of oppression that the latter has advanced" (McNally, 2017: 111). He, then, declares that "to be equal to the tasks of the moment, a dialectically reconstructed social reproduction theory is vital if we are to understand the 'unity of the diverse' that is the shape of our world – and if we are to change it" (McNally, 2017: 111).

---

45   For an epistemological analysis of the relationship between theory and practice, see Part 1 of this book where I discuss the matter in detail through a close reading of *Theses on Feuerbach*.

Thus, McNally predicates political vitality and viability of social reproduction theory on its unitary theoretical status, which in turn is predicated upon the dialectical overcoming of intersectionality because it attains correct political conclusions through an incorrect theory. Consequently, social reproduction theory assumes the formalistic task of aligning correct theory with correct political conclusions – rather than analyzing the gaps, misalignments, and excesses that necessarily exist between understanding and action that spring from people's everyday praxes as the products of lived social contradictions. During the carrying out of this (re)alignment, however, social reproduction theory conflates various theoretical and political positions in service of justifying a set of *a priori* propositions and positions, thereby rendering both theory and practice instrumental and bereft of internal coherence and significance.

For instance, McNally writes that "like dual systems approaches, intersectional theorists tended toward the *additive method* ... Where the dualists added together relations of class and gender, intersectionalists added a third element – race – to the mix, in efforts to arrive at a more complex picture of the social whole" (McNally, 2017: 108). However, in an earlier text, 'Capital, Labour-Power, and Gender-Relations,' with his co-author, McNally counterposes dual system theories and intersectionality. They argue that intersectionality tackles "a key problem that had plagued both the dual-systems and identity-politics perspectives: to elucidate the interrelations among distinct dimensions of social experience and the institutions and practices that shape them" (Ferguson and McNally, 2013: XXXV). I do not suggest that this obvious contradiction is a shortcoming of social reproduction theory. Rather, I argue that it is part and parcel of the concept formation in social reproduction theory, the natural outcome of its progress.

Indeed, from of its inception as represented by Ferguson and McNally's introduction to the *Historical Materialism* edition of Lise Vogel's *Marxism and the Oppression of Women*, social reproduction theory is concerned with going beyond the gender-class analytics of socialist feminism. This is achieved by importing the social problem of race and racialization from intersectionality. Thus, at this particular moment of the making of the theory, the progenitors of social reproduction theory do not recognize any methodological similarity between socialist-feminism and intersectionality. In fact, they use the latter to overcome the former. Later, once social reproduction theory proclaims its scientific status as a unitarian total social theory[46] and affirms this unitary

---

46 As I have previously argued in this part of the book, this transfiguration of the social scientific status is achieved through the threefold analytical movement: an ontological entrenchment of a quasi-transcendental, or metacritical structure; an epistemological

theory as the revolutionary framework that is commensurate to the exigent political demands of our time, the overcoming of intersectionality becomes imperative. As a result, social reproduction theorists suddenly recognize the same 'methodological' flaw (i.e., additive method), in intersectionality, which has previously constituted their rationale for the overcoming of dual systems approach of socialist-feminism.

I suggest that it is only by analyzing this sequence of the making of social reproduction theory that one might understand the significance of the above contradiction. I thus examine McNally's argument that both the dual systems approach of socialist-feminism and intersectionality employ an 'additive method'[47] as inviting a threefold important conceptual consideration:

1) Social reproduction theory reduces the *methods of analysis* in social sciences to the *research methods* of social sciences.[48] Therefore, 'methods' may be argued to be easily deployed in different frameworks – much like, semi-structured interviews, surveys, focus groups, etc. are deployed in different research projects. This reduction constitutes one of the most important characteristics of social reproduction theory. For it is produced through the separation between methodology and theoretical system, which social reproduction theory customarily and constantly performs.[49]

---

deployment of a unitarian phraseology; and a resultant methodological circuit that conjugates all social phenomena into the metacritical structure by the use of unitarian phraseology.

47 Not being a mathematician myself, I must confess that I do not know the difference between addition, aggregation, integrals, sums, calculus, and whatever else there may be. And when I see a mathematical sum (e.g., say 500) in the course of my everyday life, I do not think of it as the aggregation of smaller numerical parts (e.g., 150+250+100). Nor do I try to find out how many different mathematical expressions and combinations amount to the same sum. Although there are popular science books arguing that analogy is "the fuel and fire of thinking" (see, Hofstadter, Douglas R., and Sander, 2013), I do not think that mathematical analogies and metaphors are fruitful ways of thinking about social science methodologies. They introduce more confusion than clarification, especially when they are not explained with any expert knowledge in mathematics and, instead, when only used to appeal to the certitude and authority that the ancient and cardinal discipline provides. Therefore, in the following discussion, I refrain from further metaphorizing mathematics and limit myself to the analysis of 'additive method' as and when it conceptually operates in social reproduction theory.

48 While methods of analysis in social sciences considers the relationship between ontological and epistemological propositions of a given analytical framework by way of conception formation, the research methods of social sciences refer to tools that are used to conduct qualitative and quantitative social research.

49 Intersectionality and socialist-feminism are not alone in being subjected to this separation. Hegel and Marx too are subjected to this separation. While their method, dubbed as

2) If such a reduction is argued to have not been committed, it means that socialist-feminism and intersectionality have indeed the same additive theoretical framework. This, then, necessarily suggests that the initial overcoming of dual systems approach had actually not been achieved. As a result, then, the very conceptual tenability of social reproduction theory collapses.

3) If employing the same method, irrespective of the theoretical system in which it operates, can be soundly interpreted as constituting a valid ground for dialectical overcoming, anti-additivity itself ought to be subjected to the same interpretative rule. Then, one must remember that one of the strongest anti-additive responses to intersectionality have been administered by the U.S. District Court for the Eastern District of Missouri. In the summary judgement, the district court rejects the plaintiffs' attempt "to bring a suit not on behalf of Blacks or women, but specifically on behalf of Black women" (Crenshaw, 1989: 141). This attempt has arisen from the plaintiff's grievance that they have been discriminated against on the basis of both race *and* gender – contrary to Title VII of the Civil Rights Act of 1964, which *"prohibits employment discrimination based on race, color, religion, sex and national origin"* (The U.S. Equal Employment Opportunity Commission, 1964: n.p). The court states that "[t]he prospect of the creation of new classes of protected minorities, governed only by the mathematical principles of permutation and combination, clearly raises the prospect of opening the hackneyed Pandora's box" (Crenshaw, 1989: 142). This anti-additive convergence between the U.S. district court and social reproduction theory means that critiquing the additive, algebraic, and aggregative method of intersectionality does not guarantee a revolutionary political outcome. As a result, then, the political claims of social reproduction theory are undermined.

This threefold analysis reveals that social reproduction theory's adamant focus on critiquing the 'additive method' is merely oriented towards establishing itself as the sublated alternative of intersectionality that represents a coincidence and unity between correct theory and correct politics. However, upon the above consideration, it becomes clear that such a coincidence cannot be evinced to exist. More importantly, this focus does not offer a more adequate way of comprehending the nature of embodied social relations. By shifting the focus from embodied social relations to the ways in which their connection

---

'dialectic' though left unelaborated, is said to have been kept by social reproduction theory, the remainder of their thought remains dispersed, piecemeal, and unsystematized in this theoretical framework.

is represented in thought (i.e., addition, aggregation, integration, etc.), social reproduction theory essentially obfuscates the real question: how is intersectionality possible in the first place? In other words, how have embodied social relations such as race, gender, and sexuality become the categories of everyday praxis in contemporary class societies and the making of history?

This line of social inquiry, however, requires that social reproduction theory recognize the problem of additivity as belonging less to intersectional methods than to its own selection and articulation of social problems and concept formation. For, contrary to its claim of being a total unitary social theory, it does not explain a) the relationship between social relations and subjects, who stand in those relations but whose formation of subjectivity exceeds these relations, b) the sociation of and passage between these social relations, c) the nature of society in which this particular set of social relations constitutes the social. Rather, social reproduction theory accepts these social relations as social facts; inherits gender from socialist-feminism and race from intersectionality; and multiplies the 'rest' (*et cetera*) from the integration of these two social relations. In so doing, social reproduction theory displays the very additivity that it shuns in dual systems approaches and intersectionality. What is most interesting is that while dual systems approaches and intersectionality provide a social and sociological rationale for their focus on gender and race,[50] social reproduction theory integrates social relations into its roster simply upon external charges of lacking and omitting these relations, and justifies this integration as the internal necessity for having room for all undetermined aspects of an undefined totality.

This integration and multiplication of social relations does not mean much on conceptual grounds because the whole by virtue of being a totality already includes all these social relations in essence and prior to their appearances. Although McNally principally accepts that "changes in one subset of relations presuppose changes in all the others and in the system as a whole" (McNally, 2017: 111), this principle, to be conceptually meaningful, demands an explanation of the ways in which these relations constitute distinct 'subsets,' whence they come into the totality, and where they go once outside the totality. In other words, social reproduction theory still needs to develop an account for the above questions regarding the nature of social relations, subjects, subjectivity, society, and the social.

---

50   In socialist-feminism, the rationale is to analyze women's specific relationship to the capitalist mode of production as a social group; in intersectionality, it is to analyze the oppression of historical group identities in the seeming equality of liberal bourgeois legal personhood.

XVII   Liberalism, Ontological Atomism, Social Newtonianism, and Intersectionality according to Social Reproduction Theory

Instead of engaging in this necessary line of social inquiry to help develop social reproduction theory as a marxist social theory, McNally contributes yet another argument battling the metaphor of intersections to the already considerable arsenal of social reproduction theory on this front. According to McNally, the spatial metaphor of intersections betrays a 'social Newtonian theoretical model' on intersectionality's part. In what follows, I demonstrate that this argument too, like many other social reproduction theory propositions, operates within the quasi-transcendental theoretical and political structure of social reproduction theory. In this structure, neither theoretical nor political arguments are brought to their logical conclusions; rather, they are used to conceal one another's shortcomings.

McNally notes that despite various attempts, intersectional theorists "have repeatedly resorted to describing multiple oppressions with spatialized terms such as *lines, locations, axes,* and *vectors*" (McNally, 2017: 96, emphases in original). He, then, declares that "the conceptual image" (McNally, 2017: 96) of intersections "has haunted intersectionality theory" (McNally, 2017: 96) because intersectionality is "plagued by the ontological atomism inherent in ... [its] founding formulations" (McNally, 2017: 96). Having thus charged intersectionality with ontological atomism because of the continual use of a metaphor, McNally reminds us of the Newtonian influence on the atomism of classical liberalism:

> Classical liberalism, particularly in the realm of political economy, adapted this mechanical philosophy to social life. For theorists like Adam Smith, the social universe is composed of self-moving atomic parts (self-seeking individuals) whose colliding movements are regulated by morality, law and, crucially, the market. In the hectic pell-mell of collisions among self-interested individuals, a stable social order thus emerges, one that can be analyzed in much the same way Newton deciphered the order amid the flux of the physical world. Smith's 'invisible hand' of the market, which generates harmony out of the chaotic, self-interested behavior of individuals, is a deliberate analogue to the unseen forces that harmonize Newton's physical world.
>
> MCNALLY, 2017: 98

After establishing this firm relationship between liberalism and Newtonianism, McNally explains that "[i]n suggesting that intersectionality theory is haunted by social Newtonianism" (McNally, 2017: 99), he refers "precisely to the idea that different axes and vectors of difference can be mapped in social space as ontologically separate and autonomous 'bits' that enter into external relations with other 'bits'" (McNally, 2017: 99). Although the relationship established between ontological atomism, liberalism, and social Newtonianism evidently suggest that intersectionality espouses a liberal politics, McNally does not state this conclusion explicitly. Indeed, he registers that "[w]hile intersectional theorists tend to work with locations and vectors rather than the atomic individuals of liberal theory, they confront a similar methodological problem" (McNally, 2017: 99), but then he adds that "[t]hey too are challenged when it comes to deriving some kind of social order or system from these parts" (McNally, 2017: 99).

I argue that this equivocation is not only the logical outcome of McNally's argument but also necessary for the coherence of social reproduction theory. Firstly, intersectionality's relationship to liberalism is suggested but not stated because such overt acknowledgement undermines social reproduction theory's importation of race and racialization as a social problem, which as I have shown, appeals to the epistemic authority of intersectional scholars. And, because social reproduction theory conflates intersectionality and Black feminism, such a blanket political and theoretical correspondence between intersectionality and liberalism cannot be supported. An intimation of this correspondence, on the other hand, helps represent social reproduction theory as a politically and theoretically more advanced alternative to intersectionality.

Secondly, this equivocation allows McNally to make an argument not about a relationship of identity but, rather, about that of the similarity between intersectionality and liberalism. Demonstrating the former relationship necessarily requires the production of knowledge claims that are valid, whereas the latter might be argued simply through a series of associatively linked ideas. This constitutes a great advantage because the discussion of 'social Newtonianism,' by definition, cannot produce any sound knowledge regarding the limitations of intersectionality, and how social reproduction theory can overcome those limitations. For 'social Newtonianism' is about the relationship between the individual and society[51] so as to ascertain the modes of social existence and the

---

51 This may be easily discerned in the long McNally quotation above. McNally himself acknowledges this to be the case about social Newtonianism in his earlier writings as well. For instance, he writes that "[t]he problem of communication is for [Adam] Smith one of social harmony. Unless they can communicate their sentiments, thoughts, and experiences to one another, how can independent individuals – especially ones who are self-seeking – cohere to form a unified social whole? This is the central problem of

ontological primacy of these modes,[52] which is no doubt an interesting and well-established area of sociological research, but does not correspond to the main problematic that helps clarify the relationship between intersectionality and social reproduction theory (viz., the nature of social relations, subjects, subjectivity, society, and the social).

To date, McNally's discussion of 'social Newtonianism' constitutes the most developed and sophisticated critique of intersectionality that social reproduction theory offers. Moreover, it arguably makes the best case about the need for social reproduction theory to dialectically overcome intersectionality. Put simply, what is conceptually at stake in McNally's discussion of 'social Newtonianism' in relation to intersectionality is the social scientific status of social reproduction theory as a unitary social theory. Therefore, I suggest that a thorough examination of the discussion of 'social Newtonianism' is imperative to ultimately determine social reproduction theory's status. Thus, below I conduct this examination.

XVIII   An Alternative Outlook on the Relationship between Intersectionality and the Critical Import of Newton's System into Liberal Bourgeois Social Thought

Drawing on the work of David John Manning (Manning, 1976), Immanuel Wallerstein systematizes the relationship between liberalism and Newtonianism in three main tenets. These are "the principle of balance, the principle of spontaneous generation and circulation, and the principle of uniformity" (Wallerstein, 2011: 7). According to Wallerstein, these tenets socially correspond to the following propositions: "First, the stability of the world 'depend[s] upon its constituent parts remaining in balanced relationships.' Second, 'any attempt to transform the self-moving society into the directed society must necessarily destroy the harmony and balance of its rational order.' Third, 'we may expect democratic institutions to materialize in human societies whenever they reach the appropriate level of development, just as we may expect any physical phenomenon to materialize given the principle of its sufficient condition for its occurrence'" (Wallerstein, 2011: 7).

Other scholars emphasize orderliness, individuality, automatism, and normativity as the significant tenets of social Newtonianism. The philosopher

---

'social Newtonianism': what principle of attraction binds the atoms of human society?" (McNally, 1988: 180).

52   For the rich history of this debate in sociology, see Sztompka, 2013: 287–344.

Alexandre Koyré writes that social Newtonianism reduces "society to a cluster of human atoms, complete and self-contained each in itself and mutually attracting and repulsing each other" (Koyré, 1950: 268). The philosopher George H. Sabine emphasizes that social Newtonianism regards "institutions and their history as scientifically irrelevant because they are reducible to habits of thought and action which can be fully explained by rather simple laws of individual behaviour" (Sabine, 1960: 686). The historian of science Patricia Fara explains that the social implications of Newton's system gives rise to the efforts to "deduce general laws describing human behaviour and morality" (Fara, 2002: 156). Focusing on the conception of society, the sociologist Daniel W. Rossides argues that social Newtonianism is marked by "the tendency to think of society as a great, self-equilibrating machine" (Rossides, 1998: 101). Finally, the literary theorist Anne Janowitz states that "until the 1780s, Newton's natural philosophy served as the sanctioned model for social and moral theory as well, a 'social Newtonianism' whose central cultural claim was to simplicity and system" (Janowitz, 2005: 472), according to which social order was synonymous with social happiness.

As it ought to be clear from the above references, 'social Newtonianism,' or the critical import of Newton's system into liberal bourgeois social thought, is oriented towards examining the social problem of the relationship between the individual and society. Subsequently, it considers the consequences of this relationship with regard to social institutions and the state. However, in his hauntological discussion regarding the 'social Newtonianism' of intersectionality, McNally separates, what he deems to be, the social Newtonian method from the social problem that 'social Newtonianism' addresses. This separation, as noted above, is the characteristic analytical move that social reproduction theorists perform in relation to every body of knowledge it engages with – as though, method is not integral to the ontological and epistemological propositions that are constructed to address social problems under consideration.

In any case, strictly speaking, "the idea that different axes and vectors of difference can be mapped in social space as ontologically separate and autonomous 'bits' that enter into external relations with other 'bits'" (McNally, 2017: 99), and the image of "[a]tomic individuals ... collid[ing], or avoid colliding, in social space" (McNally, 2017: 99), do not constitute a methodology. In fact, according to the historian of science I. Bernard Cohen, who is also the co-translator of the authoritative translation of *Philosophiæ Naturalis Principia Mathematica* (Newton, 1999), such a methodology, in its proper sense, in social sciences does not exist. He writes that:

> Did anyone ever attempt to found a system of social science or economics on the level of identity with Newtonian rational mechanics or the Newtonian system of the world? In my research, I have never found such an example. The reason is that the Newtonian system of the world, the application of Newtonian rational mechanics, does not lend itself to a mechanical model or a visualization in the human mind that can easily be transferred to an image of society at large or to economics.
>
> COHEN, 1994: 61

As opposed to any employment of methodological identity, social sciences make use of Newtonian science through metaphorical, analogical, and homological applications (Cohen, 1994: 56–64).

Reconsidered not in separation from but in relation to the system and problem that social applications of Newtonian science comprise and address, and in the light of the lack of methodological identity between social sciences and Newtonian science, intersectionality cannot be argued to have been 'plagued' or 'haunted' by 'social Newtonianism.' This is the case because intersectionality does not share the above premises on which social applications of Newtonian science are predicated. For instance, the concept of the subject that intersectionality employs is not the autonomous, universal, and self-same atomistic subject of rationalism.[53] It is one whose mode of existence is determined by the multiple collectivities to which it belongs. In other words, unlike atomistic social theories, according to which the coming-together of subjects accounts for the constitution of society, the intersectional collective subject is produced by society within a set of historical power dynamics, such as race and gender.[54]

Moreover, intersectionality does not affirm an existing social balance and harmony, nor justify an optimal social order that legislative, executive, and judicial institutions maintain, nor legitimize the *status quo* as the moral end of society. To the contrary, intersectionality demonstrates that these notions of social balance, harmony, order, and morality are themselves made possible by the claim that the liberal (bourgeois) state is capable of addressing and redressing social inequality through the management of grievable categories

---

53 For a brief history of this conceptualization of the subject, see Edgar, 1999.
54 To be sure, this does not mean that the conceptualization of the subject in intersectionality is beyond critique. It solely means that the charge of 'social Newtonianism' is misplaced unto intersectionality. Although it is not the focus of my discussion here, I would argue that the intersectional concept of collective subject is overdeterministic in relation to history; reductionist in relation to social ontology; and simplistic in relation to phenomenology of embodied social relations.

of embodied social relations. However, because this institutional capacity commonly operates through a single-axis (i.e., race-only, gender-only) management strategy at the expense of the 'intersections' of these axes, in which social inequality is lived and reproduced, intersectionality demonstrates that this claim – and all that it legitimizes – is nothing but a convenient fiction. To be sure, other political conclusions might be drawn from intersectionality's approach to the liberal (bourgeois) state and its institutions. Some of these conclusions might be construed as 'reformist,' arguing that the state can accommodate most, if not all, intersections. However, I do not think it productive to venture into a set of hypothetical considerations as to the possibility of such accommodation. Given the contemporary proto-fascistic turn of neoliberalism, one might soundly argue that the (il)liberal (bourgeois) state and its institutions do not seem to be interested in engaging in such accommodation. I believe that the above-quoted U.S. district court statement represents the real difficulty of actualizing such 'reforms.' As the misogynistic invocation of the myth of Pandora suggests, the district court equates the accommodation of intersections with bringing "grim cares upon mankind [sic.]" (Hesiod, 1988: 39). However, considering that such grim cares have already been sprung upon the vast majority of peoples and the only remaining content in Pandora's jar is Hope, forcing the jar open against the wishes of the ruling classes and their representatives might not be such a terrible idea.

Therefore, even if one allows that intersectionality and liberalism "confront a similar methodological problem" (McNally, 2017: 99) that 'social Newtonianism' epitomizes, it does not follow from this that such 'similarity' ought to be accepted as evidence that the former also accepts the latter's foundational premises. In fact, McNally's analysis simply demonstrates that Cohen's argument, which is that "Newton's physics did not ever produce any useful analogies or homologies for the social sciences" (Cohen, 1994: 79), is correct. Furthermore, it confirms that Cohen's conclusion is more the case when the analogization is twice removed and pushed to its limits, as the already metaphorical application of 'social Newtonianism' is rendered even more tenuous through a second analogy that depends upon a separation between method and system.

To be clear, however, I do not mean to call for a blanket interdiction on researching the relationship between intersectionality and 'social Newtonianism.' What I critique is the hasty judgement that 'intersectionality is social Newtonian,' which does not at all offer a better way of understanding embodied social relations and merely serves to justify social reproduction theory as a unitary social theory by way of theoretical and political allusions and derivative methodological analogies. Otherwise, I readily admit that a rigorous research agenda proposing the study of Newton's influence on sociological thought and social philosophy in general, and on intersectionality in particular, is not only worthwhile but also exciting.

In fact, I suggest that to be commensurate to the task it sets up for itself, such an agenda ought to, at least, begin with: first, Galileo's influence on Hobbes and, following this influence, Hobbes' challenge to the Aristotelian system of theoretical, practical, and productive sciences; second, examine Mandeville's, Shaftesbury's, and Locke's reaction to Hobbes as setting the stage for understanding the debates present in the Glasgow and Edinburgh schools of the Scottish Enlightenment; third, focus on Hutcheson's mathematical overcoming of the aporias produced in thought of the above thinkers between benevolence, virtue, self-love, and vice in a Newtonian manner, Hume's philosophical reworking of Hutcheson's system of moral philosophy, and Smith's application of both Hutcheson's and Hume's ideas on moral sentiments, order, and productivity; fourth, identify Hume's and Smith's influence on Bentham's utilitarian philosophy and social science, and in turn Bentham's influence on J.S. Mill. Having covered this history of thought comprising the ground of liberalism, this research agenda may then move onto "the United States [as] the most Newtonian society of all" (Foley, 1990: 199) to scrutinize if "the postbellum dream of an American science of social Newtonianism would be realized in the synthesis propounded by Dewey, Mead, Cooley, and many others of a coordinated 'social process' embodying the 'attitude of the engineer'" (Block, 2002: 149). Finally, the research agenda that proposes to illuminate the relationship between liberalism, 'social Newtonianism,' and intersectionality, may turn to intersectionality in particular and demonstrate whether intersectionality, as well as its predecessors in the tradition of Black feminism, has been influenced – and, if so, in what specific ways – by the above traditions, and the various revisions and mutations of them. Even then, I must acknowledge, this elementary suggestion for a research agenda would be inadequate and incomplete. However, I believe that it, at least, represents the very minimum amount of scholarly labour needed to establish the desired connection in a manner that could be argued to possess a modicum of social scientific validity and soundness. For it to be less inadequate and incomplete, it needs to address the relationship between the Scottish Enlightenment and the French Enlightenment in terms of their philosophical and sociological outcomes; Marx's great reworking of Western thought in explaining the making of history, constitution of society, and sensuous human praxis;

and the relationship between Kantianism, neo-Kantianism, and American pragmatism.[55]

xix The Pitfalls of the 'Methodology' of Analogical Argumentations and Battling Metaphors

Social reproduction theorists' analogical argumentation and their battling with intersectional metaphors, however, cannot substitute such a rigorous study of concept formation, the sketch of which I provided above. Nor does social reproduction theory's approach produce any reliable knowledge about the nature of embodied social relations beyond offering an undefined and nebulous unitary account of these social relations that is justified in a forceful yet inaccurate theoretical and political quasi-transcendental structure of explanation. In fact, if the strategy of analogical argumentation and battling with metaphors is not merely an aspersion on intersectionality, but may also be argued to have social scientific validity and can be used legitimately to read other texts as well, then it ought to be noted that this method of argumentation leads to the most confounding theoretical and political conclusions.

For instance, in his famous 1890 letter to Joseph Bloch, Engels cautions against any economistic interpretation of marxism, explicating that "[a]ccording to the materialist conception of history, the *ultimately* determining element in history is the production and reproduction of real life. Other than this neither Marx nor I [Engels] have ever asserted. Hence if somebody twists this into saying that the economic element is the *only* determining one, he [sic.] transforms that proposition into a meaningless, abstract, senseless phrase" (Marx, Engels, and Lenin 1972: 294, emphases in original). In the same letter, Engels continues to write that:

> [H]istory is made in such a way that the final result always arises from conflicts between many individual wills, of which each in turn has been made what it is by a host of particular conditions of life. Thus there are innumerable intersecting forces, an infinite series of parallelograms of forces which give rise to one resultant – the historical event. This may again itself be viewed as the product of a power which works as a whole *unconsciously* and without volition. For what each individual wills is

---

55 In the construction of this cursory research agenda, I have drawn on the following sources: Baldin, 2020; Berry, 2020; Rendall, 1978; Wickman, 2015; Lowry, 2012; and Ross, 1992.

obstructed by everyone else, and what emerges is something that no one willed. Thus history has proceeded hitherto in the manner of a natural process and is essentially subject to the same laws of motion. But from the fact that the wills of individuals – each of whom desires what he is impelled to by his physical constitution and external, in the last resort economic, circumstances (either his own personal circumstances or those of society in general) – do not attain what they want, but are merged into an aggregate mean, a common resultant, it must not be concluded that they are equal to zero. On the contrary, each contributes to the resultant and is to this extent included in it.

  MARX, ENGELS, AND LENIN 1972: 295, emphasis in original

Reading Engels' above lines through social reproduction theory's customary method of analogical reason and battling with metaphors, one would have to reach the rather preposterous conclusion that one of the crispest and clearest summary articulations of historical materialism actually epitomizes a 'social Newtonian' methodology and a liberal theory and politics –simply on account of Engels metaphorical use of the language of atomism and individualism, intersecting forces,[56] parallelograms of forces,[57] vectors, laws of motions, and aggregates.

---

56 This line is translated as "conflicting forces" in the Marx-Engels Collected Works volume. Notwithstanding the difference in word choices in translation, it is clear that in his discussion Engels stylistically relies on spatial idioms drawn from physics. Therefore, this difference due to translation does not alter my argument above. For an easy comparison of the two translations, I reproduce the alternative translation here in its entirety: "history is made in such a way that the ultimate result is invariably produced by the clash of many individual wills of which each in turn has been made what it is by a wide variety of living conditions; there are thus innumerable conflicting forces, an infinite number of parallelograms of forces, productive of one result – the historical event which itself may be seen as the product of a power operating *unconsciously* and involuntarily as a whole. For what each individual wants is obstructed by every other individual and the outcome is something that no one wanted. Thus, the course of history up till now has been like a natural process and has, indeed, been subject to much the same laws of motion. But the fact that individual wills – each of which wants what it is driven to want by bodily constitution and extrinsic and, in the final analysis, economic (whether personal or general social) circumstances – do not attain what they want but merge into an overall mean, a common resultant – does not justify the conclusion that they are nonentities. On the contrary, each one contributes to the resultant and is, to that extent, part and parcel of it" (Marx and Engels, 2001: 35–36, emphasis in original).

57 Having laid out the three laws of motion in "Axioms, or the Laws of Motion," Newton states the Corollary 1 as follows: "*A body acted on by [two] forces acting jointly describes the diagonal of a parallelogram in the same time in which it would describe the sides if the forces were acting separately*" (Newton, *The Principia: Mathematical Principles of Natural Philosophy*,

The truth, however, cannot be farther from this conclusion. Engels is a thinker who is acutely aware of the limitations of Newton's thought in its own terms, not by way of analogies. For instance, in the notes and fragments of his *Dialectics of Nature,* Engels powerfully observes that "Newtonian attraction and centrifugal force – an example of metaphysical thinking: the problem not solved but only *posed,* and this preached as the solution" (Marx and Engels, 1987: 551, emphasis in original). However, despite his conceptual critique, he searches for a way of exposition that clarifies a most-maligned aspect of his and his comrades' thought (i.e., so-called economic reductionism) and finds an appropriate expression in the *idiom* of the physical and natural world that corrects this wide misapprehension. In short, I suggest that as opposed to representing an instance of epistolary looseness of form, Engels' letter bears an important lesson for not only marxists but also all social scientists that one must resist hastily criticizing forms of expressions – and metaphors and idioms used therein – and focus on concept formation in the production of knowledge.

xx   Towards a Marxist Social Theory of Embodied Social Relations

Over a century and thirty-some years after Engels' letter, we are still wrestling with the same problematic of innumerable intersecting and conflicting individual and social forces and their relationship to the making of history and the constitution of society. As I see it, this problematic cannot be adequately analyzed unless we can produce a marxist understanding of embodied social relations because much of these innumerable intersecting and conflicting individual and social forces in our time are articulated in and through the social organization of embodied social relations in class societies. Introducing

---

63, emphases in original). Explaining the use of parallelograms in Newton's Principia, Subrahmanyan Chandrasekhar writes that: "[f]rom the manner in which this 'parallelogram law of forces' is proved, it is clear that the law applies equally to *velocities, motions,* and *accelerations*; and Newton does use the law in these other contexts" (Chandrasekhar, 1995: 24, emphases in original). Engels, on his part, is well-aware of the shortcomings of the parallelogram law of forces. In Dialectics of Nature, he writes: "*Newton's parallelogram of forces* in the solar system is true at best *for the moment when the annular bodies separate,* because then the rotational motion comes into contradiction with itself, appearing on the one hand as attraction, and on the other hand as tangential force. As soon as the separation is complete, however, the motion is again a unity. That this separation must occur is a proof of the dialectical process" (Marx and Engels, 1987: 552, emphases in original).

Bakhtin into the discussion of 'social Newtonianism' (Morson, 2010: 162–163), Gary Saul Morson brings to the fore the most important question for the marxist social theory, which is the conceptualization of human beings. I argue that a marxist understanding of embodied social relations cannot be satisfied with conceptualizing human beings neither as the universal self-same subject (as in liberalism), nor as the embodiment of a multitude of particular identities (as in intersectionality), nor as the differentiated instantiations of a unitarian totality (as in social reproduction theory). I suggest that Bakhtin's following reminders must be kept in mind in any attempt to construct a marxist social theory examining embodied social relations. That is, "[a]n individual cannot be completely incarnated into the flesh of existing sociohistorical categories" (Bakhtin, 1981: 37); "[t]here always remains an unrealized surplus of humanness, there always remains a need for the future, and a place for this future must be found" (Bakhtin, 1981: 37); and, finally, "[a] man [sic.] never coincides with himself [sic.]. One cannot apply to him [sic.] the formula of identity $A = A$ ... [T]he genuine life of the personality takes place at the point of non-coincidence between a man [sic.] and himself [sic.]" (Bakhtin, 1984: 59).

To conclude, I have shown in Part II of *Grounding Critique* that social reproduction theory can neither accommodate the non-coincidence of embodied social relations, nor can it account for the excesses of them. For it receives the social problem of embodied social relations externally as an importation, and merely to fulfill a lack in its unitarian structure. Instead of integrating this social problem into its framework by undertaking intellectual labour at the level of concept formation, social reproduction theory resorts to creating a political impression of being the sublated version of intersectionality and socialist feminism by way of battling the metaphors employed in these traditions and building a quasi-transcendental structure of explanation. Thus, I submit that social reproduction theory does not constitute a marxist social theory that can further our understanding of embodied social relations. Rather, it remains as a (marxist) feminist political economy.

Coda: A Long Day's Evening

I   A Critique of Concept Formation

As in a long day's evening, at the end of a book too, it is necessary to rehearse the constitutive moments of its formation and making, so that the anticipation and hope of what is to come may be attended to with self-reflexivity. I began this book project with the knowledge, which I try and test against any dogmatization in an ongoing fashion, that Marx's social thought surpasses all existing philosophies in establishing a framework to explain the relationship between history, society, and the subject. My abiding interest has been in the conceptual place that social relations occupy in this framework – especially, that of embodied social relations, as those social relations through which subjects recognize their sensuous practical human activity in the making of history. However, during the course of my research, I discerned that contemporary marxist social thought tends to either treat these concepts in economistically reductionist ways, or de-conceptualize the concept altogether by naturalizing the constitution and organization of society as a function of our social being. Thus, in *Grounding Critique*, I undertook a critique of the concept formation of embodied social relations under capitalism in contemporary marxist-feminist thought and social reproduction theory through a methodological close reading of their critiques of intersectionality.

II   Through Intersectionality to Concept Formation in Contemporary Marxist Social Thought

Intersectionality, due to its capturing of the political and intellectual imaginary of our time, provided the impetus for contemporary marxist-feminism and social reproduction theory to clarify their understandings of embodied social relations. As I showed in Part I, in subjecting intersectionality to a marxist critique, contemporary marxist-feminist thinkers actually articulated their own interpretation of the core concepts of marxist social thought. And in Part II, I demonstrated that in order to become a unitary social theory, social reproduction theory needed to dialectically overcome intersectionality. Because the objective of this book was not to assess the validity and truth contents of the critiques of intersectionality produced by these bodies of knowledge, I did not directly engage with intersectionality as such. I limited my engagement with brief commentaries when they were needed to clarify contemporary marxist-feminism's and social reproduction theory's critiques of intersectionality, so that I could better illuminate the methodological unfolding of their concept formation. In *Grounding Critique*, I argued that a marxist engagement with intersectionality ought not to take the form of analyzing its adequacies and inadequacies and then, decide whether, or under what conditions, it could be made to co-exist with marxism. Rather, I forwarded that a more productive engagement with intersectionality needed to ask the question of 'how is intersectionality possible in the first place?' by examining embodied social relations under capitalism.

III Dissolving Intersecting Lines in Favour of Parallel Planes Bereft of Social Existence and Life

In Part I, I argued that contemporary marxist-feminist contributions to the *Science and Society*'s Symposium on intersectionality were not conceptually able to produce an account of embodied social relations that would help us understand sensuous human practical activity through which we make history. Through a methodological close reading, I demonstrated that these thinkers' works created a diremption between history, society, and the subject. In their scheme, history became knowable through the concept of the mode of production; society through social formation; and embodied social relations through ideology. Thus, contemporary marxist-feminist thought dissolved intersecting lines in favour of parallel planes that are bereft of social existence and life. To connect these planes, they summoned a marxist class politics. However, I showed that this move stymied the real political possibilities and reach of marxist politics. And it did not solve the conceptual problems that produced this separation in the first place because these problems belonged not to Marx's social thought, but to the antinomies of classical sociological reason.

IV Conceptual Conditions of Dialectically Overcoming Intersectionality

In Part II, I analyzed whether social reproduction theory could be argued to constitute a unitary social theory of exploitation and oppression. I argued that any proposition of being a (unitary) social theory was necessarily predicated upon the existence of an account of embodied social relations. Through tracing the concept formation in social reproduction theory, I emphasized that the social problem of race and racialization occupied a singularly important place in this novel and popular framework. Social reproduction theory's focus on race and racialization was used to distinguish itself from earlier feminist political economy analyses, thereby justifying the upward mobility in its scientific status as a unitary social theory. However, I demonstrated that social reproduction theory did not form its concepts of race and racialization, but it imported these concepts into its framework from intersectionality. In order to issue validity for this importation, on which the imputed unitarian character of the theory depends, social reproduction theory embarked upon dialectically overcoming intersectionality. Part II concluded that social reproduction theory did not meet the conceptual conditions of such overcoming, and that the arguments of their theorists simply operated in a quasi-transcendental structure of explanation in which ontological and political propositions were used to cover over one another's shortcomings while, at the same time, creating an appearance of such overcoming.

v   The Finality of Conceptual Judgement?

Having rehearsed the constitutive moments of *Grounding Critique*, it is now time to attend to the anticipation of what is to come. This is especially necessary when conducting a study of concept formation within a given body of knowledge. Close and deep reading practices, as required by the study of concept formation, sometimes produce an impression of finality in the reader. While this impression is not wholly mistaken, it is rather defenseless against the theoretical attitude of totality and its attendant political derivations – precisely those prevalent modes of marxist social theory that I have problematized in this book. Therefore, here I would like to offer an explicit discussion, clarification, and qualification of the meaning of this finality.

The meaning of the finality impressed upon the reader in this book is that the critique I conducted both of contemporary marxist feminism and of social reproduction theory has achieved its termination by tracing the spiral revolution of concept formation within the grooves of these respective bodies of knowledge through the following questions: How did the theories and theorists under consideration turn to embodied social relations as the object of their study? What was the point of these orientations? What was the manner in which the reaction-formation to intersectionality integrated within the analytical framework of these enterprises? How were these integrations represented in conceptual terms? How were these representations expressed in political terms? And, finally, did these integrations, representations, and expressions produce the knowledge of embodied social relations necessary for a marxist transformation of society, or did they merely appeal to the authority of a marxist politics instead?

To be sure, the marxist-feminist theorists I engaged with in Part I do not exhaust marxist-feminism as a field of ongoing social inquiry. Nor is social reproduction theory limited to the works of the theorists I focused on in Part II. Taken not in their singularity but in the inter-relationality of their works, these theories are the exemplary surfaces on which the grooves of these schools of thought are etched. As other engravings on the same groove and surface will produce the same sound, it is possible to turn the turntable infinitely. However, I considered that my critique achieved its termination when I brought the above heretofore unexplored and unelaborated questions to the foreground. Therefore, the finality of the analysis in Part I and Part II is not a foreclosure, but a saturated discernment.

VI Tarrying with Marxist-Feminism and Social Reproduction Theory

Put in more concrete terms, the reader, having studied *Grounding Critique* thus far, might ask whether we are to repudiate and expel the theories I discussed in Part I and II from the symbolic universe of marxism. The answer to this question would be a categorical no! Such a foreclosure is not what I argue in this book. For one thing, the suggestion of repudiation and expulsion runs counter to the methodological structure of the book, as well as against its politics of knowledge production. In fact, it is this very logic of foreclosure that I critique in this book. Enacted upon intersectionality, this logic of foreclosure resulted in a return of the unacknowledged heritage of sociological reason and antinomies for marxist-feminists I discussed in Part I. Moreover, it resulted in a conceptual inability to work through social problems in their concrete determinations for social reproduction theory in Part II. In both cases, this logic produced a hasty theoretical overcoming of that which is repudiated. And, in the process of this claim to overcoming, both set of theorists and theories separated history, society, and subject, thereby rendering embodied social relations unknowable and inexplicable.

These serious problems notwithstanding, I argue that applying the same logic of foreclosure to marxist-feminism and social reproduction theory ought not be entertained because this foreclosure of foreclosure would neither cancel each other out as formal logic might suggest, nor would it constitute a negation of negation as dialectical logic might suggest. It would merely replicate the problems of the initial foreclosure, thus making access to embodied social relations doubly impossible. As I pointed out elsewhere, concepts are the congealed representations of various different "orientations to construct empirical and theoretical objects of knowledge and expresses the concrete reconstruction of the social formation in which these orientations and objects coincide" (Tanyildiz, 2023: n.p.). It is, therefore, through the use of concepts in social analyses that we can render embodied social relations, within the capitalist mode of production, knowable and explainable again. This is why, in this book, I modelled a way of tarrying with marxist-feminism and social reproduction theory by studying their concept formation, rather than mirroring the foreclosures these theories performed, or generating another quasi-transcendental structure of explanation with the claim of having sublated their previous overcomings.

Thus, this tarrying was conceived to offer a contrapuntal to the hasty theoretical alternatives asserted by the two bodies of knowledge I analyzed in the book (viz., contemporary marxist-feminism and social reproduction theory). Only through this contrapuntal examination could we discern the ways in which the concepts of marxist social theory – often taken for granted and rarely explained – are used to understand embodied social relations, through which contemporary social subjects organize, contest, and express their worlds and lives. This required, throughout Part I and II, a threefold methodological labour of: 1) an attunement to the tones and moments of repudiation and expulsion of the social phenomena intersectionality represents from the symbolic universe of marxism, 2) discovering the conceptual form and content of this purified (for the marxist-feminists of Part I) or sublated (for the social reproduction theorists of Part II) symbolic universe, 3) assessing the analytic capacity of these universes to reckon with the contemporary embodied social relations and the social problems they pose.

The finality that the completion of this methodological labour produces, therefore, is a discernment of the gap between the contemporary conceptual practices of marxism and the lived social world from which these practices are launched and to which they return. When it comes to understanding embodied social relations, I believe this gap to be the necessary condition of knowledge production, as the self-sameness of thought and world (i.e., the world as thought, thought as the world, and thought thinking itself) can only consider sensuous human activity in objectified forms, not in its animating subjectivity. Thus, not only discovering this gap, but also discovering the ways in which this gap has been covered over by marxist-feminists of Part I and social reproduction theorists of Part II has been imperative for the task I set out for myself in this book. It is, therefore, the discernment of these discoveries and the demonstration of their saturation in the repeated and systematic efforts to cover over this gap that constitutes the meaning of finality in *Grounding Critique*.

VII   Quo Vadis Social Reproduction?

If the meaning of the finality, which might have been impressed upon the reader, is the termination of critique that discovers a saturated discernment of the ways in which the gap between the conceptual practices effected within a reconstructed marxist symbolic universe and the lived social world of sensuous human praxis, this very gap demands that the termination apparent initially in the meaning of finality must be recast as a determination. This is because subjective sensuous human activity is always in the middle of living and existing in the social world, without an origin or an end. Thus, conceptual attempts made to understand this activity cannot be argued to have been terminated at any point in history. Since subjective does not mean singular or arbitrary but expresses the form in which human existence is lived, picking and choosing concepts, or repudiating and expelling them are simply puerile and voluntaristic acts for the marxist sociologist, with whose predicament this book began. Instead, the project of having a marxist account of embodied social relations requires the further determination of the gap, whose discovery and covering over has been achieved upon the termination of the study of concept formation in this book.

While the proper carrying out of this determination necessitates another book, I should like to gesture towards what this might look like so that the foreclosure I methodologically negated finds a positive expression as well. This determination necessarily follows from the mode of exposition undertaken in this book. It begins where the present critique terminated because this was the moment in which the covering over of the gap between a repositioned symbolic universe of marxism and the lived social world was discovered with the clearest illumination. This covering over in social reproduction theory was effected by the way in which the concept of social reproduction activated within a quasi-transcendental structure of explanation. Here every social phenomenon was conjugated into this structure via the concept of social reproduction. In turn, as I have shown, this conjugation created a methodological circuit between infinite regress and ever-expanding tautology in not being able to anchor the discussion of the reproduction of labour-power in a robust discussion of the possibility of society, the nature of the social, the principle of sociability, and the forms of sociation.[1] As a result, the initially conceptual question of 'if labour produces capitalist value, then, what reproduces labour (-power)?' came to be a flat cartographical surface on which the sites, bodies, and activities involved in social reproduction were grafted. Produced in the key of and read in the legend of labour-power, this surface merely demonstrated the extent of the economic subsumption of life under contemporary capitalism. However, because this demonstration was achieved through the nomothetized facticity of social relations, it was unable to engage with the lived social world; rather, it turned this world into a unitarian representation of the symbolic universe that social reproduction theory created.

However, in line with the earlier methodological negation of foreclosure, this does not mean that social reproduction as a concept can no longer be used in marxist social inquiry. Rather, the particular use of the concept in social reproduction theory helps us reorient by asking where social reproduction goes and where we can go with it. Put differently, what happens if we did not work with a notion of life as produced by social reproduction, thereby not relying on a chain of infinite regression? What if we were to not allow the social reproductive structures of intentionality directed at the production of labour-power to expand to all of life? What if we divested from taking it for granted that the worker shows up at their workplace everyday with their labour-power is properly reproduced? What if we began entertaining that the capitalist actually exploits what the worker does not have, thus reproducing their non-being daily? What if we focused on the struggle between the worker's production of their being and non-being as depending upon the social relations in which

---

[1] I am grateful to Susan Ruddick who, in response to another publication where I problematized this methodological circuit (Tanyildiz, 2023), reminded me of Pierre Macherey's discussion of Spinoza's contrasting of "the partisans of finalism with those who seek to see things such as they are, in their immanent necessity" through the following fictious dialogue: "a man is dead from the drop of a stone that has fallen from a roof on his head; why has the stone fallen? Because the wind blew at the moment that he was passing. Why did the wind blow at that moment? Because he got up the day before, as the sea began to foment, and the man was invited by friends, et cetera." Macherey calls this "*et cetera* ... the veritable passageway of ignorance" and emphasizes the need to "renounce the ambition of an exhaustive knowledge of particular things, that is, their global linkages, which is by definition inaccessible: the infinite cannot be apprehended through the finite, in a movement of totalization, or else it loses its intrinsic necessity in order to become a pure possible, that is, a formal fiction" (Macherey, 2011: 152–153). Even though the sociological import of Macherey's discussion requires further elaboration and qualification, this discussion is illustrative of the serious philosophical problems that the methodological circuit present in social reproduction theory pose, as well as of the importance of the recognition and determination of the gap that the study of concept formation discovered in this book.

they stand? In short, what if we used the concept of social reproduction as a method that helps us understand how capitalist life is lived, and how it is lived differently in its collective constitution by sensuous subjective human praxis? Then, where would social reproduction go, where would it take us?

VIII   Social Reproduction Qua Method

One of the approaches we could take is what I call *social reproduction qua method*. While it is not possible to provide a full account of this approach here,[2] I wish to note that 'method' in social reproduction qua method refers to the manner in which a study of concept formation traverses, back and forth, between the gap I identified above.[3] Therefore, rather than operationalized as life-making, whereby social reproduction superimposes the symbolic universe of theory on the lived social world in order to create a unitary system of explanation, social reproduction qua method marks neither the intersection nor the union between these sets of ideal object of knowledge (i.e., symbolic universe of theory) and the real object of knowledge (i.e., lived social world). Instead, it fixes its analytical attention on the relative and absolute complements between these two sets of objects of knowledge. In other words, social reproduction qua method navigates the gap between and outside them. This traversing back and forth of the two sets of objects is animated by *social reproduction qua method*'s singular focus on the sensuous subjective human praxis.

What must be emphasized here is the shift that this traversing back and forth effects – the shift from the objects of knowledge to subjective sensuous human praxis, from the sedimented and rigidified to the unsettled and latent. I argue that this shift that social reproduction qua method effects has the double advantage of providing both an entry point into demonstrating economy as the ideological double of life and the conceptual tools producing the knowledge for social transformation. This is so not because one should not study the

---

2   For another brief discussion of social reproduction qua method, see: Tanyildiz et al., 2021.

3   This usage derives from the original Greek usage of method and methodology. J.M. Bochénski reminds us that methodology means "a speaking of the (right) going-along-the-way" (Bochénski, 1965: 9). Julián Marías emphasized that in order to rationally interpret the real, "[t]here must be a way or path, μέθοδος (méthodos) both coming and going – what Heraclitus called 'the road up and the road down,' ὁδός ἄνω καὶ κάτω (hodòs áno kaî káto)" (Marías, 1971: 9). To be sure, the way up and down for Heraclitus is one and the same. However, a fully articulated account of *social reproduction qua method* problematizes the initial identity offered in his formulation when we consider the different experiences of the knower traversing the way up and the way down.

object, objective, sedimented, and rigidified, but because only in the contexts and through the complements can we understand the objectified and ideological forms that capitalist life takes. Therefore, in turning our analytical attention to the gap between the objectified and ideological forms of life and knowledge, social reproduction qua method offers a way of examining the excess inherent in the making of history and the constitution of society.

I concluded Part II with a brief discussion this excess, and here I wish to mark the most significant contemporary articulation of this excess in Himani Bannerji's work, which examines the social spaces of capital as follows:

> It is always being and becoming at once, and generating an excess in the process, which gives a sense of disjuncture, as well as one of unspent life energy. This energy and productivity display the potentiality latent within human capacities, and cannot become fully absorbed by capital either in what it produces or how it produces. This excess becomes a source of politics, and holds the potential for critique of capital because it marks a separation between life and activities of the producers and the goal of the capitalist. The 'convergence of multiple determinations' that concretize life and the production process of commodities does not have the same destination. Though dominance and exploitation prevail, simultaneously disobedience thrives in rebellion against the exploitive process continually. It is impossible in the languages of social sciences to express the always-at-once kind of concreteness of this reality, and theorization only aggravates the problem by directing sequentiality, seriality and empiricism.
>
> BANNERJI, 2021: 25

I suggest that social reproduction qua method helps us to examine this excess by demonstrating not only how subjective sensuous human praxis lives the capitalist life, but also how it unlives the other lives that have been rendered impossible in the process of objectification and rigidification of capitalist life. For this excess is generated by the lives unlived and the one we are forced to survive, and finds its contemporary expression in embodied social relations. This is why rather than expelling the concept of social reproduction, I forward that we ought to divest social reproduction from unitarian theoretical desires and constructions and begin thinking through the ways in which we can re-envision social reproduction as a method of producing a marxist account of embodied social relations through further studies in concept formation.

IX Returning to Marx to Study Embodied Social Relations

After the constitutive moments of the book and the anticipation of social reproduction qua method, it is now time to close the book with hope – that excessive element without which no work begins or ends. I hope that with this book I was able to contribute to delineating the conditions for the possibility of returning to Marx to study embodied social relations. The conceptual universe of existing marxist social thought – including contemporary marxist-feminism and social reproduction theory – forecloses such a return by rigidifying the analytical meaning of the concepts it uses, and by offering an unexamined equation between its own usage and that of Marx.

As I have demonstrated in *Grounding Critique*, these offerings must not be taken at their face value, but ought to be subjected to rigorous critical scrutiny. For these concepts often have theoretical genealogies that overdetermine their further use, even in self-identified marxist analytical frameworks. With this book, I forward that concept formation, methodology, and the selection and articulation of social problems are not optional extras, but integral parts of any social inquiry that produces knowledge for social change. I believe that the historical moment we inhabit demands that we understand embodied social relations not derivatively, nor reductively, but on their own terms because the genuine contradictions of contemporary capitalism express themselves through these relations. I hope that *Grounding Critique* contributes to such a transformative understanding in service of the much larger political project of abolishing all classes and creating a classless society in which freedom is the embodied principle of social existence.

Afterword

Speaking typologically, the writer of the Afterword of any book is its first reader. It may be that she has been involved with the earlier stages of its making. But when the scattered and dishevelled notes and texts come together to form the 'book,' many of its aspects come to the fore that lay unnoticed in its texturation. So it is with this book for me, and my readerly task then becomes not one of continuing the conclusion, or polishing the already stated, but of capturing the impressions and evocations that the book may suggest in its reading.

I think that *Grounding Critique: Marxism, Concept Formation, and Embodied Social Relations* asks a basic question, that of the relationship between reality, the mundane daily life of actual people, and the ways in which they try to make sense of it or grasp it in various modes of representation and reflection. Some do it more intellectually than others, but all engage with greater or lesser sophistication in the task of holding up a mirror to the world. This book examines some of these efforts, especially made by critical intellectuals contributing to an epistemology for transformative social change. In other words, it draws attention to a second set of making, with a mental sort of labour, which makes the world incrementally understandable to us through the forging of mediating concepts. Of course, as the material lived world changes through human history-making, thereby accumulating multiple and complex determinations, so does the world of ideational makings which ceaselessly informs that world of living people. The desire of representing and reflecting is also ceaseless. What is important, Tanyildiz tells us, is not to convert multiple determinations into singular categorical over-determinations. *Grounding Critique*'s efforts are to avoid the ideological dead-ends of empiricist materialism, as well as ungrounded theories and intellectualisms.

What the author keeps in sight or reminds us is the embodied nature of our social relations. This is right because all things cease in the situation of disembodiment. The human factor, the modes of continuance of embodiment are of the essence. This is a reminder that history does not make itself, in fact history becomes 'history' through the necessary, almost involuntary, human efforts of remembering, recording, narrating, and analyzing. That is, the concept of history is people's gift to themselves in the course of endless generations of living. In this discourse of concept formation, of searching for an epistemological device of referentiality to life as active living, *Grounding Critique* holds its core of Marxism. Concepts, as stated in the book, are not substitutes of life, not to be conflated with whatever it is that we can never fully encompass and yet know to be reality. Nor can concepts unaided sort and confer shapes and boundaries to life processes with their changing relationship with sociality.

To say what we say above is of course not to deny but rather affirm, that we live within given modes of production and reproducible social relations at any given time. The activities signalled thus are neither temporary nor arbitrary and do shape and control the contours of our daily life. This is the point at which, or where, concepts such as social production and reproduction provide language for how to describe what we do or need to do under given socio-economic and political circumstances. But, as *Grounding Critique* demonstrates, precisely for this reason our conceptual practices must be approached cautiously, consciously, lest they become, felt or seen as 'natural' or superior because they are associated with the mind, the intellect, the clean hands of reason. The danger of reification arises here, we submit to our creation with reverence in acts of fetishism. This is the intellectual's religious deificatory moment when god as absolute intellect assumes the creator status by naming and codifying what exists. It is forgetful of the fact that people and reality will continue to exist even after the death of such gods. There is always something left over of life and living that will not fit into the box of theory as a body of axioms and content. Thus, hegemony is complete only as content, but never as a process just as the creation of the world is not complete at a given moment either. Thus, language will always have to chase after reality, theory after life. But we should use and innovate the best language and intellection we can, by best meaning that which can provide the best self-reflexivity and access to the world that we inhabit. *Grounding Critique* gives us a glimpse of what such an effort looks like.

Himani Bannerji
York University, Canada

Bibliography

Adorno, Theodor W. *Introduction to Sociology*. Stanford, California: Stanford University Press, 2000.

Aguilar, Delia D. "Intersectionality." In *Marxism and Feminism*, edited by Shahrzad Mojab, 203–20. London: Zed Books, 2015.

Ahmed, Sara. "Declarations of Whiteness: The Non-performativity of Anti-racism." *Borderlands* 3, no. 2 (2004): n.p.

Ahmed, Sara. "How Not to Do Things with Words." *Wagadu: A Journal of Transnational Women's and Gender Studies* 16 (2016): 1–10.

Ahmed, Sara. "The Nonperformativity of Antiracism." *Meridians* 7, no. 1 (2006): 104–26.

Althusser, Louis. *For Marx*. London: New Left Books, 1977.

Anker, Elizabeth S. and Rita Felski. *Critique and Postcritique*. Durham: Duke University Press, 2017.

Arruzza, Cinzia. "Functionalist, Determinist, Reductionist: Social Reproduction Feminism and Its Critics." *Science & Society* 80, no. 1 (2016): 9–30.

Avanessian, Armen. *Future Metaphysics*. Cambridge: Polity Press, 2020.

Bakan, Abigail B. "Marxism, Feminism, and Epistemological Dissonance." *Socialist Studies/Études Socialistes* 8, no. 2, 2012.

Bakhtin, Mikhail. *The Dialogic Imagination: Four Essays*. Austin: University of Texas Press, 1981.

Bakhtin, Mikhail. *Problems of Dostoevsky's Poetics*. Minneapolis and London: University of Minnesota Press, 1984.

Baldin, Gregorio. *Hobbes and Galileo: Method, Matter and the Science of Motion*. Berlin: Springer, 2020.

Banaji, Jairus. "Modes of Production in a Materialist Conception of History." *Capital & Class* 1, no. 3 (1977): 1–44.

Bannerji, Himani. "But Who Speaks for Us? Experience and Agency in Conventional Feminist Paradigms." In *Thinking Through: Essays on Feminism, Marxism, and Anti-Racism*. Toronto: Women's Press, 1995.

Bannerji, Himani. "In the Matter of 'X': Building 'Race' into Sexual Harassment." In *Thinking Through: Essays on Feminism, Marxism and Anti-racism*. Toronto: Women's Press, 1995.

Bannerji, Himani. *Inventing Subjects: Studies in Hegemony, Patriarchy, and Colonialism*. London: Anthem Press, 2001.

Bannerji, Himani. "On the Dark Side of the Nation: Politics of Multiculturalism and the State of 'Canada.'" In *The Dark Side of the Nation: Essays on Multiculturalism, Nationalism, and Gender*. Toronto: Canadian Scholars Press, 2000.

Bannerji, Himani. "The Factory and the Family as Spaces of Capital," In *Rethinking Alternatives with Marx: Economy, Ecology, and Migration*, edited by Marcello Musto, Cham, Switzerland: Palgrave Macmillan, 2021.

Bannerji, Himani. "The Paradox of Diversity: The Construction of a Multicultural Canada and 'Women of Colour.'" In *The Dark Side of the Nation: Essays on Multiculturalism, Nationalism, and Gender*. Toronto: Canadian Scholars Press, 2000.

Bannerji, Himani. *Thinking Through: Essays on Feminism, Marxism, and Anti-racism*. Toronto: Women's Press, 1995.

Barker, Colin. "Social Reproduction Theory: Going Beyond 'Capital.'" *Pluto Press*. Accessed 07.02.2019 https://www.plutobooks.com/blog/social-reproduction-beyond-marx-capital/.

Beetham, David. *The Legitimation of Power*. Hampshire: Palgrave MacMillan, 2013.

Benton, Ted. *Philosophical Foundations of the Three Sociologies*. London and New York: Routledge, 2014.

Benton, Ted and Ian Craib. *Philosophy of Social Science: The Philosophical Foundations of Social Thought*. London: Palgrave Macmillan, 2011.

Berry, Christopher. *Social Theory of the Scottish Enlightenment*. Edinburgh: The Edinburgh University Press, 2020.

Bhattacharya, Tithi. "Introduction: Mapping Social Reproduction Theory." In *Social Reproduction Theory: Remapping Class, Recentering Oppression*, edited by Tithi Bhattacharya, 1–20. London: Pluto Press, 2017.

Bhattacharya, Tithi. *Social Reproduction Theory: Remapping Class, Recentering Oppression*. London: Pluto Press, 2017.

Bhattacharya, Tithi, Sara R. Farris and Sue Ferguson. "Social Reproduction Feminisms." In *The SAGE Handbook of Marxism, Vol I*, edited by B. Skeggs, S. R. Farris, A. Toscano and S. Bromberg, 45–67. London: Sage Publishing, 2022.

Biggs, Michael. "Self-fulfilling Prophecies." In *The Oxford Handbook of Analytical Sociology*, edited by Peter Hedström and Peter Bearman, 294–314. Oxford: Oxford University Press, 2016.

Block, James E. *A Nation of Agents: The American Path to A Modern Self and Society*. Massachusetts: Harvard University Press, 2002.

Blumer, Herbert George. *Symbolic Interactionism: Perspective and Method*. Berkeley, Los Angeles, and London: University of California Press, 1986.

Bocheński, J.M. *The Methods of Contemporary Thought*. Dordrecht-Holland: D. Reidel Publishing Company, 1965.

Boggs, Carl. *Social Movements and Political Power: Emerging Forms of Radicalism in the West*. Philadelphia: Temple University Press, 1986.

Bohrer, Ashley J. *Marxism and Intersectionality: Race, Gender, Class and Sexuality Under Contemporary Capitalism*. Berlin: Transcript Verlag, 2019.

Bohrer, Ashley J. "Response to Barbara Foley's 'Intersectionality: A Marxist Critique.'" *New Labor Forum* 28, no. 3 (2019): 14–17.

Brenner, Johanna. "Intersections, Locations, and Capitalist Class Relations: Intersectionality from a Marxist Perspective." In *Women and the Politics of Class*, edited by J. Brenner, 293–24. New York: Monthly Review Press, 2000.

Bruce, Steve and Steven Yearley, eds. *The Sage Dictionary of Sociology*. London: Sage, 2006.

Butler, Judith. "What is Critique? An Essay on Foucault's Virtue." In *The Judith Butler Reader*, edited by S. Salih and J. Butler, 301–21. Malden, MA: Blackwell, 2004.

Butler, Judith. "Taking Another's View: Ambivalent Implications," In *Reification: A New Look at an Old Idea*, edited by Axel Honneth, Oxford University Press, 2008.

Buzuev, Vladimir and Vladimir Gorodnov. *What is Marxism-Leninism?* Moscow: Progress Publishers, 1987.

Cabral, Amilcar. "National Liberation and Culture." *Transition*, no. 45 (1974): 12–17.

Carastathis, Anna and Myrto Tsilimpounidi. *Reproducing Refugees: Photographía of a Crisis*. Rowman & Littlefield Publishers, 2020.

Carver, Terrell. *Karl Marx: Texts on Method,* Oxford: Basil Blackwell, 1975.

Cassirer, Ernst. *The Philosophy of Symbolic Forms, Volume 1*. London and New York: Routledge, 2020.

Chandrasekhar, Subrahmanyan. *Newton's Principia for the Common Reader*. Oxford: Clarendon Press, 1995.

Cohen, I. Bernard. "Newton and the Social Sciences, with Special Reference to Economics, or, the Case of the Missing Paradigm." In *Natural Images in Economic Thought: Markets Read in Tooth and Claw*, edited by Philip Mirowski, 55–90. Cambridge: The Cambridge University Press, 1994.

Collins, Patricia Hill. *Black Feminist Thought: Knowledge, Consciousness, and the Politics of Empowerment*. Boston: Unwin Hyman, 1990.

Cooper, Brittney C. *Beyond Respectability: The Intellectual Thought of Race Women*. Urbana: University of Illinois Press, 2017.

Cooper, Brittney C. "Intersectionality." In *The Oxford Handbook of Feminist Theory*, edited by Lisa Disch and Mary Hawkesworth, 385–406. Oxford University Press, 2016.

Crenshaw, Kimberlé. "Mapping the Margins: Identity Politics, Intersectionality, and Violence against Women." *Stanford Law Review* 43, no. 6 (1991): 1241–99.

Crenshaw, Kimberlé W. "Demarginalizing the Intersection of Race and Sex: A Black Feminist Critique of Antidiscrimination Doctrine, Feminist Theory and Antiracist Politics." *University of Chicago Legal Forum* 140 (1989): 139–67.

Crossley, Nick. *Making Sense of Social Movements*. Buckingham and Philadelphia: Open University Press, 2002.

Davies, Carole Boyce. *Left of Karl Marx: The Political Life of Claudia Jones*. Durham and London: Duke University Press, 2007.

Depaolis, Joshua. "Review of 'Social Reproduction Theory: Remapping Class, Recentering Oppression.'" *Marx & Philosophy Review of Books*. 25 April 2018. https://marxandphilosophy.org.uk/reviews/15746_social-reproduction-theory-remapping-class-recentering-oppression-reviewed-by-joshua-depaolis/.

Derrida, Jacques. *Theory and Practice*. Chicago and London: The University of Chicago Press, 2019.

Drucker, Peter. *Warped: Gay Normality and Queer Anti-Capitalism*. Leiden, Netherlands: Brill, 2015.

Du Bois, W. E. B. *The Souls of Black Folk*, edited by Brent Hayes Edwards. Oxford World's Classics. London, England: Oxford University Press, 2008.

Ebert, Teresa L. *Ludic Feminism and After: Postmodernism, Desire, and Labor in Late Capitalism*. Ann Arbor: University of Michigan Press, 1996.

Edgar, Andrew. "Identity." In *Key Concepts in Cultural Theory*, edited by A. Edgar and P. Sedgwick, 166–70. London and New York: Routledge, 1999.

Eisenstadt, Shmuel Noah and Miriam Curelaru. *The Form of Sociology: Paradigms and Crises*. New York: John Wiley & Sons, 1976.

Eisenstein, Hester. "Querying Intersectionality." *Science & Society* 82, no. 2 (2018): 248–49.

Encyclopedia of Marxism, https://www.marxists.org/glossary/index.htm. Accessed 19.06.2020.

Fara, Patricia. *Newton: The Making of Genius*. New York: Columbia University Press, 2002.

Fassin, Didier. "The Endurance of Critique." *Anthropological Theory* 17, no. 1 (2017): 4–29.

Felski, Rita. *The Limits of Critique*. Chicago: University of Chicago Press, 2015.

Ferguson, Susan. "Canadian Contributions to Social Reproduction Feminism, Race and Embodied Labor." *Race, Gender & Class* (2008): 42–57.

Ferguson, Susan. "Intersectionality and Social-reproduction Feminisms: Toward an Integrative Ontology." *Historical Materialism* 24, no. 2 (2016): 38–60.

Ferguson, Susan. "Social Reproduction: What's the Big Idea?" *Pluto Press*. 2017. https://www.plutobooks.com/blog/social-reproduction-theory-ferguson/.

Ferguson, Susan. *Women and Work: Feminism, Labour and Social Reproduction*. London and Toronto: Pluto Press and Between the Lines, 2020.

Ferguson Susan and David McNally. "Capital, Labour-Power, and Gender-Relations: Introduction to the Historical Materialism Edition of Marxism and the Oppression of Women." In *Marxism and the Oppression of Women Toward a Unitary Theory*, edited by Lise Vogel, XVII–XL. Leiden and Boston: Brill, 2013.

Ferguson, Sue, Genevieve LeBaron, Angeliki Dimitrakaki and Sara Farris. "Introduction: Special Issue of Historical Materialism on Social Reproduction." *Historical Materialism* 4, no. 2 (2016): 25–37.

Flynn, Bernard. *Political Philosophy at the Closure of Metaphysics*. New Jersey and London: Humanities Press, 1992.

Foley, Barbara. "Barbara Foley Replies." *New Labor Forum* 28, no. 3 (2019): 18–19.
Foley, Barbara. "Intersectionality: A Marxist Critique." *Science & Society* 82, no. 2 (2018): 269–75.
Foley, Michael. *Laws, Men, and Machines: Modern American Government and the Appeal of Newtonian Mechanics*. New York: Routledge, 1990.
Forgacs, David. *The Antonio Gramsci Reader*. London: Lawrence & Wishart, 1988.
Foucault, Michel. "Nietzsche, Genealogy, History." In *The Foucault Reader*, edited by Paul Rabinow, 76–100. London: Penguin Books, 1984.
Foursov, Andrei. "Social Times, Social Spaces, and their Dilemmas: Ideology 'In One Country.'" *Review (Fernand Braudel Center)* 20, no. 3/4 (1997), 345–420.
Frisby, David and Derek Sayer, *Society*. London and New York: Tavistock Publications, 1986.
Gandler, Stefan. *Critical Marxism in Mexico: Adolfo Sánchez Vázquez and Bolívar Echeverría*. Leiden and Boston: Brill, 2007.
Gasché, Rodolphe. *The Honor of Thinking: Critique, Theory, Philosophy*. Stanford: Stanford University Press, 2007.
Geuss, Raymond. "Philosophical Anthropology and Social Criticism," In *Reification: A New Look at an Old Idea*, edited by Axel Honneth, Oxford University Press, 2008.
Gimenez, Martha E. "Intersectionality: Marxist Critical Observations." *Science & Society* 82, no. 2 (2018): 261–69.
Goldmann, Lucien. *Cultural Creation in Modern Society*. Oxford: Basil Blackwell, 1977.
Goldmann, Lucien. *Essays on Method in the Sociology Literature*. St. Louis, MO: Telos Press, 1980.
Grosfoguel, Ramón. "A TimeSpace Perspective on Development: Recasting Latin American Debates." *Review (Fernand Braudel Center)* 20, no. 3/4 (1997), 465–540.
Habermas, Jürgen. *Legitimation Crisis*. Boston: Beacon Press, 1975.
Hall, Stuart. *A Reading of Marx's 1857 Introduction to the 'Grundrisse.'* University of Birmingham, Centre for Contemporary Cultural Studies, 1974.
Hall, Stuart. "At Home and Not at Home: Stuart Hall in Conversation with Les Black," In Stuart Hall, *Essential Essays, Volume 2: Identity and Diaspora*, edited by David Morley. Durham and London: Duke University Press, 2019.
Hall, Stuart. "Rethinking the 'Base and Superstructure' Metaphor [1977]." In *Selected Writings on Marxism*, edited by Gregor McLennan, 62–90. New York: Duke University Press, 2021.
Hancock, Ange-Marie. *Intersectionality: An Intellectual History*. New York: Oxford University Press, 2016.
Hancock, Ange-Marie. "When Multiplication Doesn't Equal Quick Addition: Examining Intersectionality as a Research Paradigm." *Perspectives on Politics* 5, no. 1 (2007): 63–79.
Harvey, David. *The New Imperialism*. New York: Monthly Review Press, 2003.

Hegel, Georg Wilhelm Friedrich. *Elements of the Philosophy of Right*. Cambridge: Cambridge University Press, 1991.

Hennessy, Rosemary. *Profit and Pleasure: Sexual Identities in Late Capitalism*. New York: Routledge, 2000.

Hennessy, Rosemary. "Toward an Ecology of Life-making: The Re-membering of Meridel Le Sueur." *CLCWeb: Comparative Literature and Culture* 22, no. 2 (2020): 1–14.

Henry, Michel. *Marx: A Philosophy of Human Reality*. Bloomington: Indiana University Press, 1983.

Hesiod. "Works and Days." In *Theogony and Works and Days*, translated by M. L. West, 35–62. Oxford and New York: Oxford University Press, 1988.

Hofstadter, Douglas R. and Emmanuel Sander. *Surfaces and Essences: Analogy as the Fuel and Fire of Thinking*. New York: Basic Books, 2013.

Honneth, Axel. *Reification: A New Look at an Old Idea*. Oxford University Press, 2008.

Hudson, Wayne. *The Marxist Philosophy of Ernst Bloch*. London and Basingstoke: Macmillan Press, 1982.

Hull, Akasha (Gloria T.), Patricia Bell-Scott and Barbara Smith. *All the Women Are White, All the Blacks Are Men, But Some of Us Are Brave: Black Women's Studies*. New York City: Feminist Press, 1982.

Israel, Joachim. "Epistemology and Sociology of Knowledge: An Hegelian Undertaking." *Sociological Perspectives* 33, no. 1 (March 1990): 111–28.

Janowitz, Anne. "'What a Rich Fund of Images is Treasured Up Here': Poetic Commonplaces of the Sublime Universe." *Studies in Romanticism* 44, no. 4 (2005): 469–92.

Johnson, Allan. *The Blackwell Dictionary of Sociology: A User's Guide to Sociological Language*. London: Wiley and Sons, 2000.

Kaiser, David. "A Mannheim for All Seasons: Bloor, Merton, and the Roots of the Sociology of Scientific Knowledge." *Science in Context* 11, no. 1 (1998): 51–87.

Kant, Immanuel. *Lectures on Logic*, translated and edited by J. Michael Young, 569–70. Cambridge: Cambridge University Press, 1992.

Karatani, Kojin. *Transcritique: On Kant and Marx*. Cambridge, MA: MIT Press, 2005.

Kim, Keong-il. "Genealogy of the Idiographic vs. the Nomothetic Disciplines: The Case of History and Sociology in the United States." *Review (Fernand Braudel Center)* 20, no. 3/4 (1997), 421–64.

Kojima, Hiroshi. "Japan." In *Encyclopedia of Phenomenology*, edited by Lester E. Embree, Elizabeth A. Behnke, David Carr, J. Claude Evans, José Huertas-Jourda, Joseph J. Kockelmans, William R. McKenna, Algis Mickunas, Jithendra Nath Mohanty, Thomas M. Seebohm and Richard M. Zaner, 367–71. Dordrecht: Springer Science & Business Media, B.V., 1997.

Koyré, Alexandre. "The Significance of the Newtonian Synthesis." *The Journal of General Education*, no. 4 (1950): 256–68.

Laclau, Ernesto and Chantal Mouffe. *Hegemony and Socialist Strategy: Towards a Radical Democratic Politics.* London: Verso, 1985.

Laibman, David et al. "Intersectionality: A Symposium." *Science & Society* 82, no. 2 (2018).

Leach, Nicole. "Transitions to Capitalism: Social-Reproduction Feminism Encounters Political Marxism." *Historical Materialism* 24, no. 2 (2016): 111–37.

Lear, Jonathan. "The Slippery Middle," In *Reification: A New Look at an Old Idea*, edited by Axel Honneth. Oxford University Press, 2008.

Lefort, Claude, Leonard Lawlor and Heath Massey. Foreword to *Institution and Passivity: Course Notes from the Collège de France (1954–1955)*, edited by Maurice Merleau-Ponty. Evanston, IL: Northwestern University Press, 2010.

Lenin, Vladimir I. *Collected Works Vol 01: 1893–1894.* Moscow: Progress Publishers, 1960.

Levine, Donald N. *Visions of the Sociological Tradition.* University of Chicago Press, 1995.

Lifshitz, Mikhail. *The Philosophy of Art of Karl Marx.* London: Pluto Press, 1973.

Lijster, Thijs. *Benjamin and Adorno on Art and Art Criticism: Critique of Art.* Amsterdam: Amsterdam University Press, 2017.

López, Daniel Andrés, 2019, *Lukács: Praxis and the Absolute*, Leiden: Brill.

Lorde, Audre. "A Litany for Survival." In *The Black Unicorn: Poems*, 31–32. New York: W. W. Norton & Company, 1995.

Lowry, S. Todd, ed. *Pre-Classical Economic Thought: From the Greeks to the Scottish Enlightenment.* Berlin: Springer, 2012.

Löwy, Michael. "Lukács and Stalinism." *New Left Review*, no. 91 (1975): 25–41.

Luft, Rachel E. and Jane Ward. "Toward an Intersectionality Just Out of Reach: Confronting Challenges to Intersectional Practice." In *Perceiving Gender Locally, Globally, and Intersectionally*, 9–37. Bingley, UK: Emerald Group Publishing Limited, 2009.

Lukács, Georg. *History and Class Consciousness: Studies in Marxist Dialectics.* Cambridge, MA: The MIT Press, 1971.

Lukács, Georg. "Reification and the Consciousness of Proletariat." In *History and Class Consciousness: Studies in Marxist Dialectics*, edited by Georg Lukács, 83–222. Cambridge, MA: The MIT Press, 1971.

Macherey, Pierre. *Hegel or Spinoza*, translated by Susan Ruddick, Minneapolis: University of Minnesota Press, 2011.

Manning, David John. *Liberalism.* London: J. M. Dent & Sons, 1976.

Marías, Julián. *Metaphysical Anthropology: The Empirical Structure of Human Life.* University Park and London: The Pennsylvania State University Press, 1971.

Marshall, Gordon, ed. *The Concise Oxford Dictionary of Sociology.* Oxford: Oxford University Press, 2004.

Martindale, Don. *The Nature and Types of Sociological Theory.* New York: Routledge, 2013.

Marx, Karl. *Capital: A Critique of Political Economy, Volume I.* translated by Samuel Moore and Edward Aveling, edited by Frederick Engels, 1887. https://www.marxists.org/archive/marx/works/1867-c1/ch33.htm#4a.

Marx, Karl. *Capital: The Process of Capitalist Production as a Whole, Volume III.* 1894. https://www.marxists.org/archive/marx/works/1894-c3/ch48.htm.

Marx, Karl. *Grundrisse: Foundations of the Critique of Political Economy.* London: Penguin Books, 2005.

Marx, Karl. *Theses on Feuerbach* (1845). http://www.marxists.org/archive/marx/works/1845/theses/theses.htm.

Marx, Karl. *Wage, Labour and Capital,* edited and translated by Friedrich Engels, 1847. https://www.marxists.org/archive/marx/works/1847/wage-labour/ch05.htm.

Marx, Karl and Friedrich Engels. *The German Ideology.* Moscow: Progress Publishers, 1976.

Marx, Karl and Frederick Engels, *Marx & Engels Collected Works Vol 04: Marx and Engels:1844–1845.* London: Lawrence & Wishart, 1975.

Marx, Karl and Frederick Engels. *Marx & Engels Collected Works Vol 05: Marx and Engels:1845–1847.* London: Lawrence & Wishart, 1976.

Marx, Karl and Frederick Engels. *Marx & Engels Collected Works Vol 25: Engels: Dialectics of Nature.* London: Lawrence & Wishart, 1987.

Marx, Karl and Frederick Engels. *Marx & Engels Collected Works Vol 49: Engels: 1890–1892.* London: Lawrence & Wishart, 2001.

Marx, Karl, Frederick Engels and Vladimir I. Lenin. *On Historical Materialism: A Collection.* Moscow: Progress Publishers, 1972.

May, Vivian M. *Anna Julia Cooper, Visionary Black Feminist.* New York and London: Routledge, 2007.

May, Vivian M. *Pursuing Intersectionality, Unsettling Dominant Imaginaries.* New York: Routledge, 2015.

McCall, Leslie. "The Complexity of Intersectionality." *Signs: Journal of Women in Culture and Society* 30, no. 3 (2005): 1771–1800.

McNally, David. "Intersections and Dialectics: Critical Reconstructions in Social Reproduction Theory." In *Social Reproduction Theory: Remapping Class, Recentering Oppression,* edited by Tithi Bhattacharya, 94–111. London: Pluto Press, 2017.

McNally, David. *Political Economy and the Rise of Capitalism: A Reinterpretation.* Berkeley: University of California Press, 1988.

McNally, David and Sue Ferguson. "Social Reproduction Beyond Intersectionality: An Interview." *Viewpoint Magazine* 5 (2015).

Merton, Robert K. "The Self-fulfilling Prophecy." *The Antioch Review* 8, no. 2 (1948): 193–210.

Meyerson, Gregory. "Rethinking Black Marxism: Reflections on Cedric Robinson and Others." *Cultural Logic: Marxist Theory & Practice* 3, no. 2 (2000).

Mézsáros, István. *Marx's Theory of Alienation*. London: Merlin Press, 1970.
Mezzadri, Alessandra. "On the Value of Social Reproduction: Informal Labour, the Majority World and the Need for Inclusive Theories and Politics." *Radical Philosophy* 2, no. 4 (2019): 33–41.
Mitchell, Eve. "I Am a Woman and a Human: A Marxist-Feminist Critique of Intersectionality Theory." 12 September 2013. http://www.unityandstruggle.org/2013/09/i-am-a-woman-and-a-human-a-marxist-feminist-critique-of-intersectionality-theory/.
Mojab, Shahrzad and Sara Carpenter. "Marxism, Feminism, and 'Intersectionality.'" *Journal of Labor and Society* 22, no. 2 (2019): 275–82.
Morson, Gary Saul. "Tradition and Counter-tradition: The Radical Intelligentsia and Classical Russian Literature." In *A History of Russian Thought*, edited by William Leatherbarrow and Derek Offord, 141–68. Cambridge: The Cambridge University Press, 2010.
Murray, Patrick. *Marx's Theory of Scientific Knowledge*. Atlantic Highlands, NJ: Humanities Press International, 1988.
Nash, Jennifer C. *Black Feminism Reimagined after Intersectionality*. Durham and London: Duke University Press, 2019.
Nassehi, Armin. "Social Relations." In *Encyclopedia of Social Theory*, edited by Harrington, Austin, Barbara L. Marshall and Hans-Peter Müller, London and New York: Routledge, 2006.
Newton, Isaac. *The Principia: Mathematical Principles of Natural Philosophy*, translated by I. Bernard Cohen and Anne Whitman, assisted by Julia Budenz. Oakland: The University of California Press, 1999.
Nowak, Stefan. *Understanding and Prediction: Essays in the Methodology of Social and Behavioral Theories*. Dordrecht: D. Reidel Publishing Company, 1976.
Oakes, Guy. *Weber and Rickert: Concept Formation in the Cultural Sciences*. Cambridge, Massachusetts, and London, England: The MIT Press, 1988.
Ollman, Bertell. *Alienation: Marx's Concept of Man in Capitalist Society*. New York: Cambridge University Press, 1977.
Ollman, Bertell. *Dance of the Dialectic: Steps in Marx's Method*. Urbana: University of Illinois Press, 2003.
Olson, Richard. *The Emergence of the Social Sciences: 1642–1792*, New York: Twayne Press, 1993.
Pashukanis, Evgeny. *Law and Marxism: A General Theory*. London: Ink Links, 1978.
Patnaik, Prabhat. "Some Comments about Marx's Epistemology." *Marxist: Theoretical Quarterly of the Communist Party of India (Marxist)* XXXV, no. 2 (April–June 2019), 7–15.
Plekhanov, George. *The Materialist Conception of History*. New York: International Publishers, 1940.

Poulantzas, Nicos. *State, Power, and Socialism*. London: New Left Books, 1978.

Rendall, Jane. *Origins of the Scottish Enlightenment, 1707–76*. London: Palgrave Macmillan, 1978.

Ritzer, George, ed. *The Blackwell Encyclopedia of Sociology*. Vol. 1479. New York: Blackwell Publishing, 2007.

Rockmore, Tom. *Fichte, Marx, and the German Philosophical Tradition*. Carbondale and Edwardsville: Southern Illinois University Press, 1980.

Rockmore, Tom. *Marx's Dream: From Capitalism to Communism*. Chicago and London: University of Chicago Press, 2018.

Rodney, Walter. *How Europe Underdeveloped Africa*. London: Bogle-L'Ouverture Publications, 1972.

Rose, Gillian. *Dialectic of Nihilism: Post-Structuralism and Law*. Oxford: Blackwell, 1984.

Rose, Gillian. *Hegel Contra Sociology*. London and Atlantic Highlands, NJ: The Athlone Press, 1981.

Rose, Gillian. *Judaism and Modernity: Philosophical Essays*. London: Verso Books, 2017 (1993).

Rose, Gillian. *The Melancholy Science: An Introduction to the Thought of Theodor W. Adorno*. London: Verso Books, 2014.

Rose, Gillian. *Mourning Becomes Law: Philosophy and Representation*. Cambridge: Cambridge University Press, 1996.

Ross, Dorothy. *The Origins of American Social Science*. Cambridge: The Cambridge University Press, 1992.

Rossides, Daniel W. *Social Theory: Its Origins, History, and Contemporary Relevance*. New York: Great Hall, INC. Publishers, 1998.

Russell, Shana A. "Intersectionality: A Young Scholar Responds." *Science & Society* 82, no. 2 (2018): 287–291.

Sabine, George H. *A History of Political Theory*. Calcutta, Bombay, and Delhi: Oxford and IBH Publishing Co., 1960.

Sayer, Derek. *Marx's Method: Ideology, Science and Critique in 'Capital.'* Sussex: The Harvester Press, 1979.

Sayer, Derek. "Pre-Capitalist Societies and Contemporary Marxist Theory." *Sociology* 11, no. 1 (1977): 150.

Sayer, Derek. *The Violence of Abstraction: The Analytical Foundations of Historical Materialism*. Oxford: Blackwell Publishers, 1987.

"Science & Society: A Journal of Marxist Thought and Analysis." *Guilford Press*. Accessed 21.09.2019. https://www.guilford.com/journals/ScienceSociety/Editor/00368237/summary.

Smith, Dorothy E. *The Conceptual Practices of Power: A Feminist Sociology of Knowledge*. Boston: Northeastern University Press, 1990.

Smith, Tony. *Dialectical Social Theory and its Critics: From Hegel to Analytical Marxism and Postmodernism*. Albany: SUNY Press, 1993.

"Social Reproduction Theory." *Pluto Press*. Accessed 24.05.2019. https://www.plutobooks.com/9780745399881/social-reproduction-theory/.

Sowa, John F. "Ontological Categories." In *Shapes of Forms: From Gestalt Psychology and Phenomenology to Ontology and Mathematics*, edited by Liliana Albertazzi, vol. 275. Dordrecht: Springer Science & Business Media, B.V., 1999.

Spirkin, Alexander. *Fundamentals of Philosophy*. Moscow: Progress Publishers, 1990.

Stark, Werner. *The Fundamental Forms of Social Thought: An Essay in Aid of Deeper Understanding of History of Ideas*. New York: Routledge, 2013.

Stavrakakis, Yannis. *The Lacanian Left*. Edinburgh: Edinburgh University Press, 2007.

Strohmayer, Ulf. "The Displaced, Deferred or Was It Abandoned Middle: Another Look at the Idiographic-Nomothetic Distinction in the German Social Sciences." *Review (Fernand Braudel Center)* 20, no. 3/4 (1997): 279–344.

Swedberg, Richard and Ola Agevall, *The Max Weber Dictionary: Key Words and Central Concepts*. Stanford, California: Stanford University Press, 2016.

Sztompka, Piotr. *Sociological Dilemmas: Toward a Dialectic Paradigm*. New York: Elsevier, 2013.

Tanyildiz, Gökbörü Sarp. "The Conjunctural Imagination," *Small Axe Salon*, no. 45, 2024.

Tanyildiz, Gökbörü Sarp. "Making Queer Anti-Capitalist Resistance Intelligible: Reading Queer Childhood in the Ruins of Neoliberalism." Unpublished Master's Thesis, 2013. https://dr.library.brocku.ca/handle/10464/4637.

Tanyildiz, Gökbörü Sarp. "Social reproduction, infrastructure, and the everyday." *Dialogues in Human Geography*, 0, no. 0. https://journals.sagepub.com/doi/10.1177/20438206231202820, 2023.

Tanyildiz, Gökbörü Sarp, Peake Linda, Koleth Elsa, et al. Rethinking social reproduction and the urban. In: *A Feminist Urban Theory for our Time*, edited by Peake Linda, Koleth Elsa, Tanyildiz Gökbörü Sarp, Narayanareddy Rajyashree, Patrick D/dp, Oxford: Blackwell and Wiley, 2021.

Tasić, Vladimir. *Mathematics and the Roots of Postmodern Thought*. Oxford and New York: Oxford University Press, 2001.

The U.S. Equal Employment Opportunity Commission (EEOC). "Title VII of the Civil Rights Act of 1964." Accessed 13.07.2019. https://www.eeoc.gov/statutes/title-vii-civil-rights-act-1964.

Vishmidt, Marina and Zöe Sutherland. "Social Reproduction: New Questions for the Gender, Affect, and Substance of Value." In *The New Feminist Literary Studies*, edited by Jennifer Cooke, 143–54. Cambridge: Cambridge University Press, 2020.

Vogel, Lise. "Beyond Intersectionality." *Science & Society* 82, no. 2 (2018): 275–76.

Vogel, Lise. Foreword to *Social Reproduction Theory: Remapping Class, Recentering Oppression*, edited by Tithi Bhattacharya, X–XII. London: Pluto Press, 2017.

Wallerstein, Immanuel. "Introduction." *Review (Fernand Braudel Center)* 20, no. 3/4, Nomothetic vs. Idiographic Disciplines: A False Dilemma? (Summer – Fall 1997): 277–78.

Wallerstein, Immanuel. *The Modern World-System IV: Centrist Liberalism Triumphant, 1789–1914*. Vol. 4. Berkeley, Los Angeles, and London: University of California Press, 2011.

Warren, Scott. *The Emergence of Dialectical Theory: Philosophy and Political Inquiry*. University of Chicago Press, 2008.

Weber, Max. *Economy and Society: A New Translation*, edited and translated by Keith Tribe. Cambridge, Massachusetts and London, England: Harvard University Press, 2019.

Weigand, Kate. *Red Feminism: American Communism and the Making of Women's Liberation*. Baltimore and London: Johns Hopkins University Press, 2001.

Wickman, Matthew. *Literature After Euclid: The Geometric Imagination in the Long Scottish Enlightenment*. Philadelphia: University of Pennsylvania Press, 2015.

Wiegman, Robyn. *Object Lessons*. Durham and London: Duke University Press, 2012.

Wight, Colin. "Realism, Science and Emancipation." In *Realism, Philosophy and Social Science*, edited by Dean, Kathryn, Jonathan Joseph, John Michael Roberts and Colin Wight, 32–64. New York: Palgrave Macmillan, 2006.

Williams, Raymond. *Keywords: A Vocabulary of Culture and Society*. London: Oxford University Press, 2015 (1976).

Williams, Raymond. *Marxism and Literature*. Oxford: Oxford University Press, 1977.

Wood, Ellen M. *The Retreat from Class: A New 'True' Socialism*. London: Verso, 1986.

Zembylas, Michalinos. "Affirmative Critique as a Practice of Responding to the Impasse Between Post-truth and Negative Critique: Pedagogical Implications for Schools." *Critical Studies in Education* 63, no. 2 (2022): 229–44.

Index

active side of experience   103, 103n31
additive method   122, 123, 123n47, 124
Adorno   4n1, 70n39, 78n2, 151, 157, 160
alienation   52, 52n20, 56, 64, 70
analytic primacy of class   27, 30, 47

Bakhtin   136, 151
base and superstructure metaphor   26, 28, 30, 32, 38, 71
bourgeois jurisprudence   49, 50, 54, 55, 62

capitalist subsumption of life by economy   29
charge of rationalism   67n36
charges of economism   46
charges of teleology   51
civil society   26, 55, 58n22
co-constitution   99, 100, 104, 118n43, 119, 120
concept formation   XVI, 8, 13, 14, 15, 16, 22, 45, 67, 70n40, 71n41, 74, 77, 78, 79, 83, 86, 89, 90, 91, 93, 95, 96, 103, 105, 107, 108, 111, 118, 119, 120, 122, 125, 133, 135, 136, 139, 140, 141, 143, 144, 145n1, 146, 147, 148, 149
contemporary marxist-feminism   15, 22, 24, 33, 54
critique   XII, 4, 9, 12, 13, 15, 16, 21, 22, 24, 24n3, 26, 33, 41, 42, 49, 49n17, 49n18, 50, 52, 53, 58n22, 58n23, 74, 77, 77n1, 78, 78n2, 80, 81, 82, 83, 85, 87n16, 91, 91n17, 92, 100, 101, 102n29, 104, 105, 111, 116, 116n42, 117, 128, 130n54, 131, 135, 139, 141, 142, 144, 147
cultural values   107, 108

description and explanation   62, 68, 69, 69n38, 70, 71
determinate abstractions   45
determinate positive concepts   38
dialectical overcoming of intersectionality   16, 110, 112, 121, 122
division of labour   30, 35, 64, 65, 67, 89
dual system theories   122

embodied social relations   XII, XVI, 10, 11, 12, 13, 14, 14n7, 15, 16, 21, 22, 25, 26, 27, 29, 30, 31, 32, 33, 34, 35, 36, 37, 38, 39, 40, 41, 47, 48, 50, 51, 52, 53, 54, 55, 56, 57, 58n24, 65, 70, 71, 72, 73, 74, 77, 78, 79, 82, 85, 86n13, 87n16, 93, 101, 104, 105, 107, 108, 110, 115, 120, 121, 124, 130n54, 131, 133, 135, 136, 139, 140, 141, 142, 143, 144, 147, 148
Engels   XV, 3, 88, 133, 134, 134n56, 135, 135n57, 158
epistemological validity   41
everyday life   69, 103n31, 123n47
experience and explanation   68

feminist political economy   79, 85, 86, 91, 95, 98, 99, 101, 104, 106, 107, 108, 110, 110n36, 136, 141

genealogy and history   57, 57n22
generalization of the categories of embodied experience   29
Gillian Rose   42, 52n20, 58n22, 67n36, 70n39, 108n34, 160

Hegel   58n22, 65n32, 123n49, 156, 157, 160, 161
Hegelian-Marxism   112, 115, 116, 117
Himani Bannerji   XIV, 31, 44n15, 44n15, 55, 56, 58n24, 58n24, 58n24, 71n41, 88, 91, 91n17, 92, 97, 104, 105, 107, 108, 147, 150, 151, 152
Hobbes   XI, 132, 151
human praxis   21, 27, 28, 29, 30, 31, 32, 37, 38, 40, 41, 44n15, 47, 51, 54, 132, 144, 146, 147

identity politics   14n6, 21, 23, 24, 26, 30, 34, 39, 48
immediate social relations   27, 32
indeterminate negative concepts   38
interpretation and change   63, 64, 65, 66, 66n34
intersectional ontology   113, 115, 121
intersectionality   13, 16, 21, 23, 24, 25, 32, 49, 58n23, 59, 61, 62, 71, 79, 93, 100

Kant   63n30, 66n35, 69n38, 156

Kimberlé Crenshaw   21, 40*n*11, 50, 102*n*29, 124, 153
knowledge production   10, 13, 14, 17, 21, 27, 36, 50, 60, 61, 85, 90, 93, 101, 105, 106, 119, 142, 143

lattice structures   113, 114*n*40, 115
Lenin   4, 5, 133, 157, 158
levels of analysis   42, 43, 44, 46, 47, 106
lived experience   32, 45, 60, 68, 94, 98, 118
logic of capital   56

Marx   XI, XII, XIV, XV, 3, 4, 6, 8, 9, 10, 11, 13, 15, 17, 21, 22, 26, 27, 28, 28*n*6, 43, 44*n*15, 47, 51, 62, 63, 65, 66*n*34, 67, 67*n*36, 69*n*37, 74, 80, 80*n*7, 81, 82, 91, 97, 97*n*23, 101, 123*n*49, 132, 133, 134*n*56, 135, 135*n*57, 139, 140, 148, 151, 152, 153, 154, 155, 156, 157, 158, 159, 160
Marx's method   XI, 43, 44*n*15, 63, 91
marxism   3, 5
marxist epistemology   15, 49, 53, 55
marxist social theory   6, 17, 22, 24, 25, 30, 32, 63, 64*n*31, 77, 95, 126, 136, 141, 143
mediated social relations   27
mereology   113
metacritique   77, 77*n*1, 78, 109
metaphysics   35, 64, 64*n*31, 151, 154
methodological close reading   13, 16, 17, 22, 77, 77*n*1, 90, 139, 140
methodology of social reproduction feminism   89

non-identity   54, 55, 63, 66

passive side of experience   102, 103*n*31
philosophies of history   51, 52, 54, 56, 58*n*22, 65*n*32
Pierre Macherey   145*n*1
post-structuralist accounts of subjectivity   40
post-structuralist feminism   29

quasi-transcendental framework of explanation   16, 47, 49*n*19, 51, 52, 53, 54, 68, 78, 103, 106, 107, 108, 121, 122*n*46, 126, 133, 136, 141, 143, 144

quasi-transcendental structure of explanation   16, 47, 52, 53, 54, 68, 107, 108, 121, 133, 136, 141, 143, 144

race and racialization   15, 16, 92, 96, 97, 106, 108, 109, 118, 120, 122, 127, 140
racial violence   56, 73
relations of economic production   6, 9

selection and articulation of social problems   16, 79, 93, 108, 125, 148
self-fulfilling prophecy   105, 106
Simmel   70*n*39
sociability   7, 8, 9, 10, 145
social action   7
social facts   107, 108, 125
social fracturation of political subjectivities   78
social Newtonianism   126, 127, 127*n*51, 128, 129, 130, 130*n*54, 131, 132, 134, 135, 136, 155, 156
social relations   5, 6, 7, 9
social reproduction qua method   146, 146*n*2, 146*n*3, 147, 148
social reproduction theory   12, 15, 16, 78, 80, 82, 84, 85, 86, 90, 91, 92, 93, 99, 101, 104, 112, 120, 124, 140
social structures of oppression   107
socialist-feminism   91*n*17, 122, 123, 123*n*49, 124, 125, 125*n*50
sociological reason   15, 22, 48, 53, 54, 57, 62, 64, 74, 103*n*30, 106, 108, 140, 142
sociology of knowledge   15, 49, 49*n*19, 50, 51, 53, 54
structures of oppression   107, 108
Stuart Hall   28*n*7, 155
sublation   XII, 109, 110, 112, 115, 116, 118, 119

unalienation   52, 56
understanding and action   63, 122
unitary social theory   15, 16, 74, 90, 101, 125, 128, 131, 139, 140

Weber   6, 7, 7*n*4, 8, 70*n*39, 159, 161, 162
Weberian sociology   8
white feminism paradigm   61
white supremacy   61, 73
whiteness   61, 72, 95

www.ingramcontent.com/pod-product-compliance
Lightning Source LLC
Chambersburg PA
CBHW070627030426
42337CB00020B/3937